Tom Hayllar and R[illegible]ialists in the field of Australian histor[illegible]ive years' experience. They have le[illegible]urses and taught more senior high school classes than they care to remember. Together they have written and co-edited a diversity of books including *Aussie Humour*, *The Untamed Fire* and *Enjoy the Earth Gently*.

Tom Hayllar created his own small piece of Australian history as an Australian adventurer. He received unique recognition in *The Guinness Book of Records*, when in 1976 he became the first person to walk around Australia. It took him a year and he wore out twenty-two pairs of Dunlop Volley sandshoes in the process.

IN THE LINE OF FIRE

Real stories of Australians at war,
from Gallipoli to Vietnam

REX SADLER and TOM HAYLLAR

MACMILLAN
Pan Macmillan Australia

First published 2005 in Macmillan by Pan Macmillan Australia Pty Ltd
St Martins Tower, 31 Market Street, Sydney

National Library of Australia Cataloguing in Publication Data:

Sadler, R. K. (Rex Kevin).
In the line of fire: real stories of Australians at war,
from Gallipoli to Vietnam.

Bibliography.
Includes index.

ISBN 1 4050 3649 4.

1. World War, 1914–1918 – Participation, Australian. 2. World War, 1939–1945 – Participation, Australian. 3. Korean War, 1950–1953 – Participation, Australian. 4. Vietnamese Conflict, 1961–1975 – Participation, Australian. 5. Australia – Armed Forces – History. 6. Australia – History, Military – 20th century. I. Hayllar, T. A. S. (Thomas Albert S.). II. Title.

994.04

Typeset in 12/15 pt Sabon by Post Pre-press Group, Brisbane, Queensland
Maps by Laurie Whiddon
Front cover photograph, 070243 supplied by Australian War Memorial
Printed in Australia by McPherson's Printing Group, Maryborough, Victoria

Introduction

The Australian character has played a major role in our military history. The stories that follow are told through Australian voices and reflect the essential values of our national identity. These compelling accounts are captured in extracts from letters, diaries, autobiographies, biographies and despatches. They are supported by photographs that often profile the harsh reality of the battlefield.

Generals commanding armies have a very different view of war from the infantry soldiers and it is for this reason that Field Marshal Wavell's dictum is particularly relevant in *In The Line Of Fire*. He said, 'When you study military history, don't read the outlines of strategy or the principles of war. Read biographies, memoirs, historical novels. Get at the flesh and blood of it, not the skeleton.' The individual testimonies of the Australian soldiers themselves provide personal insights into their endurance, courage and fighting prowess.

It was in the Gallipoli campaign that the Anzac legend was born. Here was a place for heroes. The unarmed Simpson, who with his donkey brought hundreds of wounded men down the shrapnel-swept gully to safety, became a symbol of courage. In life and in death he was known as 'the good Samaritan' or 'the man with the donkey'. Other famous heroes played their part. VC winners such as Harry Murray, Alfred Shout, Fred Tubb and Bert Jacka were there. However, the tenacity of the Anzacs holding impossible positions on the escarpment of the Gallipoli peninsula led to deeds where thousands of ordinary men did extraordinary things in critical situations. Lone

Pine, The Nek, Quinn's Post, Baby 700 and Dead Man's Ridge are places of triumph and tragedy. They showed the grim determination of the Anzacs as they fought in bloody battles against great odds and refused to yield.

As at Gallipoli, all the Australians who fought on the Western Front were volunteers. Through their words and actions, we learn of the terrible world of the trenches – bombardment, machine guns, charge, counter charge, no man's land, mud and death. Amidst these appalling conditions the Anzacs strove to maintain their dignity and humanity, while high above the trenches, Australian pilots sometimes whirled in deadly aerial combat with the best of the German air force. Behind the lines in the Casualty Clearing Stations, Australian nurses encountered the casualties and conditions that were part of the routine flow of the carnage resulting from the advances and retreats along the front line.

In the North African campaign in 1941, the Germans under Rommel referred to the Australians besieged by the Afrika Korps in the city of Tobruk, as the 'Rats of Tobruk'. The Australians were proud of this name. Their determination to stay and fight was part of the Anzac traditions forged at Gallipoli.

A strong sense of mateship not only existed at Gallipoli and the Western Front but also in the major conflicts that followed such as the New Guinea campaign fought against the Japanese. John Dougan Brooks served in New Guinea with 57/60 Infantry battalion in World War II and as a lieutenant won the Military Cross for distinguished and meritorious services in battle. One of his men said of him, 'He just didn't seem to care about his own safety, but he looked after us and was great to be with.' On the Kokoda Trail, the comradeship of the Australians was unique. Australian soldiers who survived, recall the sense of duty they felt towards their mates as they engaged the jungle fighters of the imperial Japanese Army in swamps, on mountain sides, in pouring rain with little food and with sicknesses such as malaria constantly striking down the men around them. Some historians have postulated that this mateship was one of the important factors that enabled the young Australian

Lieutenant Reg Saunders (the first Aboriginal commissioned in the Australian Army) shaking hands with Lieutenant T.C. Derrick congratulating each other on their successful graduation.

soldiers to inflict the first defeat on the Japanese in World War II. Previously it had been believed that the Japanese were invincible.

In the remarkable stories of courage and survival in this book, we constantly become aware of the triumph of the human spirit over terrible adversity. The narrative of Rawdon Hume Middleton winning the Victoria Cross is just one of the many inspirational stories of exceptional courage. In November 1942, he was the pilot of a Lancaster participating in a bombing raid on the Fiat works in Turin. He endured excruciating pain after being blinded in one eye by flack. Despite this, he managed to fly the plane back to England and save the lives of five of his crew before he lost his own life when he ditched the aircraft in the sea off the coast.

In each of the stories in *In The Line of Fire*, something is revealed that makes us proud to be Australian. Australians at war have won acclaim for their courage, sacrifice, determination and compassion. We are greatly enriched by the heritage that they have bequeathed us.

Rex Sadler and Tom Hayllar

Gallipoli

Gallipoli

On the fateful day of 28 June 1914, the heir to the Austrian throne, Franz Joseph and his wife, Sophie, were visiting Sarajevo, the capital of Bosnia. While they were travelling by car to the cathedral, assassin Gavrilo Princip, a young Bosnian student, fired two shots into the Duke's car from a distance of four or five paces. The first shot hit the Archduke in the neck and the second hit Sophie in the stomach. In thirty minutes they were both dead. The countdown to World War I had begun.

Within six weeks, the system of alliances amongst the superpowers would ensure that Europe would be plunged into war. On 28 July, Austria declared war on Serbia and on 30 July, Russia mobilised its army in support of its Slav relations, the Serbs. Germany responded by declaring war on Russia on 1 August and on France on 3 August. On 4 August, Britain entered the war, appalled by the invasion of Belgium on the previous day. The British Empire was at war.

Australia received the news enthusiastically and Andrew Fisher, the leader of the Labor party, promised that Australia would defend England 'to our last man and last shilling'. On 1 November, the First AIF and the 1st Light Horse Brigade left Australia for the Middle East. It was an army of 20,000 eager volunteers.

In December, the convoy of 36 ships arrived in Egypt. After they were joined by the New Zealand forces, the combined troops were christened the Australian and New Zealand Army Corps (ANZAC, or Anzacs, as they soon became known). English commander General Sir William Birdwood arrived in Egypt to lead the troops, who were then given intensive training on the sands around Cairo for the next four-and-a-half months.

Turkey's entry in the war on Germany's side posed a serious threat to the nearby Suez Canal, Britain's lifeline to its empire throughout the world. This threat became real in February 1915, when the Turks launched an attack on the Canal. Although the attack was easily repulsed, an ambitious plan to eliminate Turkey from the war was soon in place, with support from Winston Churchill, then First Lord of the Admiralty. The plan was to send battleships through the Dardanelles, using their huge guns to batter the Turkish forts at the entrance to the straits; an attack would then be launched on Constantinople (present-day Istanbul) in the hope that, with the overthrow of this famous city, Turkey would sue for peace. If successful, the Allies would be able to open a supply route through the Dardanelles to Russia. In theory, the plan was inspired. In practice, however, it was a naval disaster.

On 18 March, when a large fleet of British and French battleships, preceded by minesweepers, attempted to 'force the Dardanelles', two of the British battleships hit mines and sank, and three others were damaged. The beaten fleet withdrew. It was then decided to send an army of British, Anzac and French troops, with British General Sir Ian Hamilton as supreme commander, to occupy the Gallipoli peninsula and so gain control of the Dardanelles. The Anzacs would still be led by General Birdwood. By now, of course, the Turks had been alerted to the possibility of an invasion, and the element of surprise had been lost.

Just before dawn on 25 April 1915, the Anzacs landed about two kilometres north of their planned destination, the result of a navigational error. Anzac Cove, as it is now known, was the most precipitous part of the Gallipoli peninsula. Here the soldiers were faced with steep cliffs, gullies and ravines. The British and French had created a beach-head at Cape Helles to the south, but had made little progress.

As boatloads of Anzac troops reached the shores, the Turkish machine guns began to mow them down in the surf. Hundreds were shot as they made their way through the sea up to the beaches. On that day alone, more than 3000 Anzacs were killed or wounded. Amazingly, a few Anzacs had managed to reach the heights, but were driven back by counterattacks led by the young Lieutenant Colonel Mustafa Kemal (who, as Kemal Atatürk, would later become the president of modern Turkey).

When advised of the difficulty of consolidating the beach-head at Anzac

Cove, General Hamilton replied, 'You have got through the difficult business, now you have only to dig, dig, dig until you are safe.' From that day, Australian soldiers became known as 'diggers'. After the first few days, both sides had constructed an intricate maze of trenches and tunnels sometimes only metres from those of the enemy. The situation at Anzac Cove had become a stalemate.

The Gallipoli peninsula became a killing ground for snipers and bomb-throwers. Head wounds were commonplace as shells, shrapnel and bombs rained down on the troops in the trenches. Machine-gun and rifle fire exacted a terrible toll on frontal attacks launched first by the Turks and later by the Australians. On 19 May, the Turks suffered over 10,000 casualties when they counterattacked and tried to drive the Anzacs back into the sea. Such was the carnage that a truce was declared to allow for the burial of the Turkish dead. The Australians and New Zealanders fared little better three months later when they attacked the Turks at the Nek, Lone Pine and Chunuk Bair. In the attack on the Nek, for example, on 7 August, the unmounted 3rd Light Horse Brigade was annihilated by Turkish machine guns charge after charge.

In December 1915, with the coming of winter and its harsh conditions, orders were given for a secret withdrawal. One of the major difficulties was how to remove the troops from Gallipoli without the enemy knowing. It was estimated that if the Turks attacked during the evacuation, the casualty rates could be up to 50 per cent. As the result of careful planning and ingenious subterfuge, the withdrawal proved the most successful exploit of the whole campaign. By 18 December, half of the Gallipoli force – about 40,000 troops – had been withdrawn from Anzac Cove; over the next two nights, the remaining 40,000 were evacuated with only two casualties. The Turks had been entirely deceived.

The story of Gallipoli is one of horror and heroism. Over 10,000 Anzacs were killed and around 23,000 were wounded. The words of official historian C.E.W. Bean best sum up the achievement of the Anzacs at Gallipoli: 'Anzac stood, and still stands, for reckless valour in a good cause, for enterprise, resourcefulness, fidelity, comradeship, and endurance that will never know defeat.'

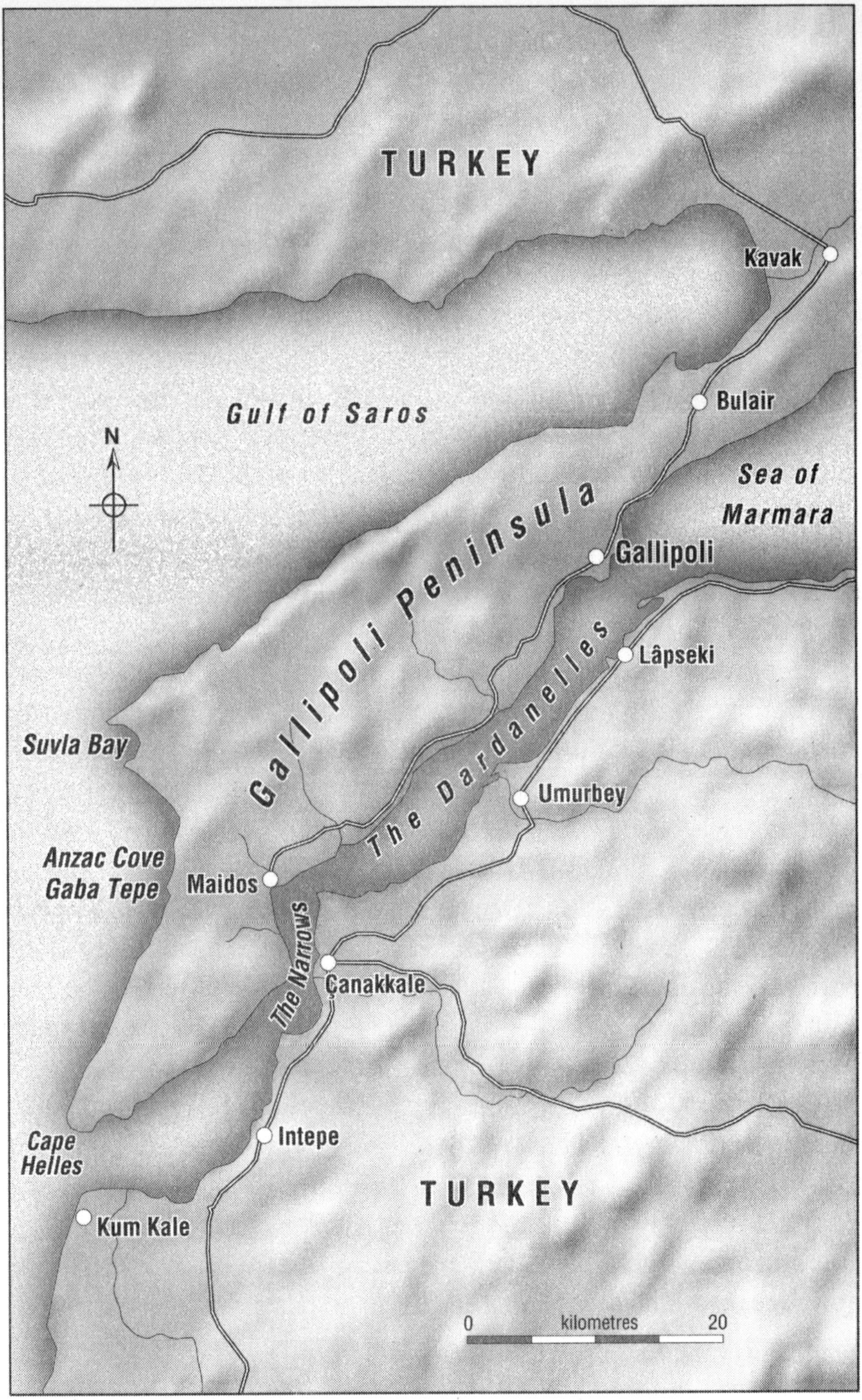

The Gallipoli Peninsula.

The landing at Anzac Cove

Albert Facey enlisted on the outbreak of war and was in the 11th Battalion on Gallipoli. In his autobiography, he graphically describes the horrors of the landing at Anzac Cove:

We left the harbour – Mudros Harbour, I had found it was called – on the afternoon of 24 April. We were nervous and excited, knowing that we were finally on our way into action. We sailed all afternoon through a calm sea. That night we turned in to sleep in hammocks. I was very tired and, despite the excitement, went to sleep.

The next thing I knew, I was being shaken awake by a corporal. The ship was moving slowly, some lights were on, and everyone was busy packing up and getting into battle dress. I noticed that stripes and rank markings had been removed from uniforms. One of the sergeants said, 'It's not far now. All portholes are blacked out and no lights on deck.'

The officers and sergeants were called to report to the Company Commander. Now excitement ran high. A few minutes later they returned and told us we were to land on the Gallipoli peninsula in Turkey.

When we were called to our sections our officer gave us a briefing on the proper instructions for landing. We were told that our ship would move as close as possible into shore but would keep out of range of the enemy's shelling. He said: 'They will throw everything they've got at us as soon as they wake up to what we're doing. Now, when the ship stops, you will be called to the side and lined up. On the side of the ship is a rope net already in place. A destroyer will come alongside and you will climb over the side and down the rope onto the deck of the destroyer when ordered. When the destroyer has enough men it will pull away and go towards where you are to land. Close to shore you will be met by a small motor boat towing rowing-boats. You will climb into the rowing-boats and the motor boats will take you as close to shore as possible. There will be sailors in the rowing-boats and they will take you into the beach. Now you are to get ashore as best you can and then line up on the beach and await further instructions.'

This was it. We were scared stiff – I know I was – but keyed up and eager to be on our way. We thought we would tear right through the Turks and keep going to Constantinople.

Troops were taken off both sides of the ship onto destroyers. My platoon and other D Company men were on the same destroyer. All went well until we were making the change into rowing-boats.

Suddenly all hell broke loose; heavy shelling and shrapnel fire commenced. The ships that were protecting our troops returned fire. Bullets were thumping into us in the rowing-boat. Men were being hit and killed all around me.

When we were cut loose to make our way to the shore was the worst period. I was terribly frightened. The boat touched bottom some thirty yards from shore so we had to jump out and wade into the beach. The water in some places was up to my shoulders. The Turks had machine guns sweeping the strip of the beach where we landed – there were many dead already when we got there. Bodies of men who had reached the beach ahead of us were lying all along the beach and wounded men were screaming for help. We couldn't stop for them – the Turkish fire was terrible and mowing into us. The order to line up on the beach was forgotten. We all ran for our lives over the strip of the beach and got into the scrub and bush. Men were falling all around me. We were stumbling over bodies – running blind.

The sight of the bodies on the beach was shocking. It worried me for days that I couldn't stop to help the men calling out. (This was one of the hardest things of the war for me and I'm sure for many of the others. There were to be other times under fire when we couldn't help those that were hit. I would think for days, 'I should have helped that poor beggar.')

We used our trenching tools to dig mounds of earth and sheltered from the firing until daylight – the Turks never let up. Their machine-guns were sweeping the scrub. The slaughter was terrible.

I am sure that there wouldn't have been one of us left if we had obeyed that damn fool order to line up on the beach.

from *A Fortunate Life* by A.B. Facey

From various perspectives, diary entries of other Anzac eyewitnesses depict the courage of the soldiers amidst the carnage of the scene:

Arrived with the rest of Fleet. It is pitch black . . . everyone is in a state of eager excitement. Transport boats are lowered. All men are lined up on deck and the orders issued: 'No rifles are to be loaded; equipment to be left unbuckled; silence to be strictly maintained in the boats. Bayonets to be fixed the moment of landing and the first line of trenches to be taken at the point of "cold steel".' At 3.10am countless numbers of small craft push off shore . . . the whole side of the mountains seem to be sending forth tongues of flame and bullets rain upon us – seven in our boat are killed and God knows how many in the others. Fifty yards from land and to wade ashore with the feeling that you are one of the first to put foot on Turkish soil . . . silent forms lay scattered on the beach everywhere: some gone to their last resting place; some writhing in their last agonies; others with their life-blood oozing out.

from an anonymous Australian soldier's diary entry

Whole boatloads vanish as a result of murderous artillery fire from the Turks' machine guns. We are ordered to wade ashore . . . Beach was littered with dead and wounded men. We discarded our packs and charged for our lives. At 6.30am we were fighting fiercely . . . Our first mountain gun spoke up at 7.30am and we cheered like one man. The butchery on both sides was gruesome but by noon we were well dug in. About 5.30pm, the enemy made another massed assault which was the worst one of the day and was repulsed with great loss.

from the diary of Private James Suggett Hagan, 3rd Battalion, AIF

We got into boats manned by midshipmen – just boys. The officer in charge of ours was 15. He was sitting with his legs hanging over the gunwale of the boat, holding his hand to his side. He called out to us: 'Go on Australians, you have them on the run and you have just captured a Krupp Gun.' With that, blood rushed from his mouth and he fell into the bloodstained sea. On the beach the sight was awful. Dead and wounded were in long rows on the strip of sand. The sea at the water's edge was red with blood . . . Two boats had all their men killed and were drifting about.

from the diary entry of Driver J.H. Turnbull

Life in the trenches

Although obviously preferable to the welcome that the Anzacs had received during the landing, life in the trenches was to provide its own hell. Detailed descriptions of the conditions the men faced are provided first by A.B. Facey, and then by Ion Idriess, a trooper of the 5th Australian Light Horse regiment.

Digging a trench with a pick and shovel was hard work. The main trench had to be from seven to eight feet deep and made in a way that it would protect us from shrapnel and rifle-fire. Every few yards a parapet was constructed so that we could get into a high position for keeping an eye on the enemy. Sand-bags were arranged to protect us while we were in the parapets on look-out duty. These bags were built up at least eighteen inches higher than a man standing, and had spaces left between, about five inches wide and six inches high. These holes were used for observations and for sniping through.

The Turks established a trench firing-line in front of ours – in some places they wouldn't have been more than twenty or so yards from our line. We had been told to always be ready for a counter-attack. During the first weeks of May, the Turks made no move in force to drive us out but subjected us to terrific shell-fire.

An invasion that did occur at about this time was body-lice – millions of them – and didn't they give us hell. Some of them were as big as a grain of wheat and they seemed to just come up out of the ground. The nuisance was made worse because we were compelled to wear cholera bands covering our kidneys and the lower parts of our body. These bands were made of a flannel material and had a strong smelling medicinal treatment in them to help combat the cholera disease. The lice didn't mind the smell at all, and used to get under the bands and give us hell until we could get off duty from the firing-line. Then we would strip everything off and crack all the lice and eggs between our nails to give ourselves some relief.

The food that we were given wasn't very good. All we had to eat was tinned meat and dry biscuits. The meat was very salty and the biscuits were so hard that we had to soak them for a few hours to be able to scrape the outside off. We would eat this and then soak them again. These biscuits were about five inches square with holes through them about an inch apart. Oh, what we would have done for a good meal.

from *A Fortunate Life* by A.B. Facey

. . . Maggots are falling into the trench now. They are not the squashy yellow ones; they are big brown hairy ones. They tumble out of the sun-dried cracks in the possy walls. The sun warms them I suppose. It is beastly . . . We have just had 'dinner'. My new mate was sick and couldn't eat. I tried to, and would have but for the flies. I had biscuits and a tin of jam. But immediately I opened the tin the flies rushed the jam. They buzzed like swarming bees. They swarmed that jam, all fighting amongst themselves. I wrapped my overcoat over the tin and gouged out the flies, then spread the biscuit, held my hand over it, and drew the biscuit out of the coat. But a lot of the flies flew into my mouth and beat about inside. Finally I threw the tin over the parapet, I nearly howled with rage. I feel so sulky I could chew everything to pieces. Of all the bastards of places this is the greatest bastard in the world. And a dead man's boot in the firing-possy had been dripping grease on my overcoat and the coat will stink forever.

from *The Desert Column* by Ion Idriess

Shells and shrapnel

Idriess is an observer of the harsh realities of war—the artillery duels, the terrible killing power of the shells and shrapnel-bullets and the horrifying head wounds. He spontaneously lays bare his own reactions to the slaughter surrounding him, and his growing respect for the fighting ability of the Turkish soldier, referred to as 'Johnny'.

What miraculous escapes! A shell has just burst in front of me; ten feet below two infantry chaps are cooking their breakfast. They were spattered with smoke and earth but refuse to leave their cooking. As I write, another shell has burst beneath them, but still the obstinate goats won't budge. Another has come and this time they grabbed their pots and ran. We all laughed. By Caesar! it is about time they *did* run. A fourth shell has come and where their fireplace was is now a cloud of smoke, ashes, earth, and fragments of shell. Shells are bursting amongst us all over the hill and up and down the tiny gully. A rumour is flying around that the Turks broke into our trenches last night. They never got out again alive, I'll bet. Johnny is

Captain L. J. Morshead looks up at corpses lying near the parapet of a Lone Pine trench.

sending his big stuff over this morning – high explosive mixed with the shrapnel-shells. A shrapnel burst in the air and sprays the ground with hundreds and thousands of bullets, according to the size of the shell. One gun alone, firing quickly, can make a regiment feel as if it were under the rifle-fire of five hundred men. But when batteries of guns get going . . . ! High explosive has its own terror. The shell itself plonks fair into the ground then explodes with a fearful crash broadcasting jagged fragments of shell.

. . . Finished breakfast under their cursed shrapnel-fire. They are 'searching' for the Indian battery now, but their creeping shells are exploding above us – unseen marksmen sending unseen death into unseen men. These artillery duels mean sheer hell for us chaps in between. Not half a stone's throw away from us, just across the gully, are the dugouts of an infantry battalion. Owing to the direction that the shells are coming [from], these poor chaps are getting it far worse than we are, for the shrapnel-bullets are pelting right into the mouths of their dugouts. One shell has exploded fair in a dugout and blown the four men up into the air. Another two are now hit. If it were not for our dugouts, we could not live. They are perfect shelters against shrapnel only, except when a shell explodes fair in or above them, or just at the angle where the bullets will strike down into the dugout. The dugout is no protection though against a direct hit by a high explosive. It is getting fearfully hot now, shells are exploding every few seconds; the row is an inferno made hellish by the hot smell of fumes. The cry is becoming continuous, 'Stretcher-bearers!' 'Stretcher-bearers!' 'Doctor!' as more and more of our poor chaps get hit. Good luck to all the medical men! We have the shelter of our dugouts, but they run out into this hail of shrapnel directly the cry goes up. The pity of it is that we cannot fire a shot in return.

Bits of earth come crumbling down from my dugout walls as I write, lying on my back. It is hard work writing that way, especially with the blasted ground rocking underneath. One poor chap opposite has just had hard luck. His mate was wounded in the leg. He knelt up, undoing his mate's puttees. A fragment of shell whizzed into the dugout and took the top of his head clean off.

. . . This horrible fire is easing off. I stopped writing, just lay flat out and shivered as those great shells sizzled, seemingly just over my nose. We have had five heart-choking hours of it. It seems longer.

from *The Desert Column* by Ion Idriess

No-man's-land

Of the 42,000 Turks who took part in their attack in mid May, 10,000 became casualties and only a few actually reached the Anzac trenches before being killed. It was sheer butchery and the Turkish commanders never again employed this kind of attack at Gallipoli. Five days later an armistice was arranged to provide for burial of the dead in no-man's-land. A.B. Facey's recollection of the inspection of the frontline by Lord Kitchener, the British Secretary of War, was accurate. After his inspection of the Gallipoli peninsula in October 1915, Kitchener decided that the 105,000 troops should be evacuated. Facey recalls this dawn attack, which attempted to push the Anzacs back into the sea:

AIF 9th Brigade gunners in action during the Lone Pine offensive in August 1915.

On about 17 May we noticed the Turks becoming very active at night. We could hear their carts rattling down the roads, travelling towards the British positions to our right. There also seemed to be Turkish troops massing in and along our front, and during the daytime we could see, by looking through field-glasses and telescopes, quite large numbers of troops moving about. After this we received a message to the effect that a mass attack was expected at any time and every man was required to stand by.

On the evening of 18 May, the Turks bombarded us heavily for a time. Then in the early hours of the morning, before daylight, the attack came, and every available man was in position. The Turks had to come over a small rise and our trenches were just below this, so that when the enemy appeared they showed out clearly to us. They were running but we were able to shoot them down as fast as they appeared. When daylight came there were hundreds of dead and wounded lying in no-man's-land, some only a few yards in front of our firing-line. The Turks hit our line in places for what seemed like a couple of hours. My section was rushed a couple of times but we stopped them before they reached us – not one Turk got in our trench. Finally the Turks called it a day and word came through to the effect that we had defeated them all along the line.

No-man's-land was now littered with bodies. Attempts were made to remove these for burial but enemy fire made this impossible. Many of our men were hit trying to bring in the bodies. The weather was very hot during the day and before long the corpses began to rot. The smell from this became almost unbearable, particularly when there was no breeze blowing.

At this time we had a distinguished visitor – a high-ranking British officer. He came along our main frontline trench with several of our Staff Officers and Commanding Officers. He got a whiff of the smell coming from no-man's-land and asked the Australian officers, 'Why don't you bury the bodies?' Our Commanding Officer explained that the Turks opened fire every time this was attempted and that we had lost men trying. The officer's reply to this shocked all of us who heard him. He said, 'What is a few men?' He was standing only about ten feet from me when he said this and I was disgusted to think that life seemed to mean nothing to this man. We referred to him as 'Lord Kitchener' from then on.

Later the Turks sent an officer in under a white flag – he was blindfolded and on horseback. He was taken back from our lines to Headquarters to see our Command. Later, we received word that an armistice had been arranged for the twenty-fourth of May to enable both sides to bury the dead.

I will never forget the armistice – it was a day of hard, smelly, nauseating work. Those of us assigned to pick up the bodies had to pair up and bring the bodies in on stretchers to where the graves were being dug. First we had to cut the cord of the identification disks and record the details on a sheet of paper we were provided with. Some of the bodies were rotted so much that there were only bones and part of the uniform left. The bodies of men killed on the nineteenth (it had now been five days) were awful. Most of us had to work in short spells as we felt very ill. We found a few of our men who had been killed in the first days of the landing.

This whole operation was a strange experience – here we were, mixing with our enemies, exchanging smiles and cigarettes, when the day before we had been tearing each other to pieces. Apart from the noise of the grave-diggers and the padres reading the burial services, it was mostly silent. There was no shelling, no rifle-fire. Everything seemed so quiet and strange. Away to our left there were high table-topped hills and on these were what looked like thousands of people. Turkish civilians had taken advantage of the cease-fire to come out and watch the burial. Although they were several miles from us they could be clearly seen.

from *A Fortunate Life* by A.B. Facey

Simpson and his donkey

One of the heroes of the Gallipoli campaign was Private J.S. Kirkpatrick, known as James Simpson, of the 3rd Field Ambulance. Each day after the landing, Simpson and one of his donkeys would carry wounded men down to the beach to receive medical help, enduring enemy fire all the while. On

19 May 1915, he was killed by a bullet while carrying two of the wounded to safety.

C.E.W. Bean, who had been appointed official war correspondent of the AIF, described Simpson and the events leading to his death:

It was the evening after the Turkish attack of 19 May. Some of us were sitting yarning that evening when someone passing said, 'I suppose you've heard that the man with the donkeys is dead?' It came as a real shock. Everybody knew that man with the donkeys, and everybody knew that if ever a man deserved honour in this war it was he. He was a stretcher-bearer. Few people knew his name. To most he was Scottie or Murphy; those who called him the one called his donkey the other. He was really Private Simpson, of the 3rd Field Ambulance.

When first we arrived at Anzac, there were landed a number of donkeys which it was thought would be useful in carrying food and water to the firing line. Donkeys will live on a diet of little more than sticks. It was found from the first, however, that the animal for this work out and away the best is the mule. He drinks much less than a horse and the amount of work he gets through on these steep hills is an eye-opener. The donkeys are the favourites with the men on account of their temper, but there are not many of them now remaining.

It was some time during the first night of our landing that Private Simpson annexed one of these donkeys. He knew the loads they carried in Egypt and it struck him that they would be especially useful for carrying down men wounded in the line. He put a red cross brassard around the donkey's head and started business at once. He went off and camped with his donkey amongst the Indians who drive mules, and fed with them; and all day and half the night he made continual trips to and from the firing line; everyone used to meet him time and again coming down the gully with wounded men sitting on the little animal beside him. You cannot hurry a donkey very much, however close the shells may burst, and he absolutely came to disregard bullets and shrapnel. The man with the donkey became fatalistic – if they were going to hit him they would whatever his precautions.

For nearly four weeks he came up and down that valley – through

Private John Simpson Kirkpatrick of the 3rd Australian Field Ambulance with Abdul, his donkey, assisting a wounded soldier.

the hottest shrapnel, through the aimed bullets of snipers and the unaimed bullets which came over the ridges. When the shells were so hot that many others thought it wiser to duck for cover as they passed, the man with the donkey calmly went his way as if nothing more serious than a summer shower were happening. Presently he got another donkey, and started to work with two of them. He was coming down the gully on the morning of 19 May after the attack, clearing some of our 300 or 400 wounded – the Turks lost twice that many thousand – when he passed the waterguard, where he generally took his breakfast. It happened this morning that the breakfast was not ready. 'Never mind,' he said to the engineer there, 'get me a good dinner when I come back.' But he never came back. He and his two patients were nearing the end of their journey when he was shot through the heart, and both of his wounded men were wounded again.

The commander of this section of our line told me that the man with the donkey had been worth 100 men to him. The Colonel of the ambulance to which he belonged had from the first so recognised the value of his work that he was given a roving commission, and allowed to camp and work entirely on his own, almost as if he were a separate unit. All he had to do was to report once a day to his unit. The moment he fell someone else took on the work with donkeys.

The man with the donkeys was not by a long way the only stretcher-bearer who was hit at this corner. On one of the early days, two stretcher-bearers were bringing down a wounded man when a shrapnel burst right onto them at this point. One, if not both, of the bearers was hit and fell. The wounded man leapt out of the stretcher and cut for his life, and was there waiting in the dressing station when the two stretcher-bearers were carried in there.

from C.E.W. Bean, despatch in *Commonwealth Gazette* 23 July 1915

Lone Pine

The Battle of Lone Pine was conceived as a diversion to occupy the Turks while combined attacks were being launched at Suvla Bay and Cape Helles to seize the heights of Sari Bair and Chunuk Bair. The attack began at

5.30pm on 6 August 1915, and by 6pm the Australians had captured Lone Pine. Here is Bean's graphic description of the Australian defence of Lone Pine:

Noting that the Turkish bombs had long fuses, the Australians constantly caught them and threw them back before they burst. The Turks then learnt to shorten the fuses and many boys' hands were blown off, and others were blinded or killed. Hundreds of times bombs falling into the trenches were smothered with half-filled sandbags; but others burst, killing and wounding the groups behind the barricades, and the stream of wounded was continuous.

At intervals when Turks were clearly massing behind the barriers, the Australians would clear them, exposing themselves above the parapet in the process, and with rifles or a machine-gun, sweeping down the enemy. The Turks dynamited a barricade, but the Australians rushed and re-established it. The Turks set fire to the logs of the head cover. The Australians twice extinguished it. The Turks twice penetrated far into the trenches they had lost; the Australians turned them and chased them back. Jam-tin bombs, though pouring in from the 'factory' on the beach, were still in far from sufficient supply. But on both sides the dead clogged many trenches . . .

When on 10 August fighting ceased in the Pine, six Australian battalions had lost, in all, 80 officers and 2197 men, and the Turks (according to their most active commander there) 5000.

from *Anzac to Amiens* by C.E.W. Bean

The withdrawal

In December 1915, orders were given for a secret withdrawal from Gallipoli. Remarkably, after the chaos and tragedy of the landing seven months before, some 80,000 troops were evacuated from the peninsula without loss of life. Many ingenious devices were created to keep rifles firing after the troops had departed. Lance Corporal William Scurry of the 7th Battalion invented the delayed-action rifle, which operated by water dripping from a top tin into a lower tin until the weight was heavy enough to pull the trigger to which it was attached.

The following is Bean's report of the operation:

At dusk the first parties began, with padded feet, to move to the beaches. Except for a few on the flanks, who embarked from specially made piers, two wound along the well-known paths and trenches – all carefully marked for this night – to Anzac Cove and North Beach . . . After midnight the eleven miles of Anzac front were held by only 1500 men. These moved from loophole to loophole, keeping up normal fire and bombing . . . Here and there was left a rifle which, by varying devices, would fire up to half an hour after the troops had gone.

So, gradually, the Anzac front was uncovered. At 2.25 the withdrawal began from the southern flank also. At 2.40 the last men left their loopholes at Lone Pine, and at 2.55 at Quinn's, where for seven months the bomb fight had continued every night and day. At all usual points the firing and bombing by the Turks still went on.

At 3.25 the last guard on Walker's Ridge retired and at 3.30, with a minute's interval between the explosions, the two mines on the Nek . . . were fired.

All over the dark waters, troops crowded boats moving out to larger crafts, and on ferry steamers, transports and warships, saw the brilliant orange glow twice flush for a moment the underside of low, angry clouds. A growing rattle of rifle fire spread along the Turkish line – a bullet from this stream hit a soldier in one of the boats causing one of the two Anzac casualties of that night. The last boat left North Beach about 4am. The naval transport officer and his steamboat with the last of the Anzac staff waited ten minutes for stragglers, but there were none and at 4.10 they pushed off. Four miles to the north a fire broke out – the stores at Suvla were being burnt. At 5.10 the last party left Suvla, where also the casualties were negligible. Till dawn the Turks were still sniping as on an ordinary night. At 6.45 they shelled the Anzac trenches and at 7.15 attacked – to find the position empty and the Anzacs gone. After a few shells which sent these Turks to earth, the covering British cruisers withdrew and left Anzac Cove to the enemy.

from *Anzac to Amiens* by C.E.W. Bean

The Western Front

The Western Front

All Australians who fought in the Great War were volunteers. Between 1914 and 1918, as part of the British Empire, Australian servicemen went to the assistance of the mother country that, together with France, faced the might of Germany and Austria. However, they paid a high price for their loyalty. By the end of the war, the Australian forces had suffered 226,073 casualties of which 59,258 were killed.

The Australian and New Zealand troops, many of whom had fought at Gallipoli, arrived in Belgium and France in March 1916. Field Marshal Sir Douglas Haig, the British commander-in-chief, distrusted the Anzacs because of their lack of respect for authority and regarded them as unpredictable in battle. Later in the war, however, when the Anzacs had proved their bravery and determination in the face of the enemy, Haig came to regard them as reliable and valuable shock troops. In 1918, the Australian commander, General Sir John Monash, would be knighted in battle for his brilliant leadership of the Australian troops and his use of hundreds of tanks and aircraft to smash through Amiens to the Hindenburg Line.

On arrival, the Anzacs found that the battle line of the opposing armies known as the Western Front had settled into trench warfare. This was the result of Germany's failure to achieve the capture of Paris after a lightning strike by their armies through neutral Belgium into France. The strength of the German thrust had been weakened when troops were diverted to guard the borders of the fatherland. Consequently, British and French armies halted the Germans at the Battle of the Marne, and from the English Channel to the Swiss border, the huge trench systems that were then dug prevented sweeping movements of forces along the battle front.

The Anzacs first experienced the trenches at the Battle of the Somme and soon discovered that life in them was squalid and dangerous. Rain, mud, rats and diseases such as trench foot, trench fever and typhus caused much misery; and enemy snipers and direct shell bursts claimed many lives. Sometimes either side tunnelled beneath the opposing trenches and detonated huge mines.

To the rear of the trenches, casualty clearing stations treated the wounded under shocking conditions until the men could be transported to hospitals. Australian doctors and nurses worked beside British operating teams to handle the huge numbers of wounded that almost overwhelmed the CCSs when barrages and assaults were in progress.

In the skies above the trenches, small biplanes and triplanes flew reconnaissance missions, spotted for the artillery, engaged each other in dog fights and strafed and bombed the men in the trenches, as well as the columns of troops moving up to the front. During the war, there were several hundred Australian pilots and mechanics fighting on the Western Front, with great bravery and devotion to duty.

The Australian Flying Corps had several squadrons on the front, while some Australians flew with the Royal Air Corps. General Trenchard, the RFC commander, said of the Australian pilots: 'Their work was magnificent. They bombed the German and attacked him with machine-gun fire from 50 feet, flying among treetops.'

On 23 July 1916, the Anzacs were ordered to assault the German defences at Pozieres, a village on a ridge, as part of a plan to penetrate and break through the German lines. However, although the Anzacs took the village, after sustained attacks and heavy enemy bombardments, the casualty list was high: 22,000 men had fallen. It was obvious that General Haig would not hesitate to sacrifice men for minor gains in territory.

As a result of their heavy losses on the Somme, the German high command withdrew its troops to the heavily defended Hindenburg Line, with its deep trenches, concrete blockhouses, earth ramparts and huge coils of barbed wire.

Winter conditions bogged down the trenches in a sea of mud but with the spring of 1917 the British forces were ordered to advance and they fought their way to the Hindenburg Line. The Australians were thrown against the strongly defended position of Bullecourt. A bombardment was withheld but the newly developed tanks that were supposed to roll over the barbed wire failed to reach the battle on time. Over 3000 Australians were sacrificed in vain assaults to breach the line. Further attacks on Bullecourt by Australian and British forces brought temporary success but only after over 7000 Australians had been sacrificed.

As I Anzac Corps had been terribly mauled at Pozieres, II Anzac Corps (previously in a supporting role to British and Canadian troops) was used against the enemy lines at Messines Ridge near Ypres, in Belgium. The assault involved setting and exploding huge mines in tunnels beneath the German lines on the ridge. The strategy was successful but the attackers lost approximately 26,000 men, of which some 12,000 were Anzacs.

On 31 July 1917, Haig ordered the commencement of the Third Battle of Ypres against artillery-proof concrete bunkers. The British advance was bogged down in heavy rain and mud. Following a rolling barrage, Australian soldiers engaged the enemy on 20 September and successfully stormed key German strongholds on the Menin Ridge, but at the cost of over 5000 casualties.

During October attacks by the Anzacs on Passchendaele – the ruined village and the ridge on which it stood – were repulsed with heavy losses, despite heroic efforts. Haig, needing a decisive outcome before winter, ordered the capture of Passchendaele at any cost. It was eventually taken by Canadian, Anzac and British forces the following month, but not before German barrages of shells containing mustard gas caused terrible injuries.

With the coming of spring in 1918, the German high command implemented a plan to split the British and French forces at Amiens before the arrival of American troops at the Western Front (the United States having declared war on Germany in April 1917). This became a decisive action when civil war broke out in Russia, as the Communists succeeded in overthrowing Tsarist rule and made peace with Germany. As a result, 35 German army divisions were released. Moving by railway from the Eastern to the Western Front, they massed opposite the numerically inferior British lines.

The German offensive began at dawn on 21 March 1918 with an artillery barrage from 6000 guns. Infantry then began a swift advance on Amiens. The Australian corps, held in reserve, moved to block the Germans at the town of Villers-Bretonneux. Later, in April, Australian brigades recaptured the town using surprise tactics and superior military planning.

A defensive line was established across the Somme and held against all enemy attacks, by the Australians. German casualties were so high that the commander overseeing the Somme offensive, General Ludendorff, stated, 'The enemy's resistance was beyond our powers.' However, there were still seven months to go before the end of the war, and during that time blows and counter-blows were struck and amidst the carnage, there were many more deeds of heroism by the Australian diggers.

As part of their plans for their tremendous offensive, German forces drove for the Channel ports and for Paris but British forces, sustained by Australian reinforcements, halted their progress. By the middle of summer 1918, the arrival of American and fresh French armies on the battlefields and the deployment of tanks meant the end of German plans of conquest of Europe. On 8 August (Ludendorff called it, 'the black day of the German army') overwhelming artillery barrages, hundreds of aircraft, tanks and armoured cars – and even cavalry – completely surprised the enemy.

On the Somme front, the Germans retreated to Peronne, some 50 kilometres west of Amiens, and their resistance intensified there. At the end of August, Australian troops battled to the top of Mont St Quentin, thus commanding the heights above Peronne. The Germans suffered terrible losses as they tried to hold the position but the Australian brigades broke through the old walled town to rout the defenders.

During September, the fighting shifted eastwards to the Hindenburg Line. One of the last Australian battles pierced the line at Montbrehain. The corps then went into reserve but were preparing to return to the fighting when an armistice was signed on 11 November 1918.

The Anzacs were slowly returned home. They were men who expected to be recognised as heroes in Australia, but many found that they had already been forgotten in the land of their birth.

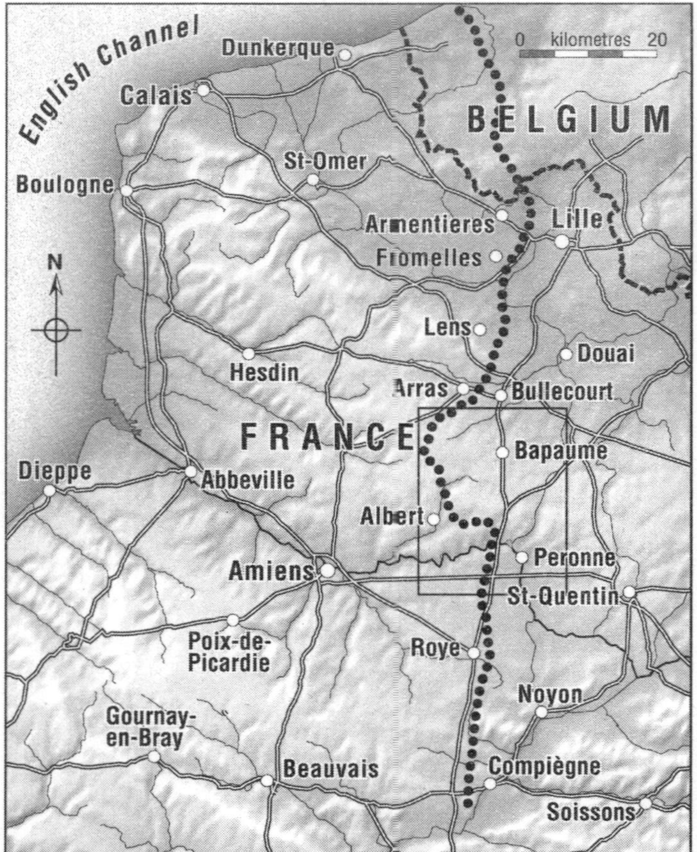

The Western Front.

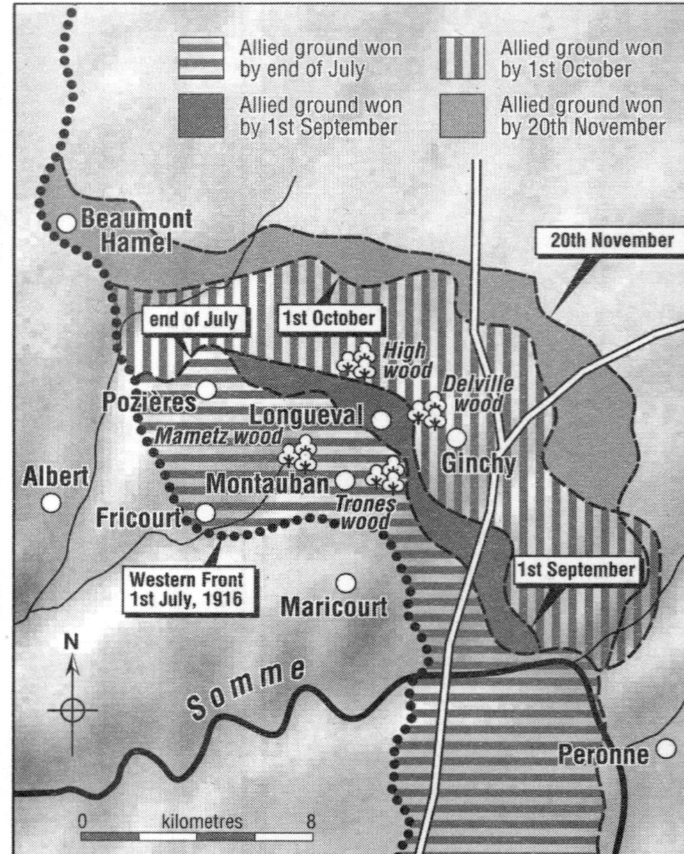

The Somme Offensive.

Harney goes to war

Bill Harney, a young Queenslander, volunteered for the war thinking that it would be a change from his life in the bush. He was looking forward to the travel and thought the whole thing would be a great adventure. After he reached Flanders and the Western Front he realised the great adventure had turned into a nightmare:

Finally our band, the battalion band, it was practising behind one of the big barns. There it's going on and – all the instruments are shined because that's a part of the job. They've gotta have them lookin' clean. They woke up afterwards that it was better to let 'em go a bit tarnished. But whatever happened, a German must have spotted 'em from one of their great Blimps; you know, their observation balloons, and he directed fire onto 'em, and over she come, a big, big shell, and it dropped right in among 'em and cleaned up quite a mob of them. And then that night we had to go and bury them. I think we buried about fifty to sixty blokes.

The first experience I ever got was burying them men. Here we are in the night, burying them, and I thought, Blimey! Blow this business. I was wishing to God I was back on the old Nicholson River with me poor horses again. You know, I reckon that was – that was paradise – blimey! By this time if they had shunted me back to Australia bare-footed and with a mob of 'Bindy-eyes' on the ground, I'd 'a been happy.

The background of it all was how frightened you become yourself. This fear. But the only thing that overcomes it is the cheerfulness of your mates. You get a great hinge with mateship in the thing, and then . . . you think of the bloke on the other side. The enemy becomes an all-efficient machine, powerful and everything. You don't look upon him as a fool or anything; he's a mighty man.

I was talkin' to a mate of mine. I said, 'By golly! I don't like these Germans on the other side, they seem to be a fairly efficient mob. By golly! It makes a man frightened on this side.'

He said, 'Always remember, Bill. The other bloke on the other side is just as frightened as you are.'

And it kinda gave me a bit of consolation. But, however, we finally went up into the line at a place called Fleurbaix. It was a big – they weren't trenches, but they were great big breast-works. And we used to go behind these big breast-works and then we'd look through periscopes and we'd see the big German lines on the other side. And that's how we were for the first time I went in the line.

It was about April, the end of April. It was a wonderful time of the year . . . all the trees was in bloom and the grass looked lovely, and birds was chirpin'. Actually, you'd never dream, and the bells used to ring every Sunday in these big steeples. It's a strange place – oh, it's a bonza place.

Well, we was there quite a while. The only thing I found out about Fleurbaix, which we called the place, is that the officers somehow told us that we hadn't to take off our clothes. We had to always be at the ready. And I'll never forget that I slept in me boots and in me clothes for about twenty days without taking 'em orf. Slept and walked in 'em. You know, I just can't imagine what it's all about. But there you are, they work accordin' to orders, and it's passed on to us, and we just do what we're told.

I found out that all initiative was gone by this time. The old days of the cattle stations where a man rounded up the cattle and used his own initiative – that's all gone. You're just a big cog in the machine and you're just moving ahead, the whole heap of us, you're a part of a big mob.

from *Bill Harney's War* by W.E. Harney (1895–1962)

Bloody Passchendaele

Passchendaele, a village in Flanders near the infamous Ypres, was of great strategic importance as it stood on a ridge commanding a view of the surrounding landscape. It was captured by the Germans in 1914 and became the scene of hopeless bravery and suffering as waves of attackers fell to shot and shell.

Alec Griffiths from New South Wales was only sixteen when he and his best mate Bob Lauchland volunteered for the army and went to the Great War. They were sent to the Western Front. Alec's job as a radio operator on the ground was to co-ordinate artillery fire using spotter aircraft of the

The morning after the first battle at Passchendaele showing wounded Australian infantry.

Australian Flying Corps. He was involved in the most terrible battles of the Western Front and, despite being wounded, survived to return to Australia but Bob did not.

A recent biography on Alec Griffiths describes his experiences on the day he was wounded at Passchendaele:

At stand-to Alec watched the day make its first movements towards dawn. Nothing stirred. The only living animals apart from the men of the battery were the vermin. In the *estaminets* [wine bars], Alec had heard the infantry talk of large rats feeding off the corpses in the trenches and in no-man's-land. Out here in the artillery batteries, though, there were no rats – the shelling was too intense for them.

After stand-down the gunners went about cleaning their guns and arranging ammunition. Something was doing. A briefing by the battery commander confirmed this to Alec: another counter-battery shoot. A German battery had been menacing the Australian infantry for many days and causing tremendous casualties. Alec cleaned his wireless equipment as best he could, had an unpalatable breakfast of hard-tack rations washed down with a few mouthfuls of water that tasted like chlorine, and thought about the brass-hats back in their chateaux poring over red-wine-stained battle maps that represented bloodstained tracts of land. He thought he felt bitter; perhaps it just saddened him. He knew that many a staff officer was killed by a shell or bomb in his headquarters, but at least back there his body could be found and given a decent burial.

The world erupted in a crash of a thousand guns. The shoot commenced not long afterwards, once an RE8 had flown over the battery from behind. The entire line was the arena for one great artillery duel. Alec did not envy the airmen. They established communications with him with difficulty as the blast of an incoming shell had blown the contact off his crystal. He prepared his canvas strips, orders were passed to the adjusting gun, the other guns prepared their ammunition accordingly. The usual messages arrived from the RE8 and the firing began. Above the bark of the lone 18-pounder, Alec heard the drone of an approaching machine. It was a red plane.

Alec's battery had been detected. Before long, a German adjusting gun was giving them some of their own back. But the shoot had to go on and they continued the laborious targeting procedure. They were slightly ahead of the Germans in the race to fire the first on-target salvo, but the Hun battery had a distinct advantage. It would soon have Alec's battery ranged and be bringing effective fire to bear, whereas in all probability the target of Alec's group was not that particular enemy battery. It would have free rein over them. Such are the fortunes of war.

A shell spiralled in and landed behind Alec's battery. Another landed in front. The Germans had them ranged. Minutes later a salvo landed. Then another, of high explosive and shrapnel. A lot of the gunners were hit. A man serving on the nearest gun to the dugout went to the aid of someone who had been hit, and was himself hit a few moments later. They died in each other's arms. Alec watched helplessly as another gunner picked pieces of shrapnel out of his screaming mate's back and carried him towards the dugout. More and more shells exploded. By the sheer weight of fire Alec felt certain there must have been more than one battery firing on them. Everywhere around him men were falling, dead or wounded. It was absolute pandemonium. The wounded gunner and the man who was carrying him were chopped down, only yards from the dugout. Neither moved again.

The battery could continue with its job only if Alec continued with his. He couldn't pause to try to help the fallen men. The incoming shells had slowed the battery's adjustment procedure, and only now were they able to fire a salvo. And then another. Men with minor shrapnel wounds continued to serve the guns. Their valour could not be described in words: Alec felt that all of them – to a man – deserved a DCM or even a Victoria Cross. But gunners were seldom awarded VCs.

Serve the guns! These words, in a gunner's heart, were more powerful than a divine order and it was almost as though the gunners knew, as Alec did, that their actions were saving many more lives in the Aussie infantry. Alec wanted to stay in the comparative safety of the dugout, but these gunners inspired him to go out in the open again. A high-explosive shrapnel shell burst nearby. Alec was hit. He was thrown to the sodden ground with the impact, and blood poured from his nose and ears and into his eyes. High-explosive shells continued to burst all around him. Everything was noise, noise, noise. Somehow he realised that blood from your nose and ears should not get into your eyes. He put his hand to his forehead and found the source of the blood. Shrapnel had snuck beneath the sentry that his steel helmet was meant to be, and sliced his forehead. He tried to mop away the blood with his arm but encountered something very hard. He felt for the cut, to find that the shrapnel had torn away most of his forehead down to the bone. The hardness he was feeling was his own skull. A wave of shock and revulsion swept over him as he tried to get to his feet.

But he couldn't move. He just sat there, trying to wipe the blood away. A couple of men whose gun had been stonkered raced over to him. One of them gave him a drink of water, while the other – as casually as if he were attending to a minor gravel graze – pushed the two remaining pieces of Alec's forehead back into place and held them there. His mate got some shell dressing and dirty sticking plaster from the dugout and stuck flaps of flesh down. 'That'll see ya right, cob,' he said matter-of-factly.

Once the shoot had finished, Alec stumbled into the relative refuge of the dugout. It was filled with the sobs and cries of the wounded and dying. Casualties were not meant to be brought in here but there was nowhere else for them to go. A jar of rum was passed around the men, though some had no hands to hold it. Despite being teetotal, Alec guzzled the rum as if it was the most soothing, calming, delicious drink on earth. That day, it was.

The shelling continued for days. The horizon was ablaze. Gunners who had served at the Somme in 1916 swore that those battles – when it came to the sheer volume and relentlessness of the shelling – could not hold a candle to this one. Gunners who had survived the Somme were now being buried by walls of earth. They yelled and pleaded to be disinterred. By the time they were, most were dead. Yet other men were blown into pieces not much larger than the shell fragments themselves. There was no respite, even at night. The groans of wounded men seeped into the darkness until the darkness itself and death dissolved them. Occasionally shells would land so close at night that Alec and the others were temporarily blinded. A handful of men were so shell-shocked that they had lost their reason. They convulsed and sang meaningless words while the others tried to sleep, trying to forget. Alec dreamed of leave. He dreamed of Effie. He dreamed of Bob. He had never come closer to prayer than now.

from *Until a Dead Horse Kicks You: The Story of an Ordinary Hero – Alec Griffiths 1900–1995* by Robert Crack

Trench warfare

As a young private with the Australian forces on the Western Front, Bert Bishop learnt what it was like to be ordered out of a trench to charge the German lines into a storm of rifle and machine-gun fire. In the Battle of Fromelles he was caught in artillery barrages and watched his mates die all around him. But Bert survived returning from behind the front line to have his first drink of rum and record his memoirs of his time at the front:

Our company went to billets in Bac St Maur. Rumour was everywhere about a stunt we were booked for. My platoon had been on a fatigue job in the village. Our sister battalion, Billy's, was billeted in the town, but I never could get time to hunt him up. Early in the afternoon our platoon was ordered to prepare to move. There was a feeling of suspense, of something unpleasant about to happen, over everything.

Before we left, Billy's battalion was paraded in a big cobblestoned yard beside the factory we had been occupying.

I thought what a splendid-looking lot of men they were. Companies were drawn up in a line abreast right across the yard. They marched in, each company taking up station-in-review order. How well they marched, wheeled and lined up. How well they sloped arms, ordered arms, stood to attention.

Their colonel stood in front centre, facing them. 'Stand at ease,' he said.

He explained the plans of the attack our division was to participate in that night. Then he became less formal.

'Remember, each one of us, that this is the first AIF battle in France. We must achieve success. Our orders are that the ground we win must be held at all cost. We will be the centre brigade of our division. We have to take two lines of German trenches and we must hold them. Good luck to all of us.'

I watched Billy's battalion march out, and a lump came into my throat. All day a barrage of our massed artillery had pounded the German front and second lines.

'That's to let them know we're coming,' Nugget had growled, 'and give them time to get ready.'

A runner came looking for our platoon officer. The platoon was not in the first wave, we had to wait till the trenches were taken, then get busy as water and ammunition carriers. We proceeded to VC Corner, near Fromelles. The first waves went across in broad daylight, five-thirty pip-emma. We could get a glimpse of the battle area here and there, and we could see that the number of men reaching the German line was far short of the number that started. A message came. The front and support German trenches were in the possession of our men. We had to get busy carrying water and ammunition across.

Loading up, we filed into a communication trench. Shells were landing all about us. We met the first wounded coming out, often two men helping each other to be mobile. Then a batch of German prisoners squeezed past us. A hold-up stopped them and we interestedly looked at each other. One big German was bared to his waist. In his top back was a hole large enough to put a fist in. Germans unable to walk were crawling along the duckboards, blood dripping from them. The duckboards were covered in blended mud and blood.

Some of the Germans could speak a little English; Nugget was having quite a conversation with one of them. A man nearby said to a German: 'Well, Fritz, what do you think of things now?'

He nearly fell over when the German replied: 'I'm quite happy, but I'm sorry for you poor bastards.'

Slipping, pushing, we slowly progressed.

Then the communication trench suddenly debouched in what had been our front line.

I stood, I saw, a queer numb feeling took possession of me. At first it was shock, then it was terror, then it was unbelief. This just could not possibly be true. We were supposed to be civilised. The most beastly and cruel animals on earth wouldn't do this to each other. I was dazed and numb, my brain wouldn't work. A thought somehow forced its way into my thinking. It was not true, it was utterly unbelievable. I was asleep, having the worst nightmare of my life. Nightmare, that was it, I clung to the thought.

'Get along there,' someone shouted. 'What the hell do you think we're here for?'

I was pushed forward. I stepped over dead bodies, I stepped over live and smashed bodies, I stepped over pieces of what had been bodies. Wounded were crying out in agony. Shell-shocked men crawled and clung to each other, some blubbering like babies. And every few seconds another shell would burst into my nightmare.

Men were trying to dig a trench across no-man's-land. We got into it, but in a few yards it fizzled out. We got out of it, and bullets hissed about us.

'Keep going on top, we've got to get our stuff over,' our officer was yelling. No-man's-land was littered with dead and wounded. We'd race a few yards, lie down, race again, down again. Our platoon was scattered, we had to do our own thinking. I had sheltered in a crater at the edge of the German wire. I studied the wire closely, looking for a passageway. My course planned, I tore my way through that wire. Bullets hissed everywhere. Not looking into the German trench, I heaved myself over their parapet, dead Germans and sandbags all jumbled together.

Tumbling over the top I landed full-length on a German body. The body grunted. Standing up I looked at him. His waxen colour meant he had bled to death. He was only a boy, his face was the most handsome I'd ever looked at. I scrambled into a trench that ran from the first German line back to their support line.

It was a shambles of duckboards, smashed men, mud, water, blood. Quite a few of our platoon were getting together again. I saw Old Chris and hurried to reach him. He was glad to see me. We reached the German support line, finding our men spread along to left and right.

Our sergeant divided us.

'You lot go along to the left as far as you can, you lot get along to the right.'

Our battalion was spread over about a hundred yards of the German trench. I was looking for machine-gunners. Coming to a Lewis gun I asked the number one man where the battalion section was.

'They are not here yet. We have to get settled in as owners of this blasted place before they come over.'

Dumping our loads we made our way back. It was safe going till we reached what had been the German front line.

Our officers appeared as we grouped together.

'There's nothing for it but to get up top. Just do the best you can.'

There was no safety now.

German machine-gunners got onto us from either flank, letting us know that our men held very little of their support line and even of the front line. We crawled, ran to shell holes, got our breath to run again, bullets zipping around us. A shrapnel shell burst above me. I turned a somersault, for some minutes I could not move.

Our own wire was only a few yards away, and having picked a track through it, I ran for my life. Out of a shell hole beside me Old Chris suddenly jumped up. He didn't run for the wire, he was man-handling another man, trying to get the wounded fellow onto his back. I helped. As Chris scrambled through our wire I wondered how his skinny legs could bear the double weight.

Our platoon officer and sergeant were waiting together to gather up the stragglers. When no more came, we were ordered to go back to VC Corner for our next load.

In the communication trench we met the battalion machine-gunners going in. Ray and I had a few minutes together, unhappy minutes. There was something about Ray's eyes that upset me. I remembered that night on the boat-deck of the *Caledonia* when we had suddenly ended our discussion of the holiday we'd have at home. Ray's eyes had a sad, sad look in them, and as we parted I felt terrible.

We loaded up again. It was dusk now, and crossing no-man's-land was easy. In the German support line I found Ray and his gun-team. Robbo was there, and we talked for a moment. I could see Robbo was worried. German fire was now coming from close on either side. Our battalion seemed stranded on only a short length of the German line. We knew this confirmed our fear that the whole operation had failed. The attack had reached its objective in the centre, but on either side had been repulsed.

'Come on, Twelve, back for another load.'

It was now near midnight. The German artillery was plastering our front line and also the area behind. Everyone had to keep to the communication trench and jamming was continuous.

We had loaded up for our next trip.

It was slow going to reach our own front line. Sappers had been trying to dig a trench across no-man's-land. We filed into it. It went only a few yards, and there we stuck. An officer got out of the sap.

'Come out of that sap,' he roared. 'We've got to cross above the ground.'

Then he dropped, riddled with machine-gun bullets. The same thing was repeated. Two officers had shown it was sudden death to get out of that sap. What was to be done?

Chris was near me. He said: 'And to think I enlisted to have a holiday.'

A few men had tried to crawl along out of the sap. None of them got far.

It was near dawn now, a hopeless dreadful dawn.

Then it came – the most heart-breaking order that troops in action ever get.

It came from the German trenches first, spreading across the area of battle.

'Get back! Every man for himself!'

Back at the corner where our loads were stacked, organising and sorting things out was going on. Our battalion's muster was being called a hundred yards along the road. Singly and in groups we collected about our allotted space. A half-hour went by, no more were coming.

Marched back to a farmyard billet, we threw ourselves onto the hay. Some slept. I could not. Ray, where was Ray, was all I could think of.

A field kitchen arrived with hot stew and tea. Then that awful muster parade after battle.

I was still dazed. I knew now it was no nightmare we had been through.

I found out the battalion machine-gunners were billeted in a barn across a field. Starting off for their barn I saw a man emerge from the billet. It looked like, yes, it was Robbo. We met in the middle of the field.

Robbo placed his hand on my shoulder. 'Thank God, you're OK. Have you heard anything – yet?'

His voice choked. Robbo was about six feet tall, a sergeant, well over thirty, a grand fellow, and tears were in his eyes.

'I've heard nothing, Robbo. But I feared something was going to happen to Ray.'

'It happened, Bert. Can you take it?'

'I've got to. Tell me, Robbo.'

'I guess when you were last over about midnight you could see how difficult our set-up was. The Germans were closing in on us from either side as well as in front. We were becoming like an island in the midst of the Germans, our position rapidly getting more hopeless. One lot of Germans were working along to get us cut off. Our officer – we all – knew what it meant.'

'"We've got to get back, and we've got to save our guns," he told us. "That group over there is our greatest danger. Will two men volunteer to take bombs and try to hold them back while we get away with the guns, then follow us?"'

A tear ran down Robbo's cheek.

'Ray and another kid volunteered. Scrambling out of the trench they made for the group of Germans. Ray's mate was killed almost at once. Then Ray was hit. He couldn't stand. He crawled closer to the Germans, threw his bombs into them, turned to come back. The men and the guns had got away. I waited. I helped Ray down into our possie. He was soaked with blood from several wounds. He was dying fast. I believe he was dead as I ran from dozens of Germans closing in.'

I walked dazedly back to my billet.

Alongside the barn was an orchard. Long green grass dotted with buttercups carpeted the ground. I sank into the soft sweet-smelling nature's mattress. All I could do was think, think, think. I tried to sleep. No, my brain kept on thinking. I heard footsteps brushing through the long grass.

'So there you are,' Chris said to me. 'There's nothing doing. I want you to drink this, then have a sleep. I'll come for you if necessary.'

He sat beside me while I drank a mess tin of hot tea well-laced with rum. It was my first drink of rum.

Making sure I finished it, Chris got up.

'Now you lie down and sleep.' And off he went.

I lay in the grass. I felt the hot drink surge through my body. It seemed to bring relaxation to my head and body, and I found myself crying. I didn't know when I had last cried and these great shaking sobs left me exhausted. I grew sleepy and, head on my arms, I went to sleep.

Chris came to call me, tea was on. I got up, slowly, like an old man would. I was calm, felt steady, but oh, so sad.

'You're quite a few years older than you were this time yesterday,' he said.

from *The Hell, the Humour and the Heartbreak – A Private's View of World War I* by Bert Bishop

'Over the Top' – a composite vista of the Western Front by war photographer Frank Hurley.

Air combat over the trenches

By October1916, the Australian Flying Corps (AFC) had a squadron of biplanes in France, on the Western Front. Australian pilots and observers flew across the devastated scenes of trench warfare machine gunning or dropping grenades by hand on enemy forces. Or, they might be engaged in deadly aerial combat with planes wearing the black crosses.

By January 1917, there were three AFC squadrons sending planes into the skies over the Western Front. Captain Harry Cobby was a fighter pilot who shot down 32 enemy aircraft in the skies over the trenches of the Western Front in 1918. With this number of 'kills', Cobby became the highest scoring pilot in the Australian Flying Corps.

On one patrol he encountered a famous German fighter group, as described by author Alec Hepburn:

High over the shell-churned morass that had once been the pleasant green fields and picturesque hamlets of rural France, ten tiny Sopwith 'Camel' fighter biplanes from No. 4 Squadron, Australian Flying Corps, buzzed about the sky like a swarm of angry bees, as they searched for enemy aircraft.

From the cramped cockpit of his colourful biplane Captain Arthur Henry (Harry) Cobby had a sweeping panorama of the vast trench network that criss-crossed the gas-stained ooze from horizon to horizon.

The young Australian flyer reflected just how different his war was from that of his fellow countrymen, slogging it out in the hellish conflict raging below. In the sky he was free of the sucking mud that covered everything, entombing the living as well as the dead. Best of all, he was above the sickening stench of death that hung like a foul cloud over the battlefield.

Yet the airman could not allow the wind that murmured gently in the rigging of his aircraft, or the warm March sun, to lull him into complacency. The horror of a terrible, fiery death was always close at hand.

The slipstream carried oil splatters from the whirling rotary engine back into his face. Cobby wiped his goggles clean with the silk stocking that trailed from the crown of his leather flying helmet like a knight's plume. He then scanned the cloud banks for signs of German aircraft and was not disappointed. Three bright red Albatros D-111s suddenly emerged from the cloud closely followed by two red Pfalz biplanes and a fourth Albatros painted in gaudy yellow and black.

Cobby was elated as he realised the German biplanes bore the flamboyant marking of the crack *staffel* commanded by the legendary 'Red Knight' – Baron Manfred von Richthofen. The Australians were about to cross swords with the boche elite. Rocking his fighter as a signal for the other 'Camels' to follow, Cobby made for the yellow and black Albatros, taking it completely by surprise. With its black Maltese Cross insignia squarely in his sights Cobby fired two short bursts that tore the wooden machine to pieces in a blinding flash of flame. The 'Camel' continued its charge right through the disintegrating German machine, entangling remnants of the flashy yellow fabric in its own wing wires.

These grisly souvenirs flapping like macabre banners in the slipstream, Cobby roared to the aid of his old friend Lieutenant Pflaum, who had dispatched a Pfalz in flames only to come under attack from two Albatros himself. Forcing his 'Camel' up on one wing Cobby pivoted the machine on its horizontal axis, coming down behind a very startled enemy. Once again he fired from point-blank range, setting the bright red German fighter on fire.

As it fell away under a shroud of black smoke Cobby leaned from the cockpit and touched his helmet in a final salute to his downed foe. The doomed aircraft was more than just a burning machine to the Australian pilot – it was also the funeral pyre of an airman much like himself. Perhaps in the next aerial duel he fought it would be his turn to die in the same manner.

The rapid destruction of their comrades was enough for the other Germans, who lost another aircraft as they fled for the safety of their own lines.

With the sky clear of enemy aircraft again, the Australian fighters re-formed and headed back to base to celebrate their victory.

from *True Australian War Tales* by Alec Hepburn

Front-line nurses

An Australian nursing sister working in a casualty clearing station gives a picture of the heartbreak, danger and tragedy endured by the nurses as they struggled to save the lives of the thousands of casualties pouring into the Australian CCSs from the fighting on the Somme.

During the battles of the Somme in the summer and autumn of 1916 the casualty clearing stations geared up to cope with the influx of casualties. The men were collected by bearers and brought first to a regimental medical officer (MO) for first aid then sent on to a field ambulance unit, and on a further few miles behind the lines to a CCS.

The Australian CCSs were attached to the Imperial Medical Service and no. 1 and no. 2 ACCSs were retained in the Ypres sector during 1916. No. 3 worked at Gezaincourt taking casualties from the Somme fighting in the last three months of the year.

No. 32 BCCS had Australian nurses attached under Sister K. Laurd who gave an informative sketch of work at an advanced unit. In May 1916, just before the Somme began, she wrote of fighting at Vimy Ridge.

Monday, 22 May 1916: A black day. Intense German bombardment and they occupied our front trenches. Our desperate attempts to regain them have filled all the CCSs and all the worst cases have come to us as we are now acting as an advanced unit. Just finished in the theatre . . . midnight. So far six have died, and more will die tonight. Still they are bringing them in. They are all being angels of patience. One who died today said that he was afraid he was a great trouble! The sad ward is very sad still. It is packed here tonight. I have been working mostly in a ghastly hut full of head cases falling off their stretchers. Two orderlies, snatches of the MO and I have ramped in and out all day when we could get away from the abdominal ward. The other sisters ramp in theirs and we meet for snatchy meals at intervals. We had a cup of tea out of a glass jampot this afternoon from the cookhouse. Just a hasty lap each (from the same jampot). Between 9 and 10pm we handed over to the night staff and lingered over supper at the billet and told each other all the funny and brave things of the day. Some of the wounds are crawling with maggots. If a man is left out without a field dressing, flies settle on the wounds and lay eggs. Many of the men are stuck fast to their stretchers. Blood is like glue if you leave it long enough. They need an anaesthetic before you can try and unstick them.'

Thursday, 25 May 1916: 'The train cleared an enormous number today, leaving us all the heads, chests and abdominals. So we still have our hands full and are getting a bit tired. It is raining cats and dogs so their field dressings will be full of wet mud.'

Ascension Day Eve: 'Jack is dying tonight, paralysed from a wound in the spine. He doesn't know, and goes on making polite little jokes and thanking us and apologising till we could all cry. The train has now not cleared for a week and we are getting heaped up. We have got to take the top of this Vimy Ridge.'

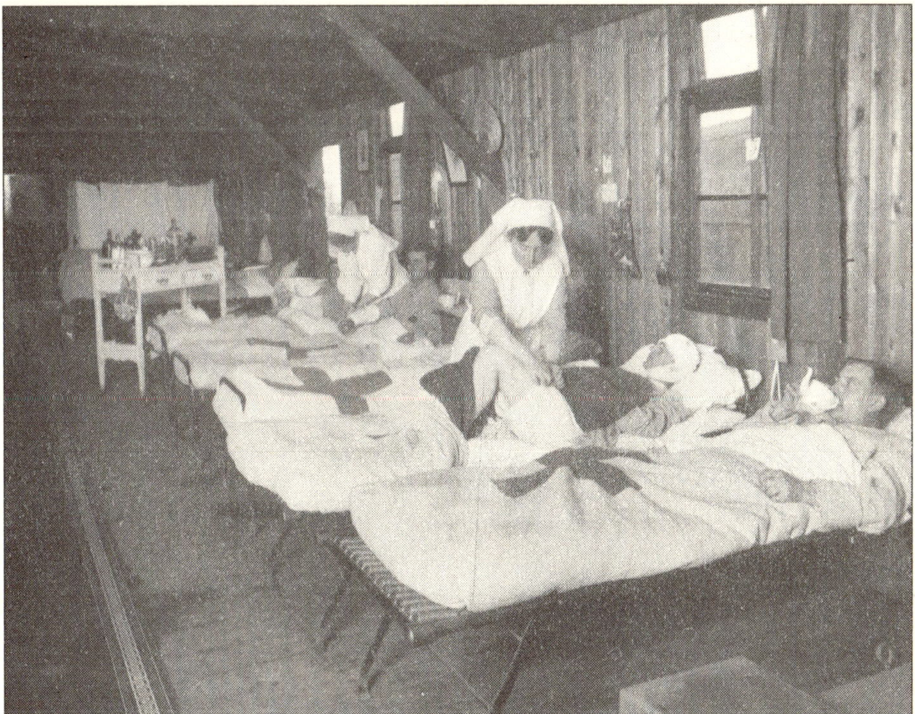

A casualty clearing station.

Friday, 2 June 1916: 'When I came on duty this morning the ward was full of wrecks. It has been a ghastly day. The train came in the afternoon and all who could possibly get to Base alive were packed up and put on. It must have been a bad load.'

Sister Luard was well aware of the difficulties confronting the sisters working on the ambulance trains: 'There have been the most appalling shell wounds I have ever seen this time. How they get here alive I don't know.'

Life at the frontline hospital had its lighter moments.

'The CO sent us off in his car to the top of the ridge and we were taken to see a battery in action. We were shown a beautiful shining gun with a HE [high-explosive] shell all ready in the breech. The sweating shirt-sleeved gunners were frightfully proud to show it off to us. They had a lot of flowers in their dugout, gathered from a ruined garden, and hideously arranged in jam tins. Facetious messages were chalked on the shells.'

from *Nightingales in the Mud: The Digger Sisters of the Great War 1914–1918*
by Marianne Barker

Letters home from the Western Front

Letters received in Australia from soldiers at the front revealed their longing for home; their misery; and, all too often, their premonition of the coming battle. The first of these three letters was written from France in August 1918 to the man's wife and son back home. Within hours the writer would be dead:

Dearest Beat and Bill,

Just a line. You must be prepared for the worst to happen any day. It is no use trying to hide things. I am in terrible agony.

Had I been brought in at once I had a hope. But now gas gangrene has set in and it is so bad that the doctor could not save it by taking it off as it had gone too far and the only hope is that the salts they have put on may drain the gangrene out. Otherwise there is no hope . . .

I got two machine-gun bullets in the thigh, another glanced off by my water bottle and another by the periscope I had in my pocket. You will see that they send my things home.

It was during the operations around Mouquet Farm . . . I was in the thick of the attack on Pozieres as I had just about done my duty.

Even if I get over it I will never go back to the war as they have taken pounds of flesh out of my buttock. My word they look after us well here. I am in the officers ward and can get anything I want to eat or drink but I just drink all day changing the drinks as I take a fancy.

The stretcher bearers could not get the wounded out any way than over the top and across the open. They had to carry me four miles with a man waving a red cross flag in front and the Germans did not open fire on us.

Well, dearest, I have had a rest. The pain is getting worse and worse. I am very sorry, dear, but still you will be well provided for. I am easy on that score.

So cheer up, dear. I could write on a lot but I am nearly unconscious. Give my love to Dear Bill and yourself. Do take care of yourself and him.

Your loving husband,
Bert.

from Lieutenant H.W. Crowle, 10th Battalion

A 1918 reinforcement, a fruiterer from Hurlstone Park in Sydney, reported on the pleasure of a successful raid:

We advanced into no-man's-land in the dark as stealthy as Red Indians and took up positions in shell holes quite close to the Hun trenches.

Then our artillery opened into the Germans and belted Hell and blazes into them. We sneaked up under the barrage and it was lovely, shells bursting and lights shooting all over the sky.

All of a sudden it lifted back a couple of hundred yards and away we charged yelling like devils right into his trenches.

Fritzey bolted and we after him. I was directly after my officer and a couple of the Germans dodged into a dugout. We fed them on bombs, etc. and on to the next.

Gee you should have been in the fun. Our boys got busy with bayonets, bombs and rifle fire.

We first bombed the dugout and finished off a couple and took a couple prisoners.

Then we climbed into it and got all the mail and so on. I got a bonzer coat and also a Fritz rifle.

It's good fun and I hope to have a bit more of the raiding stunt. It will do me . . . I really enjoyed it.

from Signaller G.H. Molesworth, 35th Battalion

Another Sydney man, this time a cashier from inner-city Glebe, was far from enthused by his experience in France. The 25-year-old would be killed in action less than three months after writing the following to his brother:

All my pals I came over with are gone. But seven out of 150 remain. It's simply scientific murder, not war at all.

I keep smiling but I tell you it takes some doing.

The premonition I had when leaving Sydney that I would never see home again still hangs about me.

One would be unnatural to go through uninjured. If I get out of it with a leg and arm off I'll be perfectly satisfied.

So you will understand what it is like . . . don't get married till after the war.

from Private E.O. Neaves, 20th Battalion

Finally, a letter that fully captures the horror of the Western Front, and war in general:

We lay down terror-stricken along a bank. The shelling was awful . . . we eventually found our way to the right spot out in no-man's-land. Our leader was shot before we arrived and the strain had sent two other officers mad. I and another new officer took charge and dug a trench. We were shot at all the time . . . the wounded and killed had to be thrown to one side. I refused to let any sound man help a wounded man; the sound man had to dig . . . we dug on and finished amid a tornado of bursting shells. I was buried with dead and dying. The ground was covered with bodies in all stages of decay and mutilation and I would, after struggling from the earth, pick up a body by me to try to lift him out with me and find him a decayed corpse . . . I went up again the next night and stayed there. We were shelled to hell ceaselessly. X went mad and disappeared . . . there remained nothing but a charred mass of debris with bricks, stones, girders and bodies pounded to nothing . . . we are lousy, stinking, unshaven, sleepless . . . I have one puttee, a dead man's helmet, another dead man's protector, a dead man's bayonet. My tunic is rotten with other men's blood and partly splattered with a comrade's brains . . .

from Lieutenant J.A. Raws, 23rd Battalion

The Australian Light Horse – Victory in the Desert

The Australian Light Horse – Victory in the Desert

The Australian Light Horse, all experienced horsemen, were mounted infantry who usually dismounted to fight. At Gallipoli, it was as infantry that they had their first encounters with the Turks. The 8th and 10th Light Horse regiments had been slaughtered at the Nek as they bravely charged the Turkish machine guns. After the evacuation from Gallipoli they returned to Egypt in December 1915, and once again assumed the role of mounted troops equipped with rifle and bayonet. Some of the Anzacs formed the Imperial Camel Corps Brigade, which fought alongside the Light Horse.

The Light Horse remained in the Middle East to defend the Suez Canal. When the Turks attacked at Romani on 4 August 1916, the British and Australian forces under the supreme command of General Archibald Murray achieved an overwhelming victory. Murray's army had suffered only 1130 casualties, while the Turks had lost 9200 men, killed, wounded or taken prisoner. It was the horsemanship and fighting qualities of the Australian Light Horse that won the admiration of the British with whom they fought. Murray said of them, 'These Anzac troops are the keystone of the defence of Egypt.'

The Light Horse now spearheaded the British advance across the Sinai desert, and by February 1917 the Allied forces had driven the Turks out of the area. General Murray's next objective was to capture the town of Gaza, which blocked the way to Palestine. The two attacks on Gaza that took place in March and April cost the Allies nearly 10,000 casualties. Gaza remained impregnable. As a result of these defeats, Murray was replaced by

General Edmund Allenby. Command of the Desert Mounted Corps was given to Lieutenant General Harry Chauvel, who became the first Australian to gain command at the corps level.

Allenby, a cavalry man, understood the importance of speed and surprise. A plan was conceived to take Beersheeba and then attack Gaza from the rear. On 31 October 1917, the Light Horse achieved legendary status when it took part in the last great cavalry charge and seized Beersheeba and its seventeen vital wells. Mounted on their much-loved Walers, the troopers of the 4th and 12th regiments thundered across five kilometres of open ground through rifle, machine-gun and artillery fire until they leaped over the Turkish trenches and dismounted to engage in frenzied hand-to-hand fighting with the defenders. Trooper Fowler of the 12th Regiment commented: 'The machine-gun and rifle fire became intense. As we came in closer to the trenches, some of the Turks must have forgotten to change the sights on their rifles as the bullets went overhead.' Because of the speed of the attack, only two of the freshwater wells were able to be detonated by the enemy. The other wells containing 400,000 litres of water remained intact to quench the thirst of the troops and the horses. Beersheeba had fallen for the loss of only 67 casualties. One week later on 6 November, Gaza was also in Allied hands. Jerusalem lay ahead.

On 12 December, under attack from the Allies, the Turks withdrew from Jerusalem. Soon afterwards, General Allenby made his dramatic entrance on foot. Jericho fell two months later and on 1 October 1918, when the 3rd Australian Light Horse entered Damascus, Turkish resistance disintegrated. After the Light Horse had reached Aleppo in Syria on 26 October, their 'Great Ride' finally came to an end – Turkey had capitulated. Allenby informed Chauvel that the Light Horse had participated in 'the greatest cavalry feat the world has ever known'.

The Walers that the troopers rode made a considerable contribution to the success of the Great Ride of the Light Horse. They were hardy stock-horses that had been bred in New South Wales, from where they derived their name. One English officer said of them, 'Their record in this war places them far above the cavalry horses of any other nation.' Sadly, of the 160,000 Walers sent overseas, only one was allowed to return to Australia.

The Australian mounted troops had shown the world beyond any doubt that they were resourceful, resilient and courageous. They had overcome the intense heat, a lack of water, a harsh terrain and an enemy they respected, in the campaigns in the Sinai desert, Palestine and Syria.

Trooper and horse

The Turkish snipers made a practice of shooting at the horses as well as the troopers to destroy the Light Horse as a mobile fighting unit.

The Waler, which was part thoroughbred and part draught horse, was capable of great endurance, speed and reliability. In the passage that follows, Ion Idriess describes the close relationship between horse and master.

The battle of Romani was touch and go. It finally hinged on the last few hours of endurance. Our horses gave that endurance. They were still on their feet when the Turkish army faded into utter exhaustion. The Australian and New Zealand walers won the battle of Romani and by saving the Suez Canal saved Egypt.

Then commenced the well organised and fighting retreat of the Turks, choosing their own ground to fight their stubborn rearguard battles at Katia, Oghratina, Bir-el-Abd, Mazar, until at last they faded back to the redoubts of Magdhaba and Rafa, on the borders of Palestine.

To us, those were nightmare days and nights, but worse for our horses. The ride throughout the night, the attack at dawn, the stubborn resistance through hell's own heat, the blistering misery of thirst, the long ride back next night because we must have water! Water! Water!

Swaying in the saddles, riding by the stars, the long black columns winding through the ghostly sandhills. The horses with bowed heads doggedly pressed on, heartened by the murmuring of their thousands of hooves, by the great breath of the tight packed columns, by the smell of sweat and humanity, by the reassuring feel of the riders. Halting instantly to the Voice, you could hear them sigh. Flopping down to the sand as the riders dismounted, lying motionless in the weariness of utter exhaustion.

Many a time have I dropped to my knees and used my old horse as a pillow, his body for warmth during that heavenly moment of time, that ten minutes rest each hour. Then the horses would hear the Voice again. We would stumble to our feet. They too would stumble to theirs and the columns were on the move again, asleep in the saddles, the horses doggedly ploughing on, on, on.

From the Canal to the borders of Palestine, two hundred miles across terrible desert, our heavily laden horses more than we, drove the Turks out of Sinai.

None of us living can forget El Arish. Riding by night, subconsciously puzzling that something was missing, and the murmuring sigh of the horse's hooves. Something had taken its place, almost a low rumbling. My old horse stumbled, giving me a shock. He had not stumbled for, it seemed, years and years. Then the horses were suddenly moving quicker with a strange excited sprightliness. My horse stumbled again; other horses were stumbling. Puzzled I stared down, the ground seemed black. Then a murmur of astonishment came whispering down the column, solid ground! For the first time in over two years our horses were again treading solid earth.

It was after Magdhaba, when many troops were four days and nights in the saddle or fighting without rest, and the equally bitter Radia battle, that our horses went mad. We felt it just before dawn. A quickening, a pricking of ears and nostrils, a stretching out of necks, then muzzles jerking to the ground. Again and again and again! Shivering with some strange excitement, for the first time we could remember our horses were breaking line, jerking our arms as they reached to the ground. For quite a time we could hardly believe that they were eating, excited voices were murmuring, 'There's grass on the ground.' Then came a beautiful dawn bringing madness to the horses for as far as the eye could see was a sea of green barley. Horses became almost uncontrollable, a ripple of laughing delight came down the column, a lark rose to sing sweetly high in the sky, excited shouts as the men pointed out the scarlet poppies, the lovely wild flowers of Palestine.

Our horses simply went crazy.

In the Palestinian plain we gradually grew into a great army that stretched right across Palestine from Gaza to Beersheeba. The spearhead of this host was Forty Thousand Horse, a wonderful sight when seen from the hills when on the warpath, clouds of horsemen as far as the eye could see. Other clouds above them growing from the lazy puffs of shrapnel and the ugly brownish-black spoutings of the high explosive. At night the horizon was a vivid lighting of the guns.

But always the horses pressed on, against deep wadis, unbroken plains, rocky hills, trenches, pits, redoubts, fortresses and fortified towns. Saddles were emptied, horses crashed to the dust, but always they went on. We knew at times they felt fear as we did, but always they went on, even when at perfect liberty to turn around and gallop back from hell. We all have seen a riderless horses lead the charge hell for leather. How often have we galloped with the riderless horses of our mates beside us!

My old horse was once wounded in the early morning. He gave no sign throughout a furious day of galloping, heat and thirst. It was only at sundown that I noticed the congealed blood under the saddlecloth. I have seen men hard pressed not to weep when their horses were killed. It was a blow when a horse was wounded or, at long last, led back to the sick lines. But within a month or so the horse would be back fresh and eager as our wounded men returned. The meeting of the horse and the friend was a reunion of true mates.

Though the big battles were frightening to the horses, it was the snipers they feared most, just as we were unnerved by them. At times the regiment would be under partial cover behind a ridge or village awaiting the order to gallop into line. A sniper would crawl around our flank, settle himself down, and then proceed to systematically shoot the horses. They *knew* that distant crack! Then the hammer blow and the squeal as a stricken horse reared and crashed down. The close smell of blood, the tense atmosphere was all absorbed by the horses. I have seen men go berserk with rage as we helplessly waited there while a distant sniper went Crack! Crack! Crack! at the horses.

from *Stout Hearts That Never Failed* by Ion Idriess

Walers and troopers on parade before departure to Egypt.

Beersheeba – The last great cavalry charge

In the Judean desert in October 1917, failure to capture the Beersheeba wells would have meant death to the horses of the Light Horse. In the last great cavalry charge, the Light Horse took Beersheeba capturing 700 Turks and gaining control of the vital water reservoirs before the enemy could detonate them. Author Frank Dalby Davison documents the charge:

The ray of the setting sun was on their fronts; a coppery glow, diffused through the dry red mist of the battlefield. They advanced.

The pace, at first, was a smart trot, with an eye to the careful alignment of the ranks. The sound of their hooves and the rise and fall of the men in the saddles were in brisk staccato.

The pace quickened to a canter, then to a gallop. The men sat firm in their seats. Sound and movement were in swinging rhythm. They had no swords, but rose with rifle and fixed bayonet balanced across the thigh; others with rifle slung across the back; bare bayonet gripped in the hand.

The Turk had seen them, and laid his guns. His shells began to burst among them. Each deafening crash drowned for a moment the roar of hooves, and seemed to defy them; but they swept on; line after line, unheeding as a shore-bound wave. Spurts of flame shot up, gapping their ranks. A long striding bay was the first to go down. He blundered, as if the hounds of death had laid him by the heels. His was a long, lurching, staggering fall; for the will to race on died hard in him. The weaving hooves of his mates swept by and over him. A sheet of flame leaped up, and before it a chestnut reared with a gaping chest and fell backward, throwing his rider from him.

The shelling increased in intensity. The ranks were thinning. Where men had ridden knee against knee they rode now with a space between them. Men dropped from their saddles and their riderless horses galloped on, shoulder by shoulder with the rest.

The pace quickened as horse laboured with horse to gain the lead, and horse laboured to keep stride by stride with his neighbour. Nostrils reddened, eyes widened, jaws gaped, and tossing heads flung spume to the air. Not one of the horses, alone, could have stood the pace and weight for half the distance; but each, like his rider, was possessed of something beyond himself.

They poured across the plain like a living flood, leaving a wide track littered with their fallen. They shook the ground as they thundered over it. The sound of their hooves was like an accelerating roll of many drums. It rose and fell and stayed, filling the space between earth and sky.

Among the men there passed a sudden shout of amazement and derision. The shells no longer fell among them, but on the ground behind. The enemy could not keep his guns on the fast-moving target!

The distance was growing short, now. They would soon be in the zone of rifle and machine-gun fire.

A ghostly whistling passed between them. A rider, sitting erect, went limp, and toppled from the saddle as if he had fallen asleep. Another and another disappeared among the welter of hooves. Horses were dropping. Bullets ricochetted and flew with wounded scream across the ranks.

The troopers could now see the men who were firing at them – head and shoulders above the trenches, right elbows pumping cartridges into rifles; red flame jetting from a traversing machine-gun.

Again that sudden surprising emergence into a deathless zone. The nerves of the enemy riflemen had failed them. They had forgotten to lower their sights! The bullets were whistling harmlessly overhead.

In the last hundred yards it seemed to the riders not that they raced to the trenches, but that the trenches were drawn to them.

There were brown clad figures that leaped from cover and ran toward the town, their arms abandoned. There were men in a clumsy grey cloth who wrestled frantically with a jammed machine-gun until the hooves were on them.

The trenches yawned abruptly; almost before the horses saw them. There was a blundering fall or two, a wrenched and sudden leaping. For the riders, looking down, there was a swift vision of men crouched fearfully in the trench bottom, and of others stabbing upward with the bayonet. Then came the staggering scramble across the parados and the race for the next trench line.

As the charging riders massed within the defences there was a minute of seeming confusion. Unable to progress, men leaped to the ground and jumped into the trenches. There were shouts in strange tongues and the clash of hand-to-hand fighting. Horses, abandoned, stood blown and sweating, or ran to and fro in alarm. Then out of the chaos came order.

The centre had gone clear across the defence. Men and horses were streaming in a packed wedge across the open ground.

From within the town sounded heavy explosion as the enemy fired his dumps.

On a hilltop stood a group of men with red-tabbed shoulders and glossy field-boots. They were all quite motionless. Each had field-glasses trained on the distant scene. The sun was gone; but the failing light was sufficient to reveal the last moments of the great charge. They saw men and horses gallop up to the buildings of the town and disappear between them.

One by one the fieldglasses came down and a murmur ran through the little group, vibrant with mirth and feeling of men who have seen cavalry sweep forward to achieve an apparent miracle.

The general was the last to lower his glasses. He said nothing but turned toward the plain. The empurpled twilight was filled with a muttering of hooves and a rumbling of wheels as brigades and batteries raced to fill the widening gap. He would rest his horses tonight, but tomorrow they must press forward to get behind Gaza and grip the enemy in his hinderparts. Waterless country must be crossed. He had need to plan anew. There was little time for jubilation in the mind that must be ever thinking forwardly. But he was satisfied. He knew now that the Turkish nerves were not proof against resolute horsemen.

The day was gone. The mood looked down on the still and silent field. In the town men laboured. The smell of water, cold and sweet was released on the dusty air. Standing weary and patient, out among the ridges, the horses smelled it, and a whinny ran from line to line.

Throughout the night the streets of the town were loud with the clatter of hooves walking. Brigade after brigade, the horses were led in, light horse and gunner, to drink with slackened girths and bitless mouths at the wells of Beersheeba.

from *The Wells of Beersheeba* by Frank Dalby Davison

Turkish retreat

After the capture of Beersheeba, the Turkish army began its retreat into Palestine and Syria. It was closely pursued by the Light Horse and Allied infantry. The following scene shows the mobility and independence of the Light Horse against a strong Turkish adversary.

Suddenly Major Bolingbroke shouted to Captain Fitzpatrick:

'The guns are escaping!'

Instantly the squadron was in the saddle, with a clatter of hooves we were plunging up over the skyline, then away. It was a wild gallop, up hills, down hills – leaping gullies – taking sun-cracked crevices in our stride – seeing in plain view two miles away the guns toiling along a road. Some of the boys whipped off their hats and laughingly smacked their neddies' rumps, for we hated using spurs on the poor thirsty beggars.

How different to yesterday! The Turks then were securely sheltered with battalions behind them, we were one hundred men in the open. Now both sides were in the open. We could see the infantry escort far ahead of the guns, hurrying their machine-guns away.

Nearer we galloped, past boxes of shell ammunition thrown hastily from the wagons – the gunners were throwing off more ammunition, thrashing their poor little teams. Along that road, a column had retreated in haste the night before. There lay hundreds of infantry packs, gas-masks, gear, rifles, baggage, bayonets all littered along the roadside.

One of the guns halted in desperation and swerved the ugly muzzle straight at us. But the squadron dug in the spurs, stood in the stirrups, waved bayonets, and roared! It was enough! The artillerymen lost their heads, a mounted officer struck in mad exasperation, then the officers leaned over their horses' necks and galloped off along the road, the artillerymen running for their lives. The squadron roared laughing. As we galloped past the first gun I saw a blood-stained Turk lying beside it.

No shells screeched from the guns' black muzzles now. Squat, solid brutes they looked, glumly silent.

We swung off our saddles, slung the reins to the horse-holders, ran out in front and knelt down: *crack-crack-crack-crack-crack-crack – rut-tut-tut-tuttuttuttuttuttut* – and the panting artillerymen must have coughed up their very hearts, for by Jove they ran until they fell! How great it was – spurts of dust kicking around their desperately moving legs. They had sweated to give us hell yesterday. But what an incomparable difference in the aim of the Light Horse trooper! The only artillerymen who escaped were those who threw up their arms, and a flying group who leapt exhausted into a ravine; they lay there panting when we galloped up.

The regiment was coming away behind with the 6th and 7th regiments spread on either hand, a long line of the dreaded 'Felt Hats'. Away behind again as a dust-storm entering Palestine thundered the Anzac ten thousand. The sky was azure blue, glinting on buzzing machine – shrapnel-puffs dissolved in lazy threads of gossamer. The irrepressible lark trilled high up, shells screamed far over the plain, red earth spouted skywards. The squadron galloped down the tell-tale road littered with the wreckage of an army. That was a great gallop; in the middle of it we plunged down into a deep wadi through a pool of clear water! How longingly our horses thrust down eager mouths! It hurt us more to force them to splash through. Then up over a low rise and a canter across bare cultivation land, to race down into a valley and suddenly gallop into dustless country.

On a hill was a commanding stone house, squat and square, built just below it a garden of fruit-trees and among them a huge stone well with a wooden water-wheel and a cement tank. The enemy were in great force just ahead – we had far outstripped the brigade – we pulled up and the horses rushed the well. The conveniences made watering quick and easy.

Bang-whee-eee-eezz-crash! and shrapnel pellets lashed the orchard-trees. But the Turkish guns could not stop us watering. Then we trotted off to the shelter of a little white hill close by. A shell burst above the house roof – out scurried the Arabs like frightened rats making for the shelter of the hills. Soon, a squadron of the 7th cantered up and away we went reinforced and quick and lively were greeted by machine-gun and rifle fire. Cantering over a ridge we gazed at a long line of Turkish infantry advancing steadily towards us.

'Dismount for Ac-tion!'

We lined the ridge – the Turks were almost on us, their numbers rapidly increasing. We simply stood and fired as fast as we could work our rifle bolts – the Hotchkiss guns shrilling one long, hot scream. Suddenly a large body of Turks appeared encircling our right – hails of bullets came from two directions – we sprang on our horses only

Palestine, April 1918: the left flank outpost of the 5th Australian Light Horse on alert at Ghoraniyeh bridgehead.

when we could plainly see the savage eyes of the leading Turks. What a gallop! Over gently sloping ground – not a leaf of cover – ten times our number furiously blazing at us. For more than a mile those vicious pests whizzed past ricochetting off the ground, flipping off a man's hat, thudding through a bandolier. How the old neddies legged it out! I began to think we would never get out of range of those high-powered Turkish rifles. At last we swerved in behind a hill, hurriedly picked our possies and waited for the Turks to come on again. They came, steadily, irresistibly. We blazed at them – we fired and fired at the splendid targets marching steadily on. They got right to the foot of the hill, their thinning rank came steadily on but other ranks were hurrying past our left and right; we even heard the thump of their feet as suddenly they doubled in on us; so close they got we saw their panting mouths as they howled when we leapt up for the saddles and away. It was a hell-for-leather go, bending over the neddies' necks, laughing with the wind in our teeth. We dismounted behind another little hill a half-mile farther back and running up near the skyline lay down and waited again, filling our emptying bandoliers with the spare bandoliers collared around the horses' necks. The Turks came steadily on – fine-looking chaps in their blue-grey uniforms. They must have been sweating hot though. We blazed into them until our rifle-bolts were blistering hot, before we rushed the horses and were away again.

And so we fought until midday, when the brigade came cantering up. That little fight was splendidly managed. The two squadrons had got into a very tight corner, we fought and retired, to fight again with very little loss to ourselves and as was proved afterwards we had seriously delayed a body of reinforcements whose strength was twelve to our one. The brigade took up a position along the rugged banks of the Wadi Hesi. The Turks halted, our glasses showed they were awaiting strong reinforcements hurrying up behind. In the midst of the excitement came news that Gaza had fallen and that the Turkish Main Army was now cut in two and in full retreat, putting up desperate rear- and flank-guard battles to allow their retreating forces a change to pour down the Ramleh, Jaffa, and Jerusalem roads. It was stirring news.

from *The Desert Column* by Ion Idriess

The Rats of Tobruk

The Rats of Tobruk

> *'The war in Africa is something different. It is simply a question of man against man, eye to eye, blow for blow. Were the battle not so brutal, one could compare it with the romantic idea of jousting among knights.'*
>
> From the diary of a German tank commander

World War II began on the back of German ambitions and the enemy was revealed as being power-hungry, ruthless and almost unbeatable. Using the combat technique soon to be known world-wide as the Blitzkrieg, the Germans swept into Poland, Norway and Western Europe halting only when they got to France, where British troops bravely resisted at Dunkirk. Before the Russian push, Hitler's ambitions were turned towards North Africa, Cairo and the Suez Canal, with an aim to being able to link up with the Japanese forces coming from the East.

In 1940, Hitler began to consider supporting Italian forces in North Africa. The ports of the southern Mediterranean assumed great importance in this kind of strategic planning and Tobruk stood out as a superbly equipped seaport.

General Erwin Rommel was ordered by Hitler to conduct a limited offensive (the Führer was preparing to use all available troops for an invasion of Russia) to aid the Italians, who were fighting and losing ground to the British desert army under the command of General Archibald.

As commander of the Afrika Korps as well as the Italian forces there, Rommel landed at Tripoli in February 1941. He was a panzer expert and was determined to capture Tobruk as a prelude to the seizure of the Suez Canal, the lifeline of the British Empire. Because of his cunning tactics, he soon earned himself the title 'the Desert Fox'.

Rommel's emphasis was on speed and power as panzers, troops and aircraft smashed through all British battlelines to reach the outer defences of Tobruk. This port could channel supplies and reinforcements to the desert battlefields and it was important for the Allies to resist its capture with all their power. Wavell appointed an Australian, Major General Leslie Morshead as the defender of Tobruk, with Major General John Lavarack as overall commander.

Morshead was ordered to hold Tobruk for at least two months. Under his command, there were some 14,000 Australian combat troops of the 9th Division and British soldiers who were mostly anti-aircraft and anti-tank gunners. Guns captured from the Italians and often used against them were called 'bush artillery' by the Australians.

'There'll be no Dunkirk here,' Morshead stated, referring to the routing the Allies had suffered in northern France at the hands of the Germans. 'There is to be no surrender and no retreat.' The commander's aggressive battle tactics would soon see him known to his troops as 'Ming the Merciless'.

German propaganda mocked the Australian effort and a broadcast by a renegade Irishman, Lord Haw Haw, described the Australians as rats caught in a trap. The 9th Division adopted the name 'the Rats of Tobruk' with pride.

By 11 April 1941, the Afrika Korps confronted the port city's defences with what seemed like overwhelming power and the reputation of having never lost a battle. Surrender terms were offered to the defenders but were refused. All through April and for months afterwards, Rommel's forces attacked with the aim of breaking through the various fortified 'rings' of the garrison that constituted its defence in depth. Tobruk was bombed and strafed every day. However, anti-tank ditches, mines, artillery action and stealthy hit-and-run night attacks by Australian patrols imposed heavy losses on the enemy in terms of troops killed or captured and tanks destroyed. Tobruk's defences held despite enemy attacks, the heat, the flies, the disease, the dust storms and the lack of water. Rommel himself was impressed by the spirit of the defenders, judging by his description of the 9th Division

A patrol leaving the defensive perimeter of Tobruk on a day-time patrol.

as 'immensely big and powerful men, who without question represented an élite formation of the British Empire'. The siege would result in the first Victoria Cross awarded to an Australian in this war – Corporal Jack Edmonson, on 13 April.

Australian involvement here lasted for nine months until the diggers were withdrawn to face the Japanese threat in New Guinea. During their tour of duty in Tobruk they had, against the odds, confronted and defeated a German army. It was the first time the Germans had suffered a defeat in World War II. Like the Anzacs of Gallipoli fame, the Rats of Tobruk had become another set of fabulous Australian heroes.

'Come on boys, up and at 'em!'

During the siege of Tobruk, Australian combat troops risked their lives on hit-and-run raids into enemy positions. The following extract describes a raid in which the ferocity and ruthlessness of the hand-to-hand fighting in the desert is revealed to the reader.

Here is the account by Sergeant R.A. Patrick, an ex-clerk from a country store, of a raid led by his company commander, Captain F.L. Bode, a Queensland amateur boxer:

> About 3000 yards out we came to the enemy minefield a little to the west of the post we were going for. We crawled through that and then moved round till we were behind the post. Still crawling, we got over the low trip-wire behind it and were within forty yards of the post, when the Ities sent up a flare and opened with a Breda. We went down flat.
>
> The firing stopped and Captain Bode said, 'Come on boys, up and at 'em!' We charged. Another flame went up behind us and the Ities must have seen us silhouetted against its light. They swung four machine-guns straight on to us and a volley of hand grenades burst in our path. For a few seconds the dust and flash blinded us, but we went on. In the confusion I ran past the machine-gun pit that I was going for, and a hand grenade – one of the useless Itie money-box type – hit my tin hat. The explosion knocked me down but it didn't hurt me. As I lay there, the fight was going on all around, and I could hear Ities shouting and screaming and our tommy guns firing and grenades bursting.
>
> I rolled over and pitched two grenades into the nearest trench and made a dash for the end machine-gun post. I jumped into the pit on top of three Italians, and bayoneted two before my bayonet snapped. I got the third with my revolver as he made for a dugout where there were at least two other men. I let them have most of my magazine. Another Italian jumped into the pit and I shot him too. He didn't have any papers so I took his shoulder-badges, jumped up and went for my life.
>
> I cleared the concertina wire in front of the post, but caught my foot in a trip-wire. Luckily it brought me down, for just then a machine-gun burst got the chap next to me. I wriggled

> over to him, but he was so badly hit I couldn't do anything to help. I took his last two grenades; crawled out through the booby-traps and then threw one grenade at a machine-gun that was still firing. As this burst, I made a dash for it, and a hundred yards out reached a shell-hole. I waited till it was all quiet again, and then came back.

Bode came out of the attack, twice wounded and nearly blinded, singing the old army song, 'My eyes are dim I cannot see . . .' After being wounded first and running out of ammunition, he had caught two Italians in a trench and was about to drag them out by the scruff of the neck when a grenade burst in front of him, so he 'banged their heads together and threw 'em back'. Reports of Australian aggressiveness in defence were changed by Axis propaganda to 'attempting to break out'.

from *Anzac* by John Vader

Here come the panzers

Frank Harrison was one of the 14,000 Australians at the siege of Tobruk. Later, as a veteran of 'the longest siege in British military history', he would relive the memory of his experiences facing the panzers.

First he describes the desert dawn and the atmosphere among the waiting, watchful troops on a May morning when the Germans attacked and broke through Tobruk's perimeter. Tense reports came in from various locations as the attack gained momentum. Schorm was a German officer who kept a diary revealing the belief of the Afrika Korps that victory would soon be theirs – until the panzer attack suddenly failed.

There is no cold like the cold of a desert dawn. It is a long, slow strangulation of sinew, blood and bone. It seeps into your bedroll more silently than a secret lover, but its squeezing of your tissues is without love. Unconscious, deep in sleep, you draw up your knees but they continue to ache, you curl into foetal form and the chill curls with you, so that you dream cold and come awake cold – into cold. You get up and hug whatever you have in the way of covering around and over you. You see monstrous shapes moving slowly in the strange, suffused light and hear muttered cursing, and you begin to see the flickering flames of sand burning inside a score of cans. On such mornings in those days, more tea was brewed than in the whole of a Lancashire day. But on May Day morning in 1941 there were no flickering flames to hasten the dawn at Ras El Medauur. German and Italian, Australian and Briton peered into the grey mush and shivered, and not only from the cold. Generals do not choose to make their attacks at dawn simply because of its deceptive visibility. They do so because men of war discovered long ago that this is the time when man is most susceptible to the terrors of his imagination.

This day's dawn had a trick of its own to play on the peering antagonists. The heavy ground mist had fused with the dust raised by the night's barrages, so that when darkness withdrew beyond Gazala the mush remained, a curtain between the eyes and the enemy. Who would see whom first? The answer might well become a final knowledge. Not for a second did the peering eyes slacken.

At 0715 hrs the curtain was raised and all was revealed. Captain Hay reported from R14 that 20 to 30 panzers were on the ridge east of Ras El Medauur. Within twenty minutes he had upgraded this to 60 tanks. By 0750 hrs 51FRG's guns were engaging enemy tanks whenever possible. From the skies above the battlefield came the first tactical reconnaissance of the day: 60 enemy tanks inside the perimeter and groups of 70, 100 and 70 approaching the perimeter along the Acroma Track. A second Tac R confirmed 60 panzers inside the wire. The wolf was on the prowl inside our house.

. . . The way was now clear for the re-scheduled drives against Maccia Bianca and the posts on the flanks of the breach. Rommel launched both soon after 0800 hrs. The panzers and their supports on the hill at Pt 209 divided into two groups: one advanced towards Wadi Giaida, the other turned south-east and began to make its way behind the rear of the perimeter posts flanking the right side of the penetration. For the next few minutes the fate of the garrison hung

Tanks waiting to advance.

in the balance. If the first group broke through, the town could fall before noon. If the second group opened up the breach, enemy reinforcements would be able to enter at will. It was not only the fate of Tobruk that depended on the outcome of those thrusts. The entire British presence west of Suez dangled on the thread of the garrison's ability to resist.

The panzers making the drive against Biana included Schorm, keeper of a diary. On the previous evening he had written: 'In the evening I drink a glass of Chianti with the Commander – our last drop. In Tobruk there is more of the stuff so we shall have to restock there.'

It was going to be as easy as that. Now Schorm was heading for Wadi Giaida where part of the 2/24th's reserve company was entrenched. Standing directly in the way were the handful of anti-tank guns of the 24AA-T under the command of Captain Norman.

Perhaps Norman and his men had some of the blood of Frobisher in their veins. Undaunted by the size of the armada sailing towards them, they stood to their 2pdr pop-guns, waited until they could perhaps see the shining of eyes through the visors and then opened fire. One gun set a panzer on fire and hit two more. Others also registered hits, but these acts of resistance proved heroic suicides; the armada sailed onwards and over these gunners.

It was now the turn of the men of the 2/24th. They watched grimly as the panzers rolled towards them, then, just when it seemed that nothing could save them from the fate suffered by the anti-tank gunners, the leading panzer slewed to one side and came to a crashing halt. Smoke bellied out from the ground beneath its tracks and began to curl upwards around it. Suddenly, the same thing was happening all along that onrushing line – not one after another, but almost simultaneously, fifteen . . . sixteen . . . seventeen panzers juddered to an explosive standstill, their tracks shredded, their sprockets splintered. Morshead's freshly sown minefield had reaped a plentiful harvest. It was not yet 0900 hrs but already Schorm's hope of Chianti was gone. Although the battle would continue through two more days of often hand-to-hand combat, in those few moments Rommel's second great attack on the fortress had been lost. All the remainder of that day the panzers which should have taken the town would squat helplessly in the minefield, saved from utter destruction only because Spowers decided not to use the artillery against them in order to preserve the minefield.

The panzer survivors hung about on the edge of the minefield for a while but 51FRG opened up on them and then the anti-tank company of 26th Bde, which had been on Forbes' Mount to the west of Bianca, appeared on the scene and joined in. Several panzers were hit, but the shells from the 25pdrs created a local dust storm and the remainder were able to get away under its cover. How did our diarist feel during these traumatic moments? 'We attack . . . tier upon tier of guns boom out from the triangular fortifications before us . . . then things happened suddenly . . . a frightful crash in front and to the right. Direct hit from artillery shell? No! It must be a mine. Five metres back a new detonation. Mine underneath to the left. Now it's all up.'

Poor Schorm! It was never like this in Poland. His luck held again, however, and he managed to get off the minefield and back through the breach. He was fast becoming the Houdini of the western desert.

from *Tobruk* by Frank Harrison

Stukas!

When Rommel's Afrika Korps locked Tobruk into its siege situation, the only route to keep the garrison alive and resisting the many German tank attacks was by sea. Vintage Australian and British warships (called 'junks') were loaded in daylight at Alexandria in Egypt and unloaded at Tobruk by night. They were stacked with cargoes that included weapons, ammunition, medical supplies, fresh troops and a great variety of foodstuffs, such as sacks of potatoes. Hence the name 'the Spud Run' that was given to this vital lifeline. Many ships were sunk but the Spud Run served its purpose by saving Tobruk from annihilation, thereby denying the use of the port as a supply base for the Afrika Korps.

While some of the old warships were destroyed by mines and others were torpedoed by U boats, Stuka bombers constantly harassed the ships. The Stukas dived vertically, sirens screaming – to drop their bombs as close as possible to their targets. These persistent German aerial attacks were referred to as 'the Stuka Parade' by the sailors. One such 'parade' is described by author Alec Hepburn:

'Stukas!'

This ominous warning echoed through the cramped decks of the little Australian sloop HMAS *Parramatta* as its anti-aircraft gunners readied themselves for a fight.

High in the bright blue Mediterranean sky a large group of Junkers JU-87 dive-bombers, the Luftwaffe's sinister terror weapon, circled around like a flock of malignant, bent-winged vultures. There were perhaps fifty of them in three separate formations, each wave of bombers manoeuvred to get the late afternoon sun at its back before beginning an attack run.

Stukas in flight.

Two days before, *Parramatta*, with the British warship HMS *Auckland*, had steamed out of Alexandria harbour in Egypt as escorts for a small transport vessel, the *Pass of Balmaha*, which was ferrying vitally needed petrol to the besieged Australian outpost of Tobruk on the north-east Libyan coast. Now, on the afternoon of 22 June 1941, the Luftwaffe was launching an all-out effort to stop them reaching their goal.

Above the ships the force of 'Stukas' jockeyed into position for the attack. The distinctively ugly, single-engined dive-bomber, with its bent 'gull' wings and spatted fixed undercarriage, had proved a very formidable terror weapon in the awesome German 'blitzkrieg' which had rolled across Western Europe with such lightning speed.

. . . As the first wave of about sixteen Stukas began their dives towards the ships, *Parramatta* and *Auckland* opened fire with every gun they could muster – a desperate bid to keep the big formations of dive-bombers away from themselves and the all-important *Pass of Balmaha*. Above the roar from the gun-turrets, and the staccato rattle of anti-aircraft machine-guns, the air was filled with the screaming sirens of the diving Junkers JU-87s as they swept in from all directions.

From the start of the battle most of the Stukas seemed to concentrate their attention on *Auckland*, which presented the largest target in the group. Only about a third of the dive-bombers bothered to attack either *Parramatta* or the transport she protected. As each Stuka pulled out of its screaming dive, an ominous black shape detached itself from the belly of the machine and whistled on towards its target. Many of the bombs that rained down about the ships fell harmlessly into the sea, which erupted in a forest of white waterspouts. However, other bombs found their mark.

Suddenly *Auckland* disappeared in a billowing cloud of thick, brown smoke as several bombs tore into her hull. The thunderous impact literally blew her stern section and aft gun-turrets to pieces, but the vessel's forward gun positions continued to fire back at her attackers. *Auckland*'s wheel was jammed hard-a-port but, for some unexplained reason, the ship itself began turning rapidly to starboard as her speed dropped to about ten knots.

As the great cloud of smoke spread across the water, those watching from aboard *Parramatta* and *Pass of Balmaha* thought that *Auckland* must surely have blown to pieces under the impact of the direct hits she had received. However, to their utter amazement, a few moments later the mortally wounded British warship emerged from the thick, brown pall and headed straight for the Australian sloop, on a collision course.

As the sea-room between the dying *Auckland* and *Parramatta* closed rapidly, the sloop frantically put her wheel hard-over and just managed to slip safely out of the way. The badly damaged British ship went by with only metres to spare. Her stern was all but blown away and the warship was heeling heavily to port, but what guns she still had operational were firing defiantly at the German dive-bombers.

Seeing that *Auckland* was almost finished the Stukas intensified their attack on her. The warship next received three direct hits, but even that did not silence her guns, which kept firing until the Junkers JU-87s had dropped their entire bombload and had withdrawn beyond ack-ack range. Now dead in the water (with smoke and flame pouring from every deck) *Auckland* began to list sharply to port, the order to abandon ship was given, and her crew quickly began launching lifeboats and rafts. Time was rapidly running out for the gallant ship.

Parramatta closed on the sinking ship and stood off to windward, where her crew immediately dropped both the whalers carried by the sloop and her skiffs, life-belts, and floats, in a desperate effort to save the British seamen already floundering in the water.

Suddenly, deep inside *Auckland* there was a terrific explosion, the force lifting the shattered vessel two metres into the air. Then, with her back broken, the dying warship settled down again with an increased list to port. Finally, *Auckland* rolled over and on her side and sank beneath the waves.

Parramatta had no time to go to the aid of survivors, for scarcely had the boiling waters closed over the British warship than the air attack was renewed. This time is was six Italian Savoia-Marchetti SM-79s that roared in to make a low-level bombing run at *Parramatta* and her charge. When both vessels managed to evade their badly handled assault, without too much trouble, the Italian pilots turned their attention to an easier prey – the survivors from *Auckland*.

The Australian sloop tried to drive them off with a withering barrage as the Italian aircraft swept in to machine-gun the helpless men in the water before turning tail and running back to their base. Luckily for the British seamen, their machine-gunning was as inaccurate as their bombing and most survived the murderous attack.

As the sun began to sink below the western horizon, even greater numbers of aircraft were spotted heading towards the ships. At first it was thought they might be British fighters coming to their aid but, as they got closer, it became clear that they were more formations of enemy dive-bombers. For more than an hour and a half, wave after wave of hostile aircraft threw themselves at *Parramatta* and *Pass of*

Balmaha, but each time the Australian sloop managed, somehow, to beat them back as tonnes of bombs churned the sea around the ships into a seething maelstrom. Miraculously both vessels survived.

Finally, night closed around the hard-pressed ships and the enemy dive-bombers were forced to break off their attack and head back to their bases.

With the darkness came aid in the shape of the Australian destroyers HMAS *Waterhen* and HMAS *Vendetta*.

The survivors from *Auckland*, most of whom had also survived the vicious Italian strafing, were quickly picked up, and with 162 rescued men on board, *Parramatta* left the transport in the charge of the destroyers and turned back for Alexandria. The battered little sloop steamed away while *Waterhen* took the badly damaged *Pass of Balmaha* in tow and, under the very noses of the enemy, delivered the transport and its cargo of 750 tonnes of badly needed petrol safely into the battle-scarred harbour at Tobruk.

from *True Australian War Tales* by Alec Hepburn

New Guinea – the Kokoda Trail

New Guinea – the Kokoda Trail

On 7 December 1941, Japan attacked the US naval base at Pearl Harbor with planes borne on aircraft carriers that were situated approximately 500 kilometres north of the Hawaiian island. As a result, much of America's battleship fleet was sunk or seriously damaged, leaving the way open for Japan to control the resources and peoples of South-East Asia, and ultimately Australia, in its 'Greater East Asia Co-Prosperity Sphere'.

The British colonies of Hong Kong, Malaya and Singapore were swiftly invaded and captured by Imperial Japanese forces, and by February 1942, Australia was under serious threat. Prime Minister John Curtin, who'd taken over from Robert Menzies late the previous year, called this time 'the gravest hour of our history'. Britain, fighting for its survival against Germany, could not send aid, and many of Australia's most experienced troops were embroiled in bitter conflict against the Afrika Korps in North Africa. Curtin made an impassioned plea for American help and recalled Australian troops from overseas to defend their homeland. Meanwhile, General Douglas Macarthur, bringing American forces and equipment, arrived and took charge of the Battle of Australia.

Japanese troops, supported by ships and planes, invaded the northern coast of New Guinea in July 1942 and soon captured the settlements of Buna and Gona, despite valiant efforts from the few hundred locals that made up the Papuan Infantry Brigade. From these new bases, columns of Japanese trained jungle troops set out to cross the Owen Stanley Range which forms the spine of eastern New Guinea, using a series of native tracks called the Kokoda Trail. Once on the southern side of the range, the Japanese aim was to capture Port Moresby and use its airfield and harbour for an attack on the Australian mainland.

The AIF from the Middle East were joined on New Guinea's southern coast by less experienced troops from Australia, and as they advanced, the Papuans, who'd been forced to retreat to the village of Kokoda on top of the range, were caught in the middle of the battles along the Trail. Nevertheless, many of the native people took on the work of carrying supplies and getting the wounded to safety, and for this they were affectionately named 'the Fuzzy Wuzzy Angels' by the grateful Australian soldiers.

The Kokoda Trail confronted the soldiers with heartbreaking climbs and descents in terrible heat and humidity on thousands of crude wooden steps or on tracks that were sometimes waist deep in mud. Torrential rain fell daily and there were many creek crossings. This meant that nothing could be kept dry, and hot food was hard to prepare. Leeches infested the jungle and swarming mosquitoes brought malaria and other fevers that, together with dysentery, caused many casualties.

Although the Papuan Infantry Brigade, a few hundred strong, tried to deny the start of the Kokoda Trail at Gona and Buna on the north coast to the Japanese, they were forced to retreat to the village of Kokoda on top of the Owen Stanley Range. Attacks and counterattacks occurred at the height of the Owen Stanleys but the camouflaged Japanese troops seemed to be everywhere, sniping and charging from the jungle. In July, the Australians were pushed back towards Port Moresby, and a month later they were running short of weapons, food and water. Macarthur began to doubt if the Australian troops were capable of throwing back the Japanese.

Then there followed a reversal in the campaign. In September the Port Moresby garrison was strengthened by further brigades of Australian troops and US infantry. America also provided aircraft that could successfully drop supplies to infantry units along the Trail.

The enemy advance was turned into a retreat, with the Australians moving north along the Trail but experiencing ferocious jungle fighting at Templeton's Crossing and Eora Creek before occupying Kokoda at the beginning of November 1942. The scattered Japanese forces were chased to the Kumusi River and back to the coast.

The Australian and American victory on the Kokoda Trail in November 1943 showed that the Imperial Japanese Army, which had been victorious in all its previous campaigns, could be beaten.

Vanimo
Manus
Kavieng
Wewak
Bismarck Sea
Namatanai
New Ireland
Marienberg
Sepik River
Rabaul
New Britain
Alexishafen
Madang
Talasea
Wide Bay
NEW GUINEA
Nadzab
Finschhafen
Lae
Kieta
Bougainville
Buin
Solomon Sea
Kikori
Wau
Huon Gulf
Morobe
Fly
River
Kerema
Buna
Kokoda
Gulf of Papua
Daru
Port Moresby
See inset
Torres Strait
N
0 kilometres 250
Samarai
AUSTRALIA
Owen Stanley Range
Kokoda
Gona
Sananada
Buna
Jumbora
Hogenahambo
Igora
Soputa
Popondetta
Sangara
Awala
Wairopi
Ilimo
Gorari
Oivi
Deniki
Kobara
Isurava
Fila
Alola
Mt Bellamy
Eora Creek
Kagi
Templetons Crossing
Efogi
Track
Menari
Mt Kenevi
Nauro
Ioribaiwa
Kokoda
Uberi
Owers Corner
Ilolo
Hiki
Koitaki
Port Moresby
0 kilometres 60
THE KOKODA TRACK

Kokoda.

Kokoda

In 1942 there was furious fighting between Australian troops and Japanese jungle fighters at Isurava on the Kokoda Trail. Among the many Australians involved was an eleven-man section that included Bruce Kingsbury, Alan Avery, Harry Saunders, Teddy Bear and 'the Professor'. After fighting in an heroic action against a very brave enemy, Kingsbury was awarded a Victoria Cross, and most of the other men in the section received decorations. Author Peter Dornan would later describe their part in the battle:

Friday, 28 August opened with a tremendous crash, shocking the apprehensive Australians into life as Japanese General Horii released the full force of his offensive. As dawn filtered through the canopy, mountain guns and mortar shells shattered the morning stillness. The frightening effects of the explosions were amplified by the closeness of

Australian troops advancing.

the jungle. Shrapnel erupted and whistled like a knife as it cut through trees and spun to the ground below. Heavy machine-guns opened up, cutting a withering path as their shells flattened the vegetation.

Then the hardened Japanese troops teemed out of the jungle, supported by a wild, screaming cacophony from the rest of their forces behind the green screen. This was the first time the men of the 2/14th had seen the enemy and they'd expected to be confronted by the popular caricature of the Japanese – little yellow men with slanted eyes and wearing spectacles. To their astonishment, these were handpicked warriors, most of them over 1.8 metres tall, and trained for years in the art of jungle warfare. They attacked on three sides in waves of about a hundred, determined to give no quarter.

But it was no pushover for them this time. Everywhere, they were met and held by strong resolve and shattering fire, as the Australians matched them physically and emotionally. They raced into an inferno of Bren and Tommy gun fire, a fusillade of rifle shots and grenade blasts, and a wall of green and khaki uniforms.

Occasionally, by sheer force of numbers, some made it to the Australian lines, where they were greeted with frantic hand-to-hand combat. The dark, mouldy leaves of the jungle floor glistened with blood as men attacked with bayonets or grappled for an advantage, fists flailing and hammering. They rolled and faltered and died as the morning sun glinted and flashed on steel.

The 11 Platoon in the Cane Field took a great deal of this attack, and very soon their commander and many of his men lay killed or wounded. Butch's friend, Lieutenant Mokka Treacy, took over command of the platoon early that afternoon and helped them to repulse several more attacks.

As the day grew longer, Butch's 10 Platoon relieved Mokka's platoon at this key position. The sugar cane patch was about the size of a normal street block, so Butch placed his men in sectional positions around it. The cane was about 1.5 metres high and the field was hot, humid and claustrophobic. George Woodward, a Tommy-gunner, and a stretcher-bearer, Lindsay Elphinstone, went to the right of the platoon, behind a log, as cover. Their position afforded a reasonably clear view 30 or 40 metres up the track through the surrounding jungle, where they could see the Japanese flitting about. From here, the platoon kept up constant fire.

The Japanese probed several points around the perimeter, trying to outflank the besieged men, but the Australians' resistance held. Time and again, successive attacks threatened to overrun the defenders as the battle continued. The enemy would melt out of the jungle, then, forming lines and yelling 'banzai', make a fanatical burst as they threw their lives away against controlled gunfire, most of them not making the Australians' territory. At one stage they tried to camouflage their attack by hiding behind billowing smoke pouring out from pyrotechnic candles. The ghostly effect was disturbing for a while, but as their forms appeared through the haze they were quickly cut down.

As night fell and the firing ebbed, the two commanders took stock of their situation. Their armies had each received a mauling but General Horii clearly was frustrated, as he had not expected this sort of resistance. He had watched the battle impatiently from a vantage point about a kilometre north of Isurava, and now realised that the weakened 39th Battalion had been reinforced by fresh and determined troops who could match his in tenacity. Not willing to lose the momentum of his offensive, he brought up his two reserve units to complement his five in-line battalions. This would allow him to make an intensive, all-out attack, hopefully to overthrow the Australians in a decisive confrontation.

Brigadier Potts had no reason to be overjoyed either. He now realised he was facing an enemy far greater in numbers and resources than Military Intelligence had previously reckoned. His request for his reserve 2/27th Battalion at Port Moresby still hadn't been authorised, and the battle was being dictated by the enemy on a ground not of Potts' own choosing. However, there was some consolation in appreciating the spirit of the troops under his command. They had met the 'invincible' Japanese in head-on confrontation and remained in some control of the situation. They estimated they had killed up to 350 of the enemy and wounded perhaps as many as 1000 of them, while they themselves had sustained less than a handful killed and about 30 wounded.

The men settled down for the night, buoyed with confidence, but keeping watch in the darkness.

At first light it began again. Their fitful sleep was shattered by the bombardment as mortars, mountain guns and hand grenades once more thundered in the air.

As the firing grew thicker, a message came through for Lieutenant Cox to take 9 Platoon further forward to reinforce 13 Platoon, which was under heavy attack. Moving forward to reconnoitre the area, Cox received a fatal wound. The platoon sergeant with him, Jock Lochhead, then went back to organise the move. At this stage the Professor, who had had to stay a day late at Myola, was reporting back to the platoon and met Lochhead beside the track. As they exchanged greetings, a mortar shell exploded near them and threw them both violently to the ground. As the Professor slowly regained his senses and crawled to his feet, he realised that the sergeant was seriously wounded, with a gaping hole in his head from a mortar fragment.

He got Lochhead to his feet and supported him back to the RAP a few hundred metres behind the lines, where he lay him on a stretcher. The orderly examined Lochhead, then bound his head wound and gave a discreet sign to the Professor that it didn't look good. Fighting to stay conscious, the sergeant whispered to the Professor: 'Tell Teddy he's now in charge. I'm not going to be much help.' He then lapsed into a coma. As the Professor made his way back to the platoon, he passed Lieutenant Cox's body lying beside the track.

Across the battalion area, as leaders were hit, the position had become confusing. It was difficult to determine responsibilities for sections, platoons and even companies. The jungle closeness and the battle noise added to the uncertainty, as men were unable to hear orders, see signals or even have contact with their section leaders. The green screen had levelled the battle into a close-fighting personal war.

When the Professor relayed the message to him, Teddy Bear had no hesitation in forming a plan as to what was needed. In fact, this type of situation was to be repeated many times over the whole battalion as the day wore on. As key officers and leaders were wounded or killed, men of lower rank quickly and ably filled their shoes. Men of certain character, with their years of training, confidently assumed a leadership role and easily led from the front.

Teddy had already realised that, unless someone took charge, his platoon would slowly be picked off one by one and any advantage they may have held would be lost. He ordered all the remaining able men of the platoon to meet him at a central point. At this stage there were only about fifteen men left, including some from other platoons who had wandered into the area.

He told him: 'You all know the situation. Coxie and Jock Lochhead have been taken out. The sarge left me in charge. My plan is simple and direct. First, go and collect as much ammo as possible and stockpile it here, so that we have a ready supply of hand grenades and bullets. Then I want you all to assemble back at this spot on the track in fifteen minutes. We're going to spread out along the track, then advance and create as much damage as we can.'

From the dead and wounded, the men salvaged Bren gun and Tommy gun magazines, .303 clips and as many grenades as they could carry. They loaded their weapons and stuffed grenades into the pouches, then stockpiled the rest.

As they moved into attacking position on the track, Alan clicked a full magazine into place on his Tommy gun, while Bruce directed a bullet into the breech of his .303. They briefly caught each other's eye and gave a dry smile. There was nothing to say – they were professionals and this was what they were trained for. Alan was on Bruce's right and Teddy moved up to Bruce's left. Jarmbe fell in on Teddy's left, with Ted Jobe next to him. Hi-Ho Silver and the Professor joined in, as did the Wilson brothers. With several others holding a spot, the line extended some 50 metres across.

Alan glanced at Jarmbe, who was waiting, sitting on a fallen log, running his thumb and forefinger up and down the sharpened blade of his bayonet. He flashed a toothy grin back, accompanied by a wink.

'Hey, Jarmba,' Alan called. 'I want you to keep smiling. It's dark in the jungle, and I don't want to lose you.' The chiacking lightened the moment as Jarmbe bared his ivory teeth in a smiling chocolate face.

Just as they were lining up in their final positions, the Bren-gunner approached Teddy. His voice was quivering, his lips and hands trembling. 'Teddy, my gun won't work.' His hands fumbling with the reload bolt. 'I don't think I can go.' The fear was palpable. Teddy took the Bren, examined it, released the safety catch and pulled the trigger. The man paled as the gun exploded into life. Realising the extent of the man's panic, Teddy said: 'Never mind, mate, I'll use this. You fall in behind and follow us up.'

Teddy told them that no man was to fire until he gave the order, and then called: 'Now, move!'

At that same instant, the Japanese decided on a break-through. Teddy could hear them crashing through the undergrowth towards 7 Section's line. There appeared to be about 50 in this wave. He gave the order to fire when they were 30 metres away.

'Now! Make every shot count!' The jungle erupted as never before – all hell broke loose. Every weapon in the confined area loosed its payload as machine-guns and rifles from both sides filled the air with screaming bullets. Everywhere men cursed, shouted or screamed as the spinning lead found its mark. My God, thought Teddy, no one is going to live through this. Bullets whistled past him, crashing into trees, ripping undergrowth apart and slashing everything to pieces in the immediate vicinity. As bullets ricocheted off trees and rocks, they emitted a terrible whining sound as they spun and funnelled dangerously out of control, adding to the terror of the firepower. Teddy gripped the handle of his Bren and, firing from the hip, slowly moved to the apex of the Australians' line.

The enemy swarmed towards the thin line, cursing, yelling and firing, only to fall to the ground, their threats choking on the blood that gurgled through great gashes in their lungs as Teddy's bullets rammed home. They continued to drop under the Bren gun's assault – four, five, six of them, clutching at their stomachs or chest as they fell.

Meanwhile, to his right, Bruce was firing and reloading his .303 as fast as he could. He was an excellent shot and didn't waste any bullets. The clinking shells ripped out from the ejection chamber as he dropped one after another of the enemy.

A few metres further to the right Alan was firing his Tommy gun from the hip at anything that moved. Two Japanese suddenly materialised from behind a clump of palms, and charged towards him. He fired a burst from his gun through one man's chest and saw the blood spurt on his clothes and run from his mouth as the man fell in a limp heap.

The other man continued over towards the Professor who, for an instant, had thought of the battle of Krythia at Gallipoli and how, as the Australians moved forward over open ground, the air had been so thick with bullets that after the battle some were found welded together, having collided in midair. Now his eye caught the movement of the charging Japanese.

Physically exhausted from his morning's exertions and a little stupefied by the pounding crescendo of the gunfire, he reacted almost too late. As the enemy lunged, the tip of the bayonet sliced through the air centimetres from the Professor's face and tore off his shoulder webbing. Shocked into action, he automatically brought his rifle butt up to protect himself. The next bayonet thrust struck the wooden stock of the butt and the blade slid along it, jamming momentarily under the depressed bolt of the Professor's .303. In the same instant, the Professor kicked the man hard in the shins, quickly gaining the advantage. As the Japanese screamed in agony, the two men were close enough for the Professor to smell the man's stale breath and his sweat-stained clothing.

The Professor wrenched his rifle free, spinning the enemy's rifle completely out of reach. This had the effect of exposing the man's throat and chest and in that eternity of a second the Japanese realised his vulnerability and the inevitability of the outcome. He was helpless. The Professor, seizing the advantage, was preparing to thrust his bayonet home when he caught sight of his assailant's coppery face.

The helpless eyes stared back at him and the Professor knew that he would see those eyes forever.

He finished the stroke off, sickening as he felt the metal crunch through the man's sternum and ribs. As the bayonet sliced into the lungs, air gurgled and blood spurted freely from the wound. The man dropped instantly to the ground without a sound, taking the Professor's rifle with him. The Professor put his foot on the man's chest to release the weapon and was beginning to shake from exhaustion and relief when he noticed another Japanese soldier racing towards him. A blast from Alan's Tommy gun dropped the charging man several metres from the Professor.

Meanwhile, Teddy was moving ahead with his Bren gun, still firing incessantly. He would empty the magazine, throw it into the bush, then replace it with a full one. Now he suddenly caught sight of blood on his shirt. Hell, he thought, I've been hit. But where? His chest seemed alright; he could breathe. He panicked a little, but eventually found he'd suffered a shrapnel wound to his nose. Amazed that he hadn't felt any pain, he continued his crusade, his machine-gun spurting at the nonstop wave of Japanese. Seven, eight, nine, ten men fell as the murderous bullets found their targets.

After half an hour of this concentrated fighting, the barrel of his Bren started to retain so much heat that he could barely hold it, so Teddy placed its two legs in the 'carry' position, parallel to the barrel. As they were still relatively cool, he held these to steady the barrel and went on fighting. The killing field by now was almost completely denuded of vegetation and cover. Tree stumps were cut off and vines were lying on the jungle floor. The bark was splintered off larger trees and palm fronds, and the canopy no longer cut out the sun.

Suddenly Teddy realised he could no longer hold the gun, as his left hand would not work. He found that a bullet had ripped through the back of his hand, which was bleeding freely. He couldn't make a fist or move the fingers. Damn!, he thought – it was useless! He put his arm inside his shirt front to support it and went on firing the gun one-handed.

Tiring now, he could still fire accurately enough, although with a lot more effort – twelve, thirteen of the enemy fell. At this stage he and the others were getting low on ammunition so he quickly detailed two men to race back to their supply dump and bring up some magazines for him and for Alan's Tommy gun. He shoved the new magazines into his haversack, loaded one into his Bren and had gone only a few steps when he realised his right leg wasn't working properly. He noticed blood pouring from his left calf muscle and seeping through the gaiter. Two bullets had penetrated it. As he could still bear weight on the leg he continued to advance, dragging the leg behind, using it as a support.

Slowly but steadily the men saw that their drive forward was telling on the enemy and making considerable ground. Teddy kept firing, producing more casualties. Finally he was staggering and realised he could go no further, but it was enough. The enemy had been badly mauled and now retreated back into the green, as quickly as they had appeared.

With the lull in the fighting, Bruce and Alan gathered around Teddy and examined his wounds. Alan took out one of his field dressings and bound the damaged hand. 'I reckon you've had enough of this blue, Teddy. You'd better go back to the RAP and see the Doc.' The other wounded men were being tended to and were also making their way back, taking advantage of the break in hostilities.

Grimacing in pain and supporting himself on Bruce's shoulder, Teddy said: 'Yeah, I think you're right. I'll go back for a spell.' He turned and said to Bruce: 'I reckon they're only having a breather – they'll be back for sure. Take my Bren. It's pretty hot, but keep firing and keep moving.'

Bruce took the Bren gun, checked it over briefly, put in a new magazine and grabbed several from the stockpile.

Teddy slowly limped back from the battlefield, utterly exhausted and beginning to feel pain, as his injuries were now starting to become inflamed and to swell. He slowly made his way back a few hundred metres to the Regimental Aid Post and Dr Duffy.

from *The Silent Men* by Peter Dornan

Entries from two war diaries

Soldiers' diary entries invariably provide a fascinating account of combat, and those from the front line in New Guinea are no exception. In the following extract from 31 August 1942 Sergeant Arthur James Traill of the 2/12th Battalion goes on to describe '14 hours of the hottest fighting one would ever wish to experience', against the Japanese at Gili Gili Wharf, Milne Bay:

During the early hours of this morning the Japs attacked number 3 strip in strong force. The militia held them from their fixed defences and were greatly assisted by a battery of artillery. We were stopped from going per barges as originally intended and were given orders to move up the jungle road along to K.B. Mission [the first defence point between the invading Japanese and the Allied airstrips] if possible and

The final assault on Buna.

occupy that area. Our forward company crossed strip 3 about 0900 hours that morning and our company crossed it about half an hour later.

From the beginning we had to contend with Jap snipers who lined the road, either lying 'doggo' along the roadside and pretending they were dead or perched up in trees or camouflaged behind bushes. We lost an officer early through a dog's trick on the part of the Japs. Lying across the strip were dozens of dead Japs, killed in the previous night's action by mortar and artillery fire. As our officer crossed in the vanguard, a Jap, apparently wounded, cried out for help. The officer walked over to aid him and as he did, the Jap sprang to life and hurled a grenade, which wounded him in the face. From then on, the only good Jap was a dead one, and although they tried the same trick again and again throughout the campaign, they were dispatched before they had time to use their grenade.

Our policy was to watch any apparent dead, shoot at the slightest sign of life and stab with bayonet even the ones who seemed to be rotten. It was all out from then on, neither side showing any quarter and no prisoners were taken. We advanced about three miles from the strip to a place called Rabbi while two companies moved on and occupied K.B. Mission. At Rabbi we threw up hasty defences and quickly worked out a fire and defence plan. At about dusk that night a detachment of about 300 Japs, apparently making for their defended positions or intending to attack K.B. Mission were more or less ambushed by us. I don't know who got the greater surprise of the two as we were more or less caught napping. Anyhow, our forward defence opened up with everything they had and just about wiped the whole of the forward platoon of about 30.

Then began what proved to be 14 hours of the hottest fighting one would ever wish to experience. Again and again the enemy tried to pierce our forward positions and each time were driven back by an ear-splitting rattle of machine-gun and rifle fire punctuated by the roar of our beautiful grenades. The fore tried to out-flank us, to assail our position by concerted rushes, to sneak to the edge of the jungle and hurl grenades and to infiltrate through singly all without avail. Never once did our forward positions falter, never once did the death-dealing Bren fail to bark out its symphony of defiance, never once did our grenades fail to roar their challenge. It was a nerve-racking experience because apart from the fact that we did not know the enemy's strength, it was darker than a dungeon and teeming with rain all the time. Moreover, there was no hope of escape for us. We knew that at the time, the Jap was not in a position to take prisoners and whatever came or went, it had to be a fight to the death.

from *War on Our Doorstep* by Gabrielle Chan (ed.)

Private Ron Berry was at Buna in 1942, part of the 2/9th infantry advance behind tanks. Here, he writes about the deadly fire directed on the advancing Australian troops by enemy snipers:

20 December
Up at dawn. Carted breakfast to Don company. The battle ground is littered with bodies of Japs and Aussies and they do stink. Heard that X was killed yesterday. He was on a stretcher bearing and a sniper shot him in both thighs and a flesh wound in the chest. Tiny Telford was with him. Tiny could not manage to carry X back alone so managed to get back for help. Tiny and his help arrived back at spot where he left X; he could not be found. Anyway they found his body this morning beside the track. He apparently crawled back to the road. On his way the sniper had another shot at him and got him through the stomach and he must have lost consciousness when he reached the road. During the night a tank went up the road and ran over X's head, finishing him off.

Joined Corporal McGill's section, 16 Platoon and Vince Donnelly is Platoon Commander. The Battalion have a system of clearing an area for about 80 yards in front and then taking up positions behind this for the night. Any enemy trying to sneak up and on trying to cross the cleared area is seen before they can do any damage. One had to be wily to compete with the bloody mongrels.

We advance. Each man trailing up a row of coconut palms and firing a shot into any likely palm hiding a sniper. The tanks go on about 10 yards ahead and fire into any likely-looking places that may be a machine gun post. A few snipers are rooted out. We halt about every 20 minutes.

The tanks get bogged every now and then and we dare not go on without them. They are a wonderful support. We have only four. In the afternoon we reach a patch of jungle. We have to advance through this. We hack our way through and proceed in file. We come to an opening caused by a bomb and are immediately fired upon by a sniper. We have to turn back.

What a hell of a business. Up to our knees in slush. We follow around the beach and cross over a creek, waist high in water. The tanks are left behind owing to the jungle and a bridge has to be made for the crossing of this creek. All at once we are set upon by mortars. Petherick cops some shrapnel in the thigh, a mortar landing about two feet from him. Cassidy cops a piece in the ribs. They are evacuated. We prepare for a counterattack from the enemy but none came. Captain Griffin received an alarm. While sheltering behind the trunk of a huge tree, a drop of blood fell on his arm. We searched the branches of the tree for a possible sniper but none could be found. While the shelling was on, one of the lads had both his feet blown off by a mortar and I think that one of his feet was hurled into the branches and the blood was dripping from it.

A sniper shot one of the platoon's mortar men stone dead. The CO arrived about this time, 4.30pm and ordered us to clear our perimeter. A Company is on our left flank. C Company is somewhere ahead of us. They return to a position slightly behind us and A Company. We clear a perimeter about 80 yards ahead. Some snipers are trying to operate and we can hear noises ahead. A Bren gunner goes forward and sprays the area with gunfire and everything quietens down.

21 December

Started out on morning fighting patrol with 16 Platoon. We advanced to the edge of the perimeter and passed about five yards into the jungle. We run across Jock Milne. He looks in bad shape and asked for water. I ask him where was he hit and he said through the shoulders. I then asked by whom and he said a sniper was in the palm above him. We searched the palms but no sniper could be seen. There were only about five palms altogether.

He explained that the Japs were digging ahead of him most of the night. He said that he could hear their silent talk and the slight scrape of the shovels. The country is sandy and makes very easy digging. Jock had laid out in no-man's-land all night. His eyes look very bright, which looked bad.

Asking him why he did not let us know he was there the previous evening, he said, 'Well, the sniper was still in the tree and I did not want to get anyone into trouble so I lay quiet.' Cam Stewart gave him a drink of water and Vince Donnelly told the rest of us to advance and get out of the area in case a sniper was about. We told someone to get a stretcher bearer and some fool yelled out at the top of his voice 'stretcher bearer'. The recs [new recruits] were giving us a lot of trouble by hanging back and that is one of the reasons why I think that so many of the old hands are getting bumped off. On the word to advance, the section leader and myself jump to it and he tells the section to advance well with him but the recs are hanging back slightly. I look through the jungle and I can see forms running towards us, the leading one disappears into what must be pits. I tell the section leader and he yells 'Japs' and there are volleys of shots from each side. (This happens about a minute from leaving Jock Milne.)

I jump to a fairly large stump as this is my only cover. McGill has a tree about six inches through and he stands up behind it and lets go with his Tommy. A machine gun opens up at my cover. Explosive bullets, for I can see the little puffs of smoke. I wonder how long my rotten stump is going to last as large pieces are falling from it. The machine gun lets up from me.

I see a Jap behind a tree with what appears to be the machine gun. I raise on to elbow and one knee in the act of rising to have a go at this Jap. A machine gun from someone else has another go in my direction, and wham! Something strikes in the vicinity of my rifle. I feel a sharp pain at the base of my thumb. I look at it . . . look at my rifle and the butt is busted off it. An explosive bullet. How lucky was I. I look for another rifle. None in sight.

I feel something warm in the vicinity of my belt and it is sticky. I look down. My shirt is all tattered at my right breast and is covered in blood. My equipment strap is only holding by a few threads. I have a slight panic and feel around my right shoulder blade – funny I cannot feel anything. I feel numb, maybe fright.

I scramble back. During the battle I see men falling. Our Bren gunner is killed and his no. 2 is wounded. Frank runs in front of me to get cover from my stump and is wounded. A couple of men to my right are wounded. Vince Donnelly drops like a stone.

Our Platoon Sergeant is yelling with pain and is holding his penis, a piece of shrapnel or a bullet has apparently gone through it. Jock Milne is left in the same place and bullets fly all around him. I scramble back about 20 yards to a big tree. Blue, the stretcher bearer, is crouching behind this tree, he goes to dress my wounds and I tell him to go to Jock.

from *War on Our Doorstep* by Gabrielle Chan (ed.)

Buna – the terrible struggle

Bill Spencer was a member of the 2/9th Battalion, which saw action in Tobruk. According to him, nothing the battalion had previously experienced was as terrible as the fighting around Buna. The Australians were forced to confront camouflaged Japanese bunkers from which accurate fire caused many casualties. However, even when the troops were exhausted and resting, sniper fire claimed many victims. Bill would later compile reports from his comrades in the action of December 1942 providing a full picture of the desperate battle:

On 18 December, after a restless night, the 2/9th was roused at 5.30am and, after a scratch breakfast, moved towards the start line. At 6.50am the Vickers guns opened up, which in unison with the artillery and mortars provided a concentrated barrage. A promised air strike did not eventuate because of bad weather.

At 7.00am I was a spellbound onlooker to actions the likes of which I had never witnessed before – or have witnessed since – as the tanks moved forward into a barbarous inferno ahead of the walking-paced infantry. The roar of their engines added to the mounting crescendo of noise from both Vickers and enemy machine guns and a wall of small-arms lead – it was like nothing the 2/9th Battalion had experienced. The sky seemed to rain debris as small pieces of undergrowth and bark floated down like confetti, and the repeated crack of bullets and chatter of automatic weapons and explosions close by, the acrid smell and eye-irritating smoke from discharging weapons and grenades, added to the extreme discomfort experienced by the men. Soldiers were dropping like sacks. There appeared to be utter confusion, but among all the chaos, the courageous men moved resolutely forward. One American general described the scene as something he had never seen before and never expected to see again, while the tank crews described the advance as 'men going in for a cup of tea' – such was the soldierly bearing of the 2/9th.

There were no sounds from the wounded, as the pain of gunshot wound comes later; sudden death was always silent. Our casualties were immediate and heavy as the thin, green, determined line moved forward. The bodies of those who had fallen became sprinkled with leaf and bark litter ripped from the undergrowth by bullets and shrapnel, which somehow softened the starkness of death. The first wounded man I saw and spoke to was Corporal Ron Fitzpatrick, a member of the Intelligence Section attached to C Company. Other wounded were leaving the scene of the conflict from all directions. The RAP soon became tragically overburdened.

The first company to reach its objective was D Company. Later Lieutenant McIntosh and his 18 Platoon, with the assistance of the tank driven by Corporal Barnett, cleaned out the enemy bunkers on their immediate front, reached Cape Endaiadere at 7.50am and consolidated. Lieutenant Syvier's 17 Platoon was having great difficulties as it had come up against a concrete bunker from which accurate fire caused many casualties. Syvier himself was killed; Sergeant Prentice took over, but was wounded; Sergeant Walters, who was sent forward to take over, also fell – shot in the head as he approached the bunker. The platoon was taken over by Lance Corporal Rudd.

It is all too easy to use the term 'bunker'. Although the bunker in question was concrete, most at Buna were made from palm logging and 44-gallon drums filled with earth. The entrances were from one or both sides and virtually impervious to artillery fire. Such bunkers varied in size and could accommodate anywhere between 10 and 20 men. They were magnificently camouflaged by earth and fast-growing frond vegetation; each bunker was protected by a number of individual foxholes to hamper the access of assailants; some were connected or approached by crawl trenches; but, most of all, the soldiers inside them were fortified by their military code of conduct – no surrender.

Moving behind, and to the centre of 17 and 18 platoons, WO2 Vince Donnelly and his 16 Platoon encountered problems of their own. As they moved forward, some positions thought to have been cleared by the forward platoons were very much alive, and this forced them to ensure that every Jap was dead before proceeding. This was a task that had to be repeated again and again throughout the Buna campaign.

D Company gained its objective and at about 8.10am was settling into its own defensive positions, attending to the wounded and forming a perimeter with the sea at its back. D Company had taken 40 casualties during the attack, winkling out Japanese in one-man weapon pits. Eighteen Platoon had only about nine men left. 'Kilcoy taken' was the code for notification on the telephone that Cape Endaiadere had been taken. The later D Company consolidation signal, 'Kilcoy held', was a great morale booster.

The position on A Company's front was even more difficult than D Company's, because A Company did not enjoy the advantage of having the sea on its right flank. And it had an additional problem – the company lost its three tanks quite early. One was burnt out, one had bellied on a log and the last was put out of action later. That crucial early tank support – of an ongoing nature throughout our fighting – cannot be overstated. Trooper Wilson described the tank role:

> The crew commander worked out with the infantry leaders a plan as follows – the infantry leader would indicate the bunker which was holding him up by firing a Very pistol at it, or throwing a grenade, or just pointing. We would advance within 10 or 15 feet so that we could line up the 37 mm cannon at the correct angle . . . using AP and HE shot to enlarge the opening. This usually took ten rounds. An infantry volunteer would then crawl forward . . . The Japs inside who survived would usually attempt to leave by the side entrance, which we would cover with out MGs. Very few escaped. This was the basic routine for a couple of hours, and then we would have to pull back about 50 yards or so to our base, refuel, and replenish ammo. The infantry often ran short of ammunition so we hung cloth bandoleers with .303 ammunition on the back of the tanks hanging down about 2 feet off the ground so they could reach up and grab some.

Captain Taylor's A Company was unable to progress any further as there was a considerable gap in the line. A pillbox holding up the company was eventually subdued when it was attacked by Captain Taylor firing through the open ports and his men throwing grenades. The enemy who ran from the bunker were bayoneted. Captain Taylor was attacked by two Japs, both of whom he held off bare-handed until one of his men killed them.

Corporal Ernie Randall relates his story of the action of 7 Platoon A Company:

> The ground was strewn with old trunks of coconut palms making it difficult for the tanks to manoeuvre. I had lost a couple of my section, killed before we got to near the Jap defences. Suddenly, my mate waved me urgently to his side. Here in an open slit trench in full battler order were ten or a dozen Japs. They were watching a tank go by and hadn't noticed us. We took care of them. Now that we had reached the pillboxes we hurled

> grenades down through the slits but they were thrown back at us. Ever try holding a grenade for a few seconds? There was so much small arms around it was not possible to tell if snipers were operating. However, during a lull in which our troops who were totally exhausted rested for a while, a sniper started to operate. Lyle Hicks was kneeling beside a coconut palm. I yelled, 'Did you see where that shot came from?' 'No,' he replied, 'but it was damn close to me.' As he spoke another shot rang out and Lyle slumped forward, shot through the temple. We up and dived for the shelter of the tank. The sniper killed more men that afternoon despite our efforts to locate him. I had a tank knock out several palms that could have been hiding him. When we went forward next morning, we found his hiding spot.

Captain Parbury's C Company on the left flank was in deep trouble right from the start. He had no tank support and had come up against heavy fire from pillboxes over the creek. His company had suffered very heavy casualties as they crossed the start line – 87 men in short order. Parbury was forced to go to ground in the short kunai grass and report his situation to Battalion HQ. At this stage of the battle Harry (the Wog) Dixon related that Parbury had instructed the orderly room corporal, Les Boylan, to call the roll. Some answered their names but many others did not – the Japanese were only 50 yards in front of them. As 'the Wog' further remarked: 'We knew the bastard was there but we couldn't see him.' Captain Parbury was instructed to try to outflank the enemy positions with a small party; Lance-Sergeant Morey's section were sent out, but were all killed after traversing only about 15 yards.

A platoon from B Company was sent to bolster Parbury's company and wait for tanks. At 2.00pm those vehicles arrived and C Company continued the attack. Captain Parbury remembered:

> I then outlined a plan to Curtiss (tank commander) for Jesse's Platoon to advance in line with the tanks, with a section between each tank and remnants of De Vantier's Platoon on

> and Lieutenant Pinwell's behind the tanks. An hour after the tanks arrived they recommenced attack, with Jesse firing Very lights into the Jap bunkers, setting several alight. Everyone seemed to be firing, creating a crescendo of noise, eventually breaking the Japanese resistance. They fled from their posts. It was a very successful action and the remnants of C Company were grateful. If only we had had the tanks for the first attack, what a difference it would have made.

Most of the Japanese fled their posts but cunningly left some men behind to catch our troops unaware as they moved forward. By 3.30pm, after heavy fighting, C Company was in control of its initial target, which was the end of the New Strip. Despite the utter confusion of the first few hours' fighting on 18 December, Lieutenant Colonel Cummings sought to maintain control of his battle under trying circumstances. If he was not certain of what was happening, he had someone out to the relevant company to ascertain the true position. He grieved deeply over the number of casualties.

B Company, supposedly in reserve, was in fact quickly committed to action. As they moved forward, the 'mopping up' role assigned to them became front-line fighting. All their platoon commanders were killed before they joined up with A and D companies at 4.00pm. B Company reached its objective with 20 men left out of 90.

That the soldiers of the 2/9th had advanced into that screen of fire and maintained their momentum was extraordinary enough, but perhaps the most startling achievement that day was their unflappable discipline while taking such crushing casualties. The battalion's level of training, discipline and esprit de corps is perhaps best illustrated by the fact that, by 10 o'clock that morning, the adjutant and seven of the 12 platoon commanders were dead. And yet those troops did not falter: as a leader was killed or wounded, courage, initiative and maintenance of the objective ruled.

Graham 'Snow' Hynard of B Company made entries in his diary at the end of each day. On 18 December he found a Japanese diary, and with a stub of a pencil graphically recorded the day's happenings:

> Friday 18 December 1942. Early morning. We moved within 50 yards of firing line, which the Yanks had held for five weeks. They had given us cigarettes and we were grateful.
>
> Seven am we moved into front line and the Japs threw everything they had at us, they were zinging over my head like hornets. We had a few tanks and moved up behind them. In the first 10 minutes my officer was killed and my corporal was cut in the head with a grenade. The first 'deadun' I saw was a Jap, who had been that way for weeks. I surprised myself by my lack of emotion. We were pinned down by a sniper who was only a few yards in front in a sangar [stone enclosure].
>
> I saw Scotty our stretcher bearer walking back with a wounded arm, he had just passed me when this sniper got him in the stomach. It was terrible to hear his groans, but we had orders not to help anyone, but keep going. We disposed of the sniper with hand grenades and moved from one coconut tree to the other. The Japs had innumerable machine gun nests in concrete sangars and they had coconuts and creepers growing over them so we could not see them until we were right on them.

The rifle companies were not the only troops under extreme pressure and fire. In the close jungle war action of Papua New Guinea, death or a wound came to anyone at any time and from literally anywhere. The Intelligence Section suffered greatly: our officer, Lieutenant Tony Worthington, was shot twice by a sniper and his place taken by Lieutenant Jackson.

Four members of the 'I Section' attached to companies became casualties.

Moving around between the companies was a macabre and at times hair-raising task. It was sickening to see the number of mutilated, dead bodies lying everywhere, together with the torn undergrowth, blood-stained clothing and discarded utensils of war. Some of the dead lay or were slumped in natural positions, appearing to be in a deep, peaceful sleep. I thought one of your lads, Jack Hardwick, was asleep, and I had to gently push him to make sure. Poor old Jack did not wake up. Any thoughts of peace were driven from your mind when you heard the sharp crack of a sniper's bullet. Although you knew that it was not the one you could hear that claimed you, you still instinctively ducked. According to Snow Hynard's diary:

> The tanks were doing a wonderful job, but even they couldn't damage sangars and we had to get at them with grenades. By midday we had gone about 500 yards and ran right into hell itself. Very seldom could you see the enemy. At this point we were told to withdraw a few yards while the tanks went in; two of my mates started to go back, and Les was hit right in the back. I was pinned under a tree with the sniper right on me for two hours and Les only a few yards away. It was hell not to able to help him, but assured him that I was staying until I could. We took the post and Pat and I got Les out. The bullet was sticking out of his back but he wasn't bad and walked out. I was completely exhausted and sick. We captured four machine guns that evening. Tom was now Platoon Commander [Corporal Tom Clarke MM] and I have never seen a man with more guts, he never took cover and was everywhere. He was wounded four times but still kept on going. We made a perimeter for the night but there were many missing faces.

Clarke miraculously survived Buna and the rest of the war. The battalion formed a perimeter on the night of 18 December 1942, deeply saddened by its sacrifice – five officers and 49 other ranks killed in action and six officers and 111 other ranks wounded in action.

On 19 December the 2/9th took stock of its gained ground, reorganised, and continued to clean out all the enemy defences encountered the previous day. Burial parties were kept busy with their sad, noisome task.

from *Footsteps of Ghosts* by Bill Spencer

Stretcher bearer, Corporal Leslie (Bull) Allen carries a comrade to safety.

Homeland Under Attack

Homeland Under Attack

The attack on Pearl Harbor seemingly established Japan as the leading power in the Pacific, controlling landmasses from Manchuria to New Guinea. Within Australia, a Labor government had gained power and John Curtin would hold office during the critical war years from October 1941 to July 1945.

When Japan entered the war in December 1941, Australia found itself confronted by one of its worst nightmares: invasion from the north by an Asian power. The defence of Britain and the battles against German troops in North Africa swiftly became of secondary importance. The British attempt to halt the Japanese advance in Malaya had resulted in the sinking, by torpedo bombers, of two great symbols of British power, the battleships *Prince of Wales* and *Repulse*. This had convinced Australia of its isolation and vulnerability.

Many Australian troops were brought back from overseas to defend Australia as part of Curtin's 'Australia First' policy, and American forces were in Australia under the command of General Douglas Macarthur when Darwin was raided by Japanese planes in February 1942. The city was unprepared. Civilians were machine-gunned in the streets. Bombs destroyed ships and buildings, and even the hospital was damaged. More raids were to follow. The federal government minimised the intensity and extent of the attacks but the Australian population was shocked to realise that Japanese power had reached their homeland.

The next shock came three months later when Japanese midget subs, released from a large 'mother' submarine off Sydney Heads, penetrated the harbour defences and caused havoc before they could be destroyed. Even Australia's largest city no longer seemed safe.

The third threat to Australia's security came with the violent, mass breakout of Japanese prisoners of war from a camp at Cowra in New South Wales. It occurred in August 1944 and was accompanied by much loss of life. To the stunned population of Australia, it seemed that a kamikaze attempt had actually occurred within their homeland.

Darwin bombed

On the morning of 19 February 1942, Commander Mitsuo Fuchida led a force of Japanese low-flying bombers and fighters in a surprise raid on Darwin. Sirens sounded only a few minutes before the planes arrived. People in the streets and buildings suddenly found themselves threatened by exploding bombs and machine-gun bullets. Fearing a Japanese invasion, many people including soldiers and airmen fled from the town. Shipping in Darwin Harbour and planes on Darwin's airfield were specially targeted. Altogether, 240 people were killed and there were hundreds of wounded.

At the time, the Commonwealth Government censored the facts for fear of causing panic among the Australian people. Still, as is clear from the following extract, the fact remains that the Northern Territory's largest town was hopelessly ill prepared for the arrival of war:

Intelligence reports had told Commander Fuchida that he could expect to find Darwin harbour an attractive target, but he could hardly believe his eyes as he came within sight of it for the first time. There below him, trapped like rabbits in a snare, were no less than forty-five ships.

He led his force in a wide sweep around the town, positioning them for the first attack and expecting at any moment to be met by a furious onslaught from the guns on the ground, but there was nothing. Not a shot was fired. Even as he came over the town and was laying his aim on the ships in the harbour he could see people apparently going about their business unconcernedly. The first bombs went away and only then did a few anti-aircraft guns come to life.

He knew exactly what his priorities were and so, if they had followed their briefing, did every member of his team. The Japanese had evolved a scheme which allowed them to bomb with great accuracy even when they were using semi-skilled air crews, and he was to use this with devastating effect on Darwin.

Each bomber had a bomb-sight, but in most cases this was not used. Instead, there was only one bomb aimer in each flight and he located the target and at the critical moment waved a flag that the crews of the other aircraft would see. This was the signal for them all to release their bombs simultaneously and it ensured a highly effective bombing pattern. If the leader's aircraft was destroyed, the crew of the plane immediately to his right would normally take over the role.

Bruce Acland, in his slit trench near the perimeter of the runway, had his first taste of a 500-pound bomb when one exploded only 75 metres away. He never imagined that an explosion could be so deafening and he experienced a partial blackout of all his senses. And then the fighters came in almost at ground level, machine-gunning aircraft and buildings with deadly accuracy. They were so low that the Australians could see the pilots' faces.

A small-arms dump, used by the RAAF, caught fire and 300,000 rounds of .303 ammunition began to explode. There were smaller fires everywhere and when the fighters had disappeared, Acland and the others ran to the aerodrome to try to put them out. But the Japanese had set the fire tender alight and they couldn't get near it.

The roar from the fires was now so loud that they could hardly hear themselves speak and a strong wind was fanning the flames towards the main administration building. The shack housing the transmitters and receivers had been hit, but the damage did not appear to be too severe. For the time being, however, they were still unusable because the power in the town had been destroyed and their emergency power supply was on fire.

There was a direct line to Darwin Radio, the AWA coastal station, and Acland was given permission by Lou Curnock to use his emergency facilities. The most urgent priority was to warn all unsuspecting civil aircraft to stay well clear of the Darwin area until further notice. For the next five days, all communications about civil air operations had to be sent through VID, adding yet another burden to the AWA staff, many of whom worked day and night without sleep to maintain contact with the outside world.

After the raid, Bruce Acland and two other DCA radio operators drove across to the RAAF base intending to offer them the use of their transmitter if they needed it. To their astonishment, the station was deserted and they could find nobody. They wandered unchallenged through the base until they came to the transmitter room. It should have been under close security, but instead they found the door swinging open and the room empty.

The transmitter seemed to be undamaged, so they opened up a watch on an emergency frequency and stayed there the rest of the day until, late that night, three RAAF wireless operators returned and took over.

The RAAF watch was with the Air Board in Melbourne, but this was fast becoming absurd because all in-coming messages were in code and all the officers who could have decoded them had run away.

By that evening, there were so many signals stacked up which none of them could read that Andrew Swan [another survivor] agreed to go in search of one of the missing decoding officers. He had no luck, but what he did find, 30 kilometres down the road at the ACH transmitting station, was a code book, which he brought back carefully hidden as he had no right to it. In this way they decoded their signals and at the same time managed to keep from the Air Board for one more day the truth about what had happened at Darwin that day.

In the town, people reacted to the raid in many ways. Some broke down immediately while others displayed courage they had probably never suspected they possessed. One elderly man, Alf Shepherd, a veteran of the Battle of Mons in the First World War, sat unperturbed on a flight of office steps and watched the raid as the planes swooped low over the town, machine-gunning and bombing, as though he were sitting on the Hill at the Sydney Cricket Ground.

He watched without expression as a man ran for safety and threw himself onto the ground centimetres ahead of a burst of machine gun fire. But his dog was fractionally too slow and it was hit by bullets and rolled over dead.

Property owner Roy Edwards, who was one of the few men in Darwin that day who had been born there, was talking to the secretary of the local Red Cross branch, and they went on chatting, watching unconcernedly as the Japanese aircraft came closer and closer. There was no alarm and Edwards was one of the many who were saying with relief, 'Thank God the Yanks are here at last!' And he added, 'If the Japs hear of this lot, they'll think twice before attacking.' Then the man he was talking to said, 'What are those silver-looking things?' and the dreadful truth suddenly dawned on Edwards.

He shouted, 'Good God! They're Japs – run for your life!' At the moment the first bomb exploded he heard a siren begin its low wailing somewhere behind him, gradually building up to a full crescendo. Roy Edwards was one of the few people in Darwin who had not worried unduly about being trapped in Darwin. Out of the civil aerodrome his little single-engined Puss Moth was waiting to take him and his wife to safety whenever the danger became too great. It never occurred to him, as it never occurred to anyone in Darwin that day, that the raid would take place without any warning. And he did not know until later that day that his Puss Moth was a smouldering ruin, machine-gunned out of existence by a Zero pilot.

Not far away in the police barracks in Mitchell Street, Constable Leo Law had just stepped under the shower when the raid began. He knew at once what was happening and, wrapping a towel around himself, he raced outside and dived into a slit trench that had been dug for public servants in one of the other government departments.

Law had taken careful note of the position of that trench because by some bizarre aberration, the acting senior police officer in the town, First Class Sergeant Bridgland, had specifically forbidden his policemen to dig slit trenches. Bridgland had told them that if there was an air raid, they would all be on duty patrolling the town and wouldn't need any slit trenches.

Throughout the town, civilians were exposed because they had not bothered to dig trenches; but nothing was quite so reprehensible as this order forbidding men who knew that they needed trenches from digging them. As it was, it was only by using the trenches that others had dug that at least five policemen were saved from certain death.

As Law dived for the trench, he heard the whistle of a falling bomb followed almost instantaneously by an almighty explosion. The bomb fell ten metres from where he was lying, and dirt and rocks showered down on him as he lay, with his hands protecting the back of his head. For a few terrifying moments he couldn't breathe and he thought he had been buried alive. But he managed to push his head clear through a metre of rubble and for the rest of the raid he stayed there, covered with dirt, which he hoped would give him a little more protection.

Through the dirt he could hear the planes screaming over the town, and behind him on the oval there was the constant hammering of machine guns from the anti-aircraft positions. As he gingerly lifted his head over the edge of the trench, he saw the ack-ack shells bursting behind, below and to the side of the Japanese planes, without ever seeming to touch them.

In the next trench was another policemen, Sergeant Bill McKinnon – though Law didn't know it until he heard McKinnon call out to an old man called Charlie Clark, who lived in a cottage next to the police barracks.

'Are you all right, Charlie Clark?' the sergeant called, and from the direction of the cottage came a muffled reply, 'Yes, I'm okay.' Charlie Clark had taken refuge under his kitchen table.

McKinnon had sent his wife to Adelaide with Guinea Airways, paying for her ticket himself rather than wait for the government to evacuate her. He was now living at the police barracks, and as his first action before going out of the trench he'd been to shake awake a constable who had been on duty the night before. McKinnon, too, had been bitterly resentful of the order that prevented the police from digging trenches. He was watching the level-bombers from the trench and saw the bombs fall away from the aircraft – 'like soap bubbles' – without at first realising what they were. He watched them all the way to the ground and saw them explode somewhere near the Administrator's residence. (Although the first run concentrated its

Darwin 1942, heavy anti-aircraft battery.

attack on the harbour, one stick of bombs, probably released too early, fell between the Darwin Hotel and the police station.)

During a lull in the bombing, McKinnon walked briskly between what was left of the police barracks and the government offices and then through the offices, calling out as he went, 'Is there anyone there?' The only reply came from a constable who had taken cover under a water tank behind the barracks. In the raid the tank was blasted right off its stand and no trace of it was ever found. The constable had looked up to find he was huddling under the open sky.

Labourer James Kerbin was due to go on the afternoon shift on the waterfront and he was asleep in the Don Hotel where he lived when the raid started. In his sub-conscious he heard the bombs falling and thought it was a thunderstorm. He got up, washed leisurely and as he looked out of the window, saw the post office blow up. He said later that his heart stopped beating.

In his cottage behind the Victoria Hotel, another waterside worker, Joe Walker, was also in bed when he heard one of the sirens, which was just outside his window, begin its slow wind up to the full alarm.

Walker, who was an assistant secretary of the North Australian Workers Union, walked to the edge of his verandah, but could see no aircraft, although he could hear the sound of the bombs exploding and the anti-aircraft guns firing frantically. Debris was falling all the time on the tin roof of his cottage.

When the dive-bombers began screaming down over the harbour he tried to take a few steps outside the cottage but he was almost hit by the falling cases from the ack-ack ammunition and he had to beat a hasty retreat. He stayed indoors until the raid seemed to be over and then walked down towards the waterfront to see what had happened. He passed some men in khaki wearing steel helmets and they told him to go back and change out of his white shirt because it would be a good target for the Japanese if they returned. He thought that idea was daft, as he put it later, but he was in no mood for an argument and, uncharacteristically for him, did as he was told.

There were few closer encounters with death than that of Thornton Hunter, who was a mess manager at one of the workmen's camps on East Point. Thornton was on his way to the hospital to have treatment for his leg in the out-patient's department when there was an enormous explosion at the end of the hospital where the military patients were housed.

He threw himself to the ground and bridged himself, keeping his stomach off the ground to lessen the effects of bomb blast. A shower of dirt and small stones poured down on him but he was not injured. Thinking that it was now clear, he picked himself up, shook off the dirt and had just started to walk towards the hospital when a Zero came after him. Hunter glanced over his shoulder and saw the fighter coming straight at him, flying at tree-top height, its machine guns blazing. With bullets ripping up the ground all around him and whistling past his feet, he didn't know whether to stand or run. As the fighter roared over his head, he fancied he could see the pilot gesturing obscenely, a broad grin on his face. The hospital was severely attacked, but whether by mistake for the Larrakeyah Barracks (which it closely resembled from the air), or deliberately was never clear. Certainly, between the aerial photographs being taken of the area by Japanese reconnaissance planes, and the raid itself, the barracks was roughly camouflaged with sandbags, piled thirteen high all around it. From the altitude of the bombers, it would have been very easy to mistake the hospital for the now camouflaged barracks. And the red crosses which were later claimed to have been very conspicuously painted on the hospital roof would have been invisible from 7000 metres.

Fuchida afterwards said that it had never been his intention to bomb the hospital, any more than he had ordered his pilots to attack a hospital ship which was anchored in the harbour. True or not, it was much less convincing to believe that the low-flying dive-bombers and the fighters were confused about their target, for they must have seen the red crosses.

In his radio room at Fannie Bay, Lou Curnock heard the explosions that rocked Darwin three kilometres away and a moment later the shock waves rattled the walls and the windows of the building. He punctiliously logged the time of the raid, 0958, and breathed a sigh of relief that at least he had given the town twenty minutes warning.

from *Darwin, 1942* by Timothy Hall

Japanese midget subs attack Sydney Harbour

On 3 May 1942, mother vessels released three Japanese midget subs, each controlled by two men, off the New South Wales coast. The subs headed into Sydney Harbour and, as it was a time of invasion fears, their appearance seemed to indicate a larger waiting force.

One of the submarines, the *M-24*, attacked with torpedoes, causing confusion, damage and loss of life in Sydney Harbour. One torpedo sank HMAS *Kuttabul*, a wooden harbour ferry converted to a RAN depot ship. Although two of the midget subs were destroyed, *M-24* escaped from the harbour and headed out to sea.

Judging by author Lew Lind's study of the incident, the results of this underwater invasion could quite easily have been far more devastating:

Japanese midget sub sunk in Sydney Harbour.

At 5.02pm on 31 May the eternity of waiting ended for Lieutenants Chuma, Matsuo, Ban and their crewmen. One by one, at intervals of nineteen minutes, the midget submarines floated free of their mother ships, the clutches were engaged and the telephone umbilical line separated. The fear of the operation being aborted was swept away by the keen wind.

Now, with the guardian heads of the enemy harbour looming like crouched lions, they would revenge a hundredfold their comrades who had died so heroically at Pearl Harbor. In two hours, the enemy battleships swinging on their buoys would erupt in fire and thunder. The attackers would be dead when the sun rose, but their spirits would exult to the million banzais which would rise higher than Fujiyama when the news of their success reached Japan.

Through the narrow radius of their periscopes they could see heavy waves swell and curl in lips of white spume at the foot of the cliffs. The beacon lights were visible at the entrance to the harbour and, on the cliff tops, the softer glow of house lights.

The three midget submarines rendezvoused at 6.55pm, a mile short off the Heads. They were partly submerged and the silhouettes of the hulls and the conning towers made small targets. As they rocked in the swell, the lights of a small collier appeared from the north. It was the *Mortlake Bank*, low in the water with a full cargo of coal from Newcastle. From time to time they sighted brightly lit Manly ferries passing close inshore to Middle Head. There was no sign of patrol boats.

M-24 is believed to have entered through the boom gate, passing under, or close to, HMAS *Yarroma.* Despite the presence of patrol boats, the midget was not detected in her passage down-harbour to the main anchorage east of Garden Island. The midget submarine passed through the destroyers and small ships and followed the shoreline of Garden Island. As she neared the north-east corner of the base, lookouts on USS *Chicago* sighted her. It was 10.30pm.

Surprisingly, the submarine did not submerge and soon came under fire from the heavy cruiser's 5-inch and close-range guns. Six minutes after this first sighting, *M-24* narrowly averted a collision with the dockyard tender *Nestor* as it rounded the knuckle of the island.

Searchlights from the ships at anchor and from shore batteries were now sweeping the surface and blinding the gunlayers. Shells screamed high over the small target and crashed into Fort Denision, the 1850s fort in the middle of the harbour.

A harbour ferry, crowded with theatre-goers returning home, was caught in this melee of gunfire and wildly flashing lights. The passengers, believing they were seeing a navy exercise, rushed to the rail and caught a momentary glimpse of the conning tower of the midget submarine 100 yards away. The ferry master was not deceived. He rang down the order 'full astern'.

The city's air-raid sirens sounded at 11pm, adding their banshee wails to the chorus of the guns. Many of the city's residents, awakened by the gunfire, hurried to the nearest air-raid shelters.

Ten minutes later the corvette HMAS *Geelong*, berthed at the northern end of Garden Island, sighted *M-24* and opened fire with machine-guns. The corvette's gunner was ashore and her 4-inch gun could not be brought into action. Bullets from the machine-guns were seen ricocheting off the submarine's conning tower.

M-24 apparently dived soon after and was next sighted from the cruiser HMAS *Canberra* at no. 1 buoy in Farm Cove. AB R.W. White, who was on watch in the cruiser, recalls: 'The objective, propelled by a propeller at a speed which was more like a midget submarine than a torpedo, dived and passed under *Canberra*.' The four patrol boats, *Steady Hour*, *Sea Mist*, *Toomaree* and *Marlean*, moored inshore of the cruiser, failed to sight the submarine.

Canberra was the third large warship to be passed at close range by *M-24*, which suggests the midget's periscope was defective or damaged. The other possibility for Lieutenant Ban not attacking on the inward passage was the powerful arc lights reflecting on the water and the mirrors of the submarine periscope. This, with the dazzling beams of the searchlights, would have effectively blinded him.

The reactions to the attack on the two largest men-o'-war in the harbour were directly opposite. Before Captain Bode returned on board USS *Chicago*, the heavy cruiser was firing wildly with her 5-inch and small-calibre armament at anything that moved on the water. Large shells screamed low over harbour ferries, chewed large lumps of masonry from Fort Denison and ricocheted wildly off the rocky foreshores of Mosman. Captain Bode disbelieved the large number of submarine sightings reported by the cruiser's company and ordered all firing to cease.

Conditions in HMAS *Canberra* remained calm and disciplined, and Captain G.D. Moore recorded in the ship's Letters of Proceedings: '*Canberra* was at No. 1 Buoy, Farm Cove and two-thirds of the ship's company was on night leave. We were able to raise steam for slow speed and kept the ship's head pointed so as not to be silhouetted against the shore lights.' The ship did not open fire, despite the passing of *M-24* under the cruiser's keel.

Shortly after 11pm Sydney radio stations interrupted their programmes to broadcast a 'general recall' to all sailors on leave. Police patrol cars were instructed to round up naval personnel in the city and return them to Garden Island. Attendants at Sydney railway stations were alerted to inform sailors of the general recall.

At 11.15pm the guns fell silent, although the nervous fingers of searchlights still probed the anchorage and the shoreline. Admiral Muirhead-Gould was at his Garden Island headquarters, studying the reports which were still arriving. Since a malfunction of the radio transmission had temporarily blacked out communications, messages from the Port War Signal Station were relayed by telephone. Irritated by the slow reporting, Muirhead-Gould called up his speedboat and at 11.26pm set out for an inspection of the defences. He went alongside *Yarroma* and spoke briefly to Lieutenant Eyers and then crossed the harbour to the Port War Signal office on South Head.

M-24 was still in the lower harbour area, but fifty minutes passed before she was sighted again. It was thought Ban took the midget down to the bottom and waited until the surface commotion subsided.

At 12.25am, on 1 June, he surfaced again. He was in open water between Bradleys Head and where USS *Chicago* was moored. *M-24* closed the range to approximately 500 yards and the first torpedo leapt out of its tube. It ran true, but the setting was too deep and it passed under the cruiser. Thirty seconds later, a great gout of water rose above HMAS *Kuttabul* and the Dutch submarine *K-9*. The second torpedo was running before the first struck; it passed five yards clear of *Chicago*'s bows and hit the shoreline of Garden Island, adjacent to the Gun Wharf, without detonating.

Kuttabul was not torpedoed. The torpedo passed under her and struck the base of the stone wall below the wharf. The blast from the explosion lifted the wooden ferry bodily out of the water and she sank in a swirl of splintered timber and debris. The sinking of *Kuttabul* was witnessed by Mr J. Donaldson, who was in a small motor launch some distance off Garden Island fishing for John Dory: 'The explosion set us swinging violently. Several of us were thrown to the deck. I thought a Jap plane had scored a near miss and I expected more bombs.'

K-9 was also lifted out of the water and rolled on her beam ends. The submarine suffered no casualties – half of the crew was ashore – but she was severely damaged. The depth gauges and light bulbs were shattered and her diesel engines lifted from their beds. She was never to be used operationally again. Several months after the attack, the submarine was transferred to the Royal Australian Navy for training anti-submarine vessels.

Controversy is still rife on *M-24*'s failure to score a hit on USS *Chicago*. One school of thought believes the torpedoes were damaged by gunfire. The author supports the damaged-periscope theory. If the periscope was damaged, Ban had no other recourse but to surface and physically line up the midget's bows with the target. The wind and waves, the wash from the many patrol boats and the tendency of the midgets to porpoise under wave conditions would account not only for the first torpedo diving deep and passing under the cruiser, but would also tend to swing the midget's bows off-line in the interval between firing and launching.

The explosion of the torpedo sounding HMAS *Kuttabul*'s death knell reverberated around the harbour and sent another wave of alarm through the now fully wakened residents of the city. Many still believed the city was under air attack, and some were sure that a Japanese invasion had commenced. Panic was taking a grip on the population.

What happened to *M-24* after she fired her torpedoes remains a mystery. Ban's desperate attempts to break through the ring of fully alerted patrol vessels may have been responsible for the reports of a fourth midget submarine in the harbour. The outward crossing of the magnetic indicator loop recorded at 1.58am may have been *M-24*, the unsatisfactory performance of the loops throughout the attack casts doubt on any such assumption.

The reader's faith in the accuracy of reports made by the defenders on that night must be shaken by the wild claims that have since been found to be incorrect. Fifty years later, the official history of the action, *Royal Australian Navy 1942–1945*, still records HMAS *Kuttabul* being sunk at 11.30pm on 31 May – the wrong time and the wrong date. The error appeared in Rear Admiral Muirhead-Gould's first report to the Australian Naval Board on 22 June. It was corrected in the admiral's second report, dated 16 July, but few had the opportunity to read it.

Ordinary Seaman T. Lawrence, a survivor of HMAS *Kuttabul*, never doubted the ship sank at 12.30am on 1 June. He recalled:

> I was in *Kuttabul* waiting to join my ship HMAS *Dubbo* and on the night of 31 May was on sentry duty at the Gun Wharf at Garden Island. My duty spell ended at midnight, but when my relief failed to arrive I walked back to the ship and woke him up. In order not to disturb the other sailors, I climbed into my relief's hammock which was close to the door. The time was approximately 12.15am and about fifteen minutes later I was wakened and stunned by a violent explosion, I threw myself out of the hammock and the water was up to my waist. I knew the ship was sinking. When I reached the shore *Kuttabul* was well down in the water. My watch, a gift from my mother, stopped when it was immersed. The time it

> stopped was 12.30. I never had the watch repaired but kept it as a grim reminder of my closest brush with death.

There were thirty survivors of the sinking, ten of whom were wounded. Two of these were ratings of the Royal New Zealand Navy and one of the Royal Netherlands Navy. Their accounts of the torpedo destroying *Kuttabul* were reported in the *Daily Telegraph* the next day.

Seaman William Willams of Inverell, one of the wounded, commented: 'Can you beat it! More than two years overseas and I don't cop it till I was back in my own home port. I've been in danger spots about England, in the Mediterranean, Indian and Pacific oceans, getting mighty close to it at times, but never like this.'

Leading Wireless Operator J.B. Donaldson said: 'I, and about 14 other men, climbed through the windows and ran down the deck. Some of us climbed across a launch while others dived into the water and swam to safety.'

New Zealander AB C.R. Whitfield was another of the wounded: 'Just got out of my hammock, I had reached the top deck to go on duty, when there was a hell of a noise. Bits of ferry flew all around me and I thought we were being bombed. I called out to my mate named Richards, "Where are you Snowy?" But there was no answer.' One of Whitfield's legs was broken and the other badly lacerated.

AB Eric Doylen said: 'I had been asleep on the lower deck when the explosion come. I was blown right through the roof to the next deck, getting wedged in some of the timbers. No matter how I struggled, I could not free myself. Soon the water was up to my head. I was pulled out, and here I am, not hurt very much.'

The devastation ashore at Garden Island was not as great as was expected. Fifty yards north of where *Kuttabul* sank the clock in the high tower of the Command Building had stopped. Each of its four faces had showed a different time, one hour apart. The blast from the torpedo had swept up the tower and lifted the four clock drives from the gear wheel. Ten yards behind the wharf, two great sliding timber doors of the rigging shed were blown fifty yards out into

Woolloomooloo Bay. The navy dental surgery, alongside the wharf, escaped with minor damage. A lower-floor window had been inadvertently left down and the blast passed through the opening and then upward, removing two sheets of asbestos roofing.

Empty oil drums, stacked four rows high on the wharf, were hurled into the air and were later found scattered hundreds of yards away. A five-ton steel boiler was tossed into the water close to Clark Island and was found next day, aground at Elizabeth Bay.

Many hours were to pass before the dockyard workforce could be checked for casualties. Night shifts on duty were scattered in naval stores and workshops over a large area. In the minutes following the explosions they had run for shelter, some joining the stream of construction workers running along 'the Burma Road' which joined the island to the shore at Potts Point. Rescue operations at the site of the sinking were just commencing and would continue through the night.

To add to the confusion, the guns on ships in the anchorage had reopened fire and shells were landing in the water close inshore. The searchlights, which earlier in the night had swept the harbour waters, were now fanning across the sky searching for enemy aircraft, believing the explosion was caused by an aerial bomb. The safety valve of a steam whistle in one of the darkened workshops had jammed in the 'on' position, so escaping steam wailed a mournful dirge for the dead sailors trapped in the twisted and battered hull of the unlucky accommodation ship.

from *Toku Tai* by Lew Lind

Breakout at Cowra

On 5 August 1944, hundreds of Japanese prisoners attacked their guards and broke out of the prisoner-of-war camp at Cowra in the central west of New South Wales. Fanatical Japanese leaders urged the prisoners 'to die like the carp', with dignity. Several hundred prisoners were killed and hundreds more escaped. Four Australian soldiers died and four were wounded.

News of the full extent of the breakout was suppressed by the government for fear of its effect on Australian morale. Much later, however, writers like Harry Gordon would tell the whole story:

The Cowra prisoner of war camp.

It was very close to midnight when Seji Ogi told the men in his hut of their mission. They were in A Group and would attack the perimeter wire to the north-east. A number of them were civilian workers attached to the army rather than pure soldiers, but none of them demurred. 'What happens if and when we do get outside?' asked one young man.

'Ideally, if enough people get through, the thought is that we should re-group and head for the infantry training battalion,' Ogi replied. 'But that will depend on many things . . . mainly on the kind of success the whole plan is having. Nobody is too clear. We shall have to make our arrangements as we go. But this whole thing, you must know, is more about dying that fighting. That's why it is so important for you to think tonight about the carp, to remember that you have to die like the carp. The whole thing could go wrong. The

Australians may annihilate us all tonight. You have to be dignified at the last moment, like the carp. This is a good time for you to think about those streamers and coloured fish that were flying over your homes in Japan just a couple of months ago. You remember them, don't you, so coloured and lively . . . a carp for every one of you?'

Most of the thirty young men nodded. A few looked steadfastly ahead. All of them were silent, though, their thoughts on families, friends, customs, countryside too many thousands of miles away.

As the minutes marched mutely towards 2am that Saturday, the prison camp at Cowra resembled a deserted fairground. The lights still blazed along Broadway and at intervals around the perimeter wire, but a great ghostly silence had finally invaded the place. Three of the four quarters of the circle had subsided into sleep; in the fourth the wakefulness – and even the occasional agonising death – was controlled and quiet.

It was Private Alfred James Rolls, lone member of the quarter-guard which had been posted from D Camp in a tent in the centre of Broadway, who first saw any sign of activity. His orders were straight-forward: to watch through the gappy wooden gates for any incident in the Japanese compound, and to telephone the D Camp guardroom immediately he had something to report.

Sometime towards a quarter to two, Rolls thought he saw a figure bobbing from one of the huts towards the gate. What had happened was that a Japanese prisoner – never afterwards identified – had found the strain too great. He had not wanted to die, and had decided to cut and run to the gate to warn the authorities. Around the time Private Rolls saw him, about 20 metres from the huts, one of his fellow-prisoners spotted him too.

'What's going on?' called Rolls, moving towards the gate with his .303 in the ready position.

The Japanese kept running towards the gate, with his hands now above his head, shouting incomprehensibly. He seemed to be trailing a blanket. The prisoner scaled the gate easily, still calling, then dashed towards Rolls. He was clearly terrified.

Rolls had waited long enough. He fired two warning shots in the air, the arranged signal for an 'incident'. Almost immediately his telephone rang. The Japanese was close now, but he had stopped running when he heard the shots, and was calling feverishly. Rolls picked up the phone.

'What the hell's happened?' asked Corporal Speerman, from the guardroom.

'I've got this Jap here,' said Rolls. 'He's in an awful state, yelling and screaming. I can't understand a word, but he's dead scared.'

'Just hang on to him,' said the corporal. 'We'll be there in a minute with an escort.'

In Hut 13, Tadao Minami had been told what had happened. 'Get that man,' he screamed. 'He's an informer.' Then he sounded a blast on his bugle. It was now about five minutes before the scheduled time of 2am.

The prisoners whose job it was to attack the gates into Broadway spilled out of their huts and headed after the informer. Seconds later, waves of Japanese shouting 'Banzai, banzai' were charging across B Compound in their prearranged directions.

Now the whole garrison was awake. The colonel and his four camp commandants were trying to find out what was going on. Others, whose task was simply to take up post as soon as they heard the two-shot warning, were already sprinting, greatcoats over pyjamas.

Private Rolls saw the two-man escort party approaching him at a jog along Broadway, from the direction of B Company headquarters. Then, running towards him in the other direction, he could see Lieutenant Thomas Aisbett, orderly officer of D Camp. They all met at the B Compound gates – the on-duty sentry Rolls, the two members of the escort party, Lieutenant Aisbett and the frightened Japanese, still with his hands clutching a blanket, above his head.

Aisbett said later that the prisoner 'kept shivering and crying'. He was trying to tell the lieutenant something, and occasionally used the words 'strike' and 'calaboose'. But he was unable to make himself understood. For a moment the group just stood there, with Aisbett trying to comprehend all that was happening. A matter of minutes ago he had been asleep; now he knew that an alert had been sounded, a strange bugle sound had blasted the icy air, and he was confronted with a terrified Japanese prisoner who was jabbering and pointed to the compound behind him.

Then Aisbett heard a growing commotion as a mass of Japanese rushed towards the gate. He looked around, quickly calculated that he and the other Australians had only three rifles between them, and made a decision. 'Run for your lives,' he yelled. The guards fired a couple of shots at what seemed a rolling, swelling, burgundy-coloured flood of human beings about to hit the gates. Then they turned tail, abandoned their prisoner, and galloped towards the gates at the southern end of Broadway, about 50 metres away.

As Aisbett and his comrades ran, the southern gates at the end of Broadway were opened to let them through. Aisbett looked around once, and saw a great surge of Japanese, ranged right across Broadway, pelting after his group. He glanced up at the tower above the southern end of Broadway where someone from his company should have been on duty with a Bren gun. It should have been raking the road behind him, cutting down his pursuers. But the tower was still silent as the Australians reached the end of Broadway and the hefty wooden gates clanged shut behind them. Further back along Broadway the Japanese would-be informer had run a few paces, then turned, stopped and run towards the side of the road, like an uncertain rabbit. Then the mob were upon him. He was clubbed and slashed, and his throat was cut. His body was kicked aside as the stampede continued, almost without interruption.

At this moment, so many other things were happening. The heart of B Compound had erupted like a spewing people-volcano. Two streams were hitting Broadway, and two coursing towards the boundary fence. The sheer weight of the force which headed after Aisbett and his party burst open the gates into Broadway, splintering the wood and squeezing out the screws which held padlock attachments.

The fires, which were to have synchronized with the onslaught immediately after Minami's bugle call, were a few minutes late. The tailor's shop erupted in flame first, then a sleeping hut. Soon the whole core of the compound would be a noisy inferno, with straw palliasses and firewood and wooded walls blazing, then fibro roofs exploding like grenades in the heat. Eighteen of the 20 huts were burnt, and inside them the bodies of some 20 Japanese who had elected to die before the break.

The main rush was towards the Vickers gun – Number Two Machine Gun Post to the garrison – which was mounted on a four-wheeled trailer and had been trained on the Japanese compound. It was situated 50 metres outside the three barbed-wire fences which surrounded the compound, beneath a searchlight and inside one last simple three-strand barbed-wire fence of a type found on most Australian farms.

The unmanned Vickers represented the finishing line in the most vital race of the whole terrible night. (The fact that it *was* unmanned on one of the last three nights before the separation of the Japanese represented an unawareness, or a complacency, that bordered on negligence.) The contestants in the race were two middle-aged, slightly short-of-breath bachelors, privates of the Australian Military Forces, both of whom were still rubbing sleep out of their eyes as they pulled greatcoats over army-issue flannel pyjamas and unlaced boots over bare feet, and some 200 desperate Japanese who had been watching that gun for many days, planning and preparing for just this contest. The Australians had to sprint about 50 metres from their beds in the B Company lines – outside and adjacent to the northern gateway to the camp; their starting gun had been the one which fired two bullets in Broadway, and roused them from their sleep. To reach the same point the Japanese had to cover about 200 metres and clamber over three separate and difficult barbed-wire barriers, about 10 metres apart and each two metres high; all of these fences carried seven spans of barbed wire, stapled into pine posts, and the second 10-metre gap – the area between the second and third fences – was filled to a height of about four or five feet with tangled barbed wire.

The middle fence was the toughest to negotiate; four coils of barbed wire festooned the whole length of it. It was a fairly daunting obstacle course, but the Japanese had the advantage of being virtually on their marks as the bugle sounded.

The Japanese did not really believe that they would reach the Vickers first. That could have been an undesirable result for them in a sense; certainly they might have been able to prevent the two-man Australian crew from taking it over, but they could not be sure that boxes of ammunition would have been easily available on the trailer. A more worthwhile result was to have the Australians win the race narrowly, and render the gun workable, even if that meant firing it into them. This was a suicide charge, with all of them prepared to die. They had the sheer weight of numbers to overpower the crew, even if the cost in lives was high. Then they would use the gun to assault the administration and sleeping huts and the guardrooms; they would be able to take possession of every round of ammunition, every rifle in the stores, the guardrooms and the huts.

Privates Ben Hardy and Ralph Jones reached the gun first. In fact boxes of ammunition were available on the trailer, and Hardy quickly began firing into the burgundy waves which were crashing and spilling over the first wire, with Jones feeding the ammunition belt.

Kiichi Ishi, the tailor from Tokyo, took part in the first assault on the Vickers gun. He carried a greatcoat and a blanket, wore a baseball glove on his left hand and grasped a nail-studded baseball bat in his right. He tossed the greatcoat and the blanket across the first high wire, which he reached on the left of a three-abreast line with Michinosuke Sawada and Buichi Sato. Sawada, beside him in the middle of the trio, was hit in the abdomen and the right leg as they attempted to straddle the wire; he was a close friend who had been captured in New Britain, and Ishi wasn't keen to leave him up high on the wire. 'Can I help?' he asked. Sawada was too far gone to reply, and suddenly Ishi was on his way again, across the wire and heading for the concertina roll ahead. On the flat, he looked around for Sato – but found no sign of him. He plunged for a few yards towards the next fence, then dived down into the tufty, frosty grass as the gunfire raked towards him.

The chattering machine-gun left 23 bodies draped on the concertina roll, punctuating and blotting the barrier grotesquely as mortally wounded men subsided onto the blankets they had thrown ahead of them. The main, high coil was like a heavy red surf, with new waves pounding down continuously, remorselessly. High on this wall of wire and blankets and dead and dying humans, Shonai Kichiro, a New Guinea veteran who had arrived at Cowra in the same convoy as the Korean informer Matsumoto, was shot in the face. He did not scream or struggle; almost as a reflex action, he buried a knife blade deep in his solar plexus. Shigeo Tairo, a non-combatant labourer, hoisted himself across the crest of the wire-wave and jumped – but twisted an ankle badly as he landed in a furrow of earth. He tried to run on, but found he could put no weight on the injured ankle. 'Stab me, Fumio', he called to a friend who landed close by; Fumio obliged, stabbing him in the chest. 'Again, please, again,' called Shigeo. Fumio stabbed again, and missed the heart again. 'I have to go,' said Fumio apologetically, 'I can't wait.' The searchlights were glaring as Fumio headed for the next obstacle, leaving his friend Shigeo weeping because he had no knife.

Six more died under the wires approaching the third high fence – among them Kazunari Okada, a regular soldier who had helped take care of Ichijiro Do at the Port Moresby hospital after they had both been captured. And still they came, across that last wire hurdle – where 15 died – and across the last 60 metres to the mounted gun, swinging their clubs and knives. Hardy depressed the gun further and further as the Japanese swarmed below and around him; men's heads were literally torn off as the Vickers pumped downwards now.

As the Japanese began to engulf Hardy's position the searchlight above the gun – and indeed all the lights of the camp – went dark. A ricocheting bullet had cut the wire that fed electricity to the unit, and suddenly people were charging about with hurricane lamps. Not that it made much difference, though; from where Ben Hardy sat behind his gun, the crackling fires and the lovely full moon provided more than enough light.

Hardy knew now that he and Jones had no hope. It was like trying to stay on a rock that was about to be submerged by a powerful wave. But he knew, too, that there were plenty of belts of ammunition unused, and that if the Japanese took over the gun they could inflict a great deal of damage on the garrison. 'Get going, Ralph,' he called to Jones – and Jones tried a frantic dive across the Japanese heads.

It is worth focussing briefly on this man Hardy in the last few seconds of his life. He was days away from his 46th birthday, and he had always lived with his mother and sister, whom he accused often and good-naturedly of mollycoddling him. He was a fisherman and an expert rifleman who shot in Saturday-afternoon contests with the Chatswood (Sydney) rifle club; one of the few real joys of his army life came from the constant study, dismantling, assembly and demonstration of weapons. He refused on principle to shoot at rabbits and game-birds, and he kept a cockatoo as a pet, trying vainly but persistently to teach it to talk. Despite his carefully clipped moustache, he was emphatically not a ladies' man; he had always preferred to mess about with fishing bait for hours in his toolshed rather then attend parties or dances. In civilian life he had become a motor mechanic. He had had his last home leave – he lived beside Sydney Harbour – three weeks before, and as his tram pulled out after that last night together he was signalling his mother and sister in the city's brown-out by switching a torch on and off. He was tall and shy, and his was not the stuff of conventional heroes. He was an unlikely, over-gentle soldier, born at the wrong time for wars – too young for the first, too old for the second. And here he was now, dressed a little ludicrously in those striped pyjamas, separated from history, in the form of rewarded heroism, by the time it takes to count to ten.

What happened up there on the trailer after Ralph Jones made his last desperate dive has never been established conclusively. There is little doubt that in those final moments, Ben Hardy tried feverishly to render the machine-gun useless to the Japanese. He removed the block, and was attempting to dismantle other vital parts when he went down, clubbed repeatedly by baseball bats. Jones was clubbed too as he vaulted from the back of the trailer, then stabbed in the chest and the back. Again he was stabbed about the body, but he broke free and staggered about 80 metres to the steps of the nearest hut in the B Company lines. 'They got us,' he gasped, and fell dead.

from *Die Like the Carp* by Harry Gordon

Australian Prisoners of War

Australian Prisoners of War

More than 35,000 Australians became prisoners of war during World Wars I and II and the Korean War of 1950–53. Many of these died in POW camps. The stories of those who survived show the triumph of the human spirit in the face of adversity.

In the Gallipoli and Middle East campaigns against the Turks, over 200 Australians became the prisoners of Ottoman Turkey. Included among these were the captain and crew of the submarine *AE2* who were captured on 30 April 1915. They were soon put to work building roads and a section of the Baghdad railway. Conditions were extremely harsh, as A.B. Wheat, one of the captured sailors, recorded in his diary: 'In this space (twenty men in 3m x 3m) we had to eat and sleep for a week. The only liberty we had was one hour per day for those well enough to take it . . . I have often been in cramped spaces in submarines where you could cut the air with a knife but never did I experience the nausea I suffered in that putrid hole and it must have been worse for the sick and weak.'

On the Western Front, 4000 Australians fighting in France and Belgium were captured by the Germans between 1916 and 1918. Some of these POWs, in contravention of the Hague Convention, were compelled to work close to the German trenches and were exposed to artillery fire. Australian soldier Tommy Taylor, captured at Bullecourt in 1917, complained bitterly of his lot as a POW of the Germans: 'For fifteen weary months we have been forced by starvation and hardship to submit to humiliation and indignities, allowed barely sufficient food to keep body and soul together, and forced to gather weeds and herbs for sustenance; gaunt, unwashed,

Warrant officer Ronald Guthrie, with beard, and Americans, British and Turkish POWs during the winter of 1952–53 in North Korea.

unshaven and devoured by vermin; knowing practically nothing of what was going on beyond our barbed-wire enclosures; seemingly dead to the world, and, for all we knew, mourned as dead.'

In World War II, after defeats in Crete, Greece, North Africa and Singapore, many thousands of Australian soldiers became prisoners of the Germans and the Japanese. Australians who became German prisoners of war were generally treated in accordance with the Geneva Convention. Those captured by the Japanese, however, had to endure brutal discipline, torture, starvation and disease. Major Kevin Fagan, who served as a doctor on the Thai–Burma Railway, describes the horrifying ordeal of a group of soldiers who had the misfortune of being prisoners of the Japanese. 'There were about 300 of us left out of about 600. From that group, none of whom were well, all of whom had malaria, were malnourished, and some of them were shivering on parade, dressed in a lap-lap [loincloth] or a pair of shorts, rarely any boots, I had to choose 100 men to march another 100 miles into the unknown, certainly to worse and not to better. I never saw any of those men again . . . It was the most terrible thing I've had to do.' A number of the stories that follow in this chapter give personal examples of the tenacity and courage of POWs enduring captivity under Nippon.

In the Korean War, 29 Australian servicemen became prisoners of the North Koreans. This number included six members of 77 Squadron RAAF. All these Australian prisoners of war experienced great suffering at the hands of the North Koreans and their Chinese allies. As well as enduring cold, hunger and beatings, these prisoners were subjected to 'brainwashing' and psychological punishments.

Massacre in the surf

Vivian Bullwinkel was an Australian Army nursing sister with the 8th Division AIF in Malaya from 1941 till early in 1942, shortly before Singapore fell to the Japanese. She was with a group of Australian nurses evacuated from Singapore on the *Vyner Brooke*, only for the ship to be bombed and sunk. Twenty-two nurses were among the survivors who floated ashore with her. Vivian was later incarcerated with a number of other western women but much had happened in between, as Betty Jeffrey records:

Vivian is a tall, slim girl, with very fair straight hair, cut short, and blue eyes. She is not an excitable person at any time, and she quietly walked in through the door of the jail, clasping an army-type water bottle, which was slung over her shoulder, to her side. We immediately saw why she did this. It was hiding a bullet hole in her uniform.

We took her into our dormitory, and as we all gathered around her she told us what had happened.

Vivian was with a group of servicemen, civilian women, and twenty-two Australian Army Nursing Service sisters. They had all gathered at this one spot on the sandy beach about two or three miles from Muntok, and had come ashore in lifeboats or had swum in. They spent the first night sitting around the fire we had all seen from the sea. There were quite a few wounded people with them, so they decided that when morning came they would search for some Japanese and see if the wounded could be cared for properly.

They waited all day, but nothing happened, and when night fell they were still there.

Next morning it was decided that a naval officer should walk into Muntok and bring back some Japanese with stretchers for the wounded, also informing them of the presence of the party on the beach.

After an hour or so of waiting, the civilian women decided to walk on to Muntok themselves and so meet the Jap party on the way along. Our sisters, with Matron Drummond of the 13th AGH in charge, stayed behind to look after the wounded members of the group.

A little later the naval officer returned, bringing a party of Japanese with him. To everybody's amazement, the men were then separated from the nurses and then taken along the beach around a bluff and out of sight.

Later the Japs returned, wiping their bayonets, and everyone realised what had happened to the men.

The nurses were told to form a line, including the wounded, and walk into the sea. They were then machine-gunned from behind. All were killed outright but Vivian. A bullet passed through her left side just above her hip and sent her headlong into the water. She floated there for some minutes, then, when the Japanese had gone away, was able to struggle ashore. She realised she was the only person to survive. She wandered into the jungle, lay down by a tree, and went to sleep.

As soon as Vivian was able to walk she went back to the beach, thinking it was the same day and she had been asleep only a few hours. On the way she found an English serviceman, who told her he had been lying there for two days. His arm was badly wounded and he had been bayoneted. She helped him to move into the shade of the jungle, then went off to look for some food and water. She found a stream and was able to bring back water in her bottle.

For about ten days Vivian looked after this sick man, going each day to a small native settlement and getting food from them and water from the stream. The natives told her to give herself and her companion up to the Japanese; they had seen white women wearing Red Cross arm-bands in Muntok. They did not want to help them. As both were feeling a little better they decided to do this and so they set off for Muntok.

On the road they heard a car coming and it tooted at them. Quite unconsciously they moved to the side of the road to allow it to pass, then it dawned on them that the car must have Japanese in it, so they waited. It pulled up and a Japanese naval officer motioned them to get in. They did so, and he gave them a banana to eat.

This officer took them to Naval Headquarters and questioned them, then later brought them to the jail to join the rest of us.

What a wonderful relief it must have been for that poor girl, only in her twenties, to see familiar faces after going through a hell like that!

Vivian's companion was desperately ill and was put into the crude hospital here. He died a few days later.

After we heard this story we decided then and there never to mention it again; it would not do for it to go back to Japanese ears. The subject was strictly forbidden.

from *White Coolies* by Betty Jeffrey

Women prisoners of war were forced to bow as a sign of respect to their Japanese captors.

The courage of 'Weary' Dunlop

Australian surgeon Colonel Edward 'Weary' Dunlop has become a national legend because of the courage he displayed when serving as a senior medical officer in the prisoner-of-war camps in Java and on the Thai Burma Railway. A constant inspiration to his men, Dunlop was described as 'A lighthouse of sanity in a universe of madness and suffering'.

In the following incident he has been arrested and placed in the hands of the Kempi, the dreaded Japanese military police, because he is suspected of having an illegal radio.

Following my arrest, I was first thrown into a small cell where, to my disgust, I found in a concealed pocket of my shirt some wireless news whose cryptic nature no longer seemed clever. This I chewed up and swallowed. Curiously my prolonged interrogation was not accompanied by a search of my gear in the lines. I hoped that it would be dispersed by friends. Some hours of patient interrogation as to my doings ensued, with whom did I exchange news, what did I know about the war, what were my movements from camp to camp, with whom had I had conversation, etc. Suddenly after some four hours, there was a dramatic violent change. The interrogating officer, 'Stone Face', jumped to his feet and pulled down a screen with Japanese characters and a tracery of connecting arrows. Pointing to a rather central character, he said, 'You are this person – we know all about you and your set – you will be executed but first you will talk.' I was clapped in manacles and he deputed two soldiers to flog me with lumps of firewood each time my answers to questions, though verbose, finished up in the negative. I thought of the dead British officers beaten to death in this way at adjacent camps where all this started. I maintained my 'innocence' under steady beating, but pined for a cyanide pill.

At last I was told patience was now exhausted and I must die. I was pushed and flogged along to a tree and my manacles changed to encircle my wrists behind the tree, with my body and arms taut about the tree, my bare belly exposed to four bayonets wielded by an execution squad of four, making the characteristic belly grunting, blood-curdling yells, working themselves up to 'the moment'. I was told by the interpreter – the one in the party with long hair – that I was to have the grace of 30 seconds, which were grimly counted in Japanese. My eyes were locked on the flinty, impassive face of the 'interrogating' officer. Strange thoughts flitted through my mind. 'This can't be me. I don't feel frightened enough. It's just unreal!' I thought with ironic amusement of a time at school when for an escapade I anticipated expulsion and disgrace. My reaction then seemed far worse, more horrendous. I speculated whether anyone would even know how I died.

The egregious voice of the interpreter – 'Now ten seconds to go. Have you last message for relatives. I shall try to convey.' I shifted my gaze to his distasteful face and said contemptuously: 'Last message conveyed by thugs like you – no thanks!' The bayonets were withdrawn and poised for the last yelling thrust when I saw a flush on the face of my executioner who raised a hand and cried, 'Stop! He will suffer a lot more than this before he dies – untie him!' The manacles were transferred to the front and I suffered a bout of heavy beating without further interrogation.

At length I was pushed into a cell, squat-legged, facing a wall to await execution and presumably meantime to improve my attitude. A guarding sentry struck me with a rifle if my erect body slumped. As a ridiculous distraction I tried to recall Keats' 'Ode to a Nightingale' and watched a small lizard enviously.

Evening and, of all things, I was suddenly hauled forth to make up a team of 'lags' to play Japanese guards at 'circlos': a species of quoit was hurled back and forth and the point was lost if it was dropped. The game on our part was to be played in dead silence whilst the Japanese made raucous laughter and derisive yells at trembling hands and, in my case, bruised limbs and hands. My old friend, Dr John Diver of St Mary's Hospital London, was particularly unsteady, and the Japanese concentrated on him, calling 'Diver! Diver!' Well, the Japanese won 6–5. There were a few frustrating opportunities in turning to attempt communication in a stage whisper out of the corner of the mouth.

Back to the cell, manacles, and wall contemplation, some flashes of Keats' ode. A conundrum – 'If I had that pill would I take it now?' More 'encouragement' to sit at attention, legs crossed. It seemed too painful to think of home, my beloved Helen, or past life.

Again I was roughly taken out for execution, the same grizzly ritual, the same tree, but this time an air of grim finality: just the sound of steady counting and the horrible grunting yells with cold steel at times meeting my skin – but again, surprisingly to me, the last-second reprieve.

This time I was taken in manacles to a small metal-framed pen which contained a Thai with, I thought, a good deal of Chinese blood. His manacles rested easily on his slim wrists, whilst mine sunk in even more deeply as my hands swelled. I rested on my back, hands raised most of the time. His conversation was to point at me pistol fashion and say, 'You – bang!', to which I wearily returned the compliment. Later, the ever present sentries pushed in rice and I envied him his monkeylike agility and mobile hands whilst I made such heavy-going attempts to eat. Knowing the type of torture which went on in the place and having heard the screams of anguish, I frankly wondered whether I had the fibre to take it. For example, handcuffs behind, hitched with a rope over a beam, standing on a high chair, chair kicked away, dangling with a double dislocation of the shoulders – real torture then begins, eyes, testicles, etc. 'Yes,' you say, 'I have the set – you can have it.' But then the Judas pit opens: 'Who gave you the set? Who supplied the batteries? With whom did you communicate?' All unthinkable. I sweated it out until the following evening with a little more rice and intolerable pain in the hands.

My impassive companion was removed and tidily shot – my turn again, now almost hoping for a quick clean end. Shooting seemed like promotion. My interrogator astounded me by resuming parley, inviting me to sit. He said, 'Colonel, you must understand that though you have not talked, that others have and we know that you are guilty.' Me: 'If they have talked, they are liars. Why don't you give me a fair trial to throw the lies in their faces.'

After a while, he looked at me in a sort of puzzlement and said: 'Is it that you really have not done these things or that you will not talk?' I laughed and said, 'Have I not spent all this time telling you that I know nothing?' Then to my utter astonishment: 'Colonel, if I were to release you this time, would you have hard feelings against the Japanese, hard feelings against me? We *kempis* do but do our duty.'

I said cautiously, 'From all I have heard of you *kempis*, I feel that I have been well treated.' I thought, have we some curious affinity? My manacles were removed and I was given beer and cigarettes. Suddenly I realised that prisoners' eyes would be on me being treated to the fatted calf, obviously as a reward for telling all, and this dimmed the surge of joy at my release. *Kempi* professionalism to the last.

I was subsequently called on once a month by *kempis* who looked me over. 'Colonel, how is your health? We *kempis* know that you are dangerous spy!'

At the fag end of the war, I faced 'Stone Face' in one of General Slim's 'identification' parades. There, without tunic or belt, holding up his trousers with one hand, face strangely grey and drawn. Our eyes locked again and I said, 'Interesting specimen that; but I have not seen him before.' However, what hope would a *kempi* officer have. 'We *kempis* do but do our duty.'

from *The War Diaries of Weary Dunlop* by E.E. Dunlop

Working on the Thai–Burma Railway

The infamous Burma-Thailand Railway ran 415km and was constructed by more than 60,000 prisoners of war during 1942–43. One out of every two prisoners who worked on the railway died and it has been said that the line was bought at the 'cost of a life for every sleeper' lain. The workers endured starvation, disease and all kinds of inhumanity. Private Roy Whitecross of the 8th division AIF was one of these soldiers who recorded his experiences:

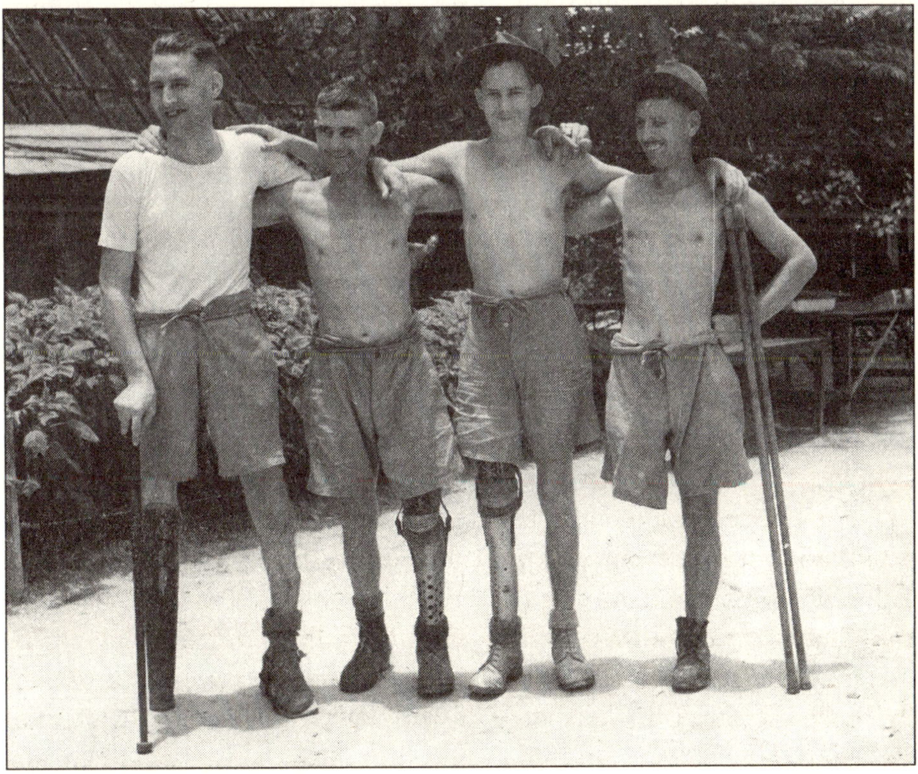

Four Australian prisoners of war amputees in Changi prison camp. They had been tropical ulcer sufferers on the Thai–Burma Railway.

Whilst we certainly found the Japanese difficult, if not impossible to understand, there were times when our behaviour confounded the Jap soldiers. They could never understand why we sang on our way back to camp after the day's work. They took it for granted that we joined together in camp and sang and held concerts on every possible occasion, but after working all day and on through the hours of darkness, when men raised their voices in song as they splashed, slipped and staggered along the waterlogged road, the guards shrugged their shoulders, pointed to us with one hand and made circular motions round their heads with the other – we had 'wheels' in our heads.

Some of the guards enjoyed our singing, and this led to trouble when we did not want to sing, as on the night after one of our men had been crushed to death on the line by a load of sleepers and rails which had slipped from the truck. That night there was no singing until the Maggot said 'All men – sing', and the man who replied 'No, not tonight' was soundly slapped. Several more were cuffed and kicked until someone commenced singing 'Abide With Me'.

Our move from the '122' to the '131' on 30 September had a few new points over the other moves. The railway truck carrying the cooks and all the kitchen gear broke an axle, which meant no meals for a day and a half.

The camp area was not muddy, but to make up for this, the huts were only half-finished. There was no thatch on the roof! As we arrived in camp the rain was falling in solid sheets, and there was no shelter at all.

I spent the first night curled up on the wet bamboo floor with my groundsheet spread over me as far as it would go. Like everyone else I was soaking wet, but at least the groundsheet kept the rain from beating on my face.

'There's one bright spot. The camp is brand new, so it should be clean and healthy,' said someone.

But even this consolation disappeared next day when we found traces of a native hut, and what had obviously been a crude latrine. Far from being a clean, healthy camp, it turned out to be one of the worst. When we left three months later, seventy-four wooden crosses stood beneath the trees beside the line. The huts were the smallest we had ever occupied. Space worked out at the rate of twenty-one men to a 'bay' measuring ten feet by twelve feet. So in yet another camp, tired men cut bamboos and built themselves bunks one above the other. Those with the lower bunks were lucky, as the top bunks kept some of the rain off them until the huts were roofed a week later.

For some weeks line-laying operations ceased. Ten kilometres further on, the line came to several small hills, through which a cutting was dug. In the usual fashion the cutting was made only just wide enough for the trucks to pass the vertical walls. But nature frustrated the Jap engineers, who had not allowed for the shale type of rock through which the cutting ran. As soon as the cutting was 'completed', tons of shale and rock fell from the sides, and this took a week for the Chinese prisoners to remove. Immediately this fall was cleared, more rock fell, making the line impassable again. This went on until the walls of the cutting were dug at an angle receding sufficiently to prevent the shale from crumbling.

During the hold-up we worked on the line putting ballast beneath the sleepers. Then the completed line was fully spiked and generally tidied up. When these jobs were finished we were sent to the Nike rail siding four kilometres away and put to work re-stacking thousands of sleepers. The job was simply to keep us working, as the sleepers were already stacked neatly, and we merely re-stacked them 200 yards from their original position. It was a rotten job. The sleepers were heavy, many of them being redwood which weighed almost twice as much as the ordinary sleeper, and it was all two men could do to carry them. The Japanese engineers were irritable, no doubt because the line was held up. No one was allowed to sit down or go back to camp if an attack of malaria came on; every man was forced to keep on working.

One of the Japs stood on the stack from which sleepers were being taken and cracked each of us on the head as we came up to it, screaming 'Faster, faster! Hurry, hurry!' Soon all the Japs were emulating him. It helped pass the time for them, I suppose. If the Japs thought any man was not working hard enough, they forced him to make several trips carrying a sleeper on his own.

I hated the trip through the cutting when it was passable, because at various points the rock was still so close to the trucks that large cuts could be seen on the face where a truck had swayed towards it and scraped along. When this happened the danger of a landslide was increased.

On 13 October 1943, we commenced line laying again. The Japs drove us at a frightful pace. They wanted to finish the work in two or three days. The working parties were still doing the two shifts, and I worked from 6am on the 14th to 12.30am on the 15th. Then out again at 6am on the 15th to work until midnight. The final frantic effort was made on the 16th. From 6am on Saturday we worked right through until 3pm Sunday – thirty-three hours without a break, when the two ends of the line were joined at the 157 Kilometre peg.

We had linked Burma with Thailand. Roughly we counted the cost, and reckoned that for every three men who had worked on the line, two now lay in lonely jungle-clad graves.

The 'rest' that had been promised was not forthcoming. We were back in camp about 4pm on Sunday the 16th, and went out to work again next morning at 6am. But the Japanese engineers seemed to have no heart for straightening spikes, so in the afternoon we spent two hours swimming in a river a few kilometres above the camp. The Japs then cleared us out of the river and dropped sticks of dynamite into the water to catch fish. We were made to stand in a line across the river to catch the stunned fish, and were amazed when the Japs set aside a small portion of the catch for us. In all we brought back to camp about three-dozen fish, which were carefully cooked for the sick men in the hospital.

When the pressure of work was relaxed a larger number of men suddenly became sick. Cases of malaria, beri-beri and ulcers increased while many men contracted a skin complaint similar to scabies. Apart from the normal malaria, several cases of cerebral malaria occurred. For those stricken with it, there was no hope. The patient quickly became delirious and then lapsed into unconsciousness. Death followed in two or three days.

The Japs weighed us all at the end of October. My weight was eight stone one pound.

The best tonic for many a long day was Captain Richards's return to the force. In less than two minutes the news raced through the camp. Men smiled at each other and said 'Thank Christ for that.'

from *Slaves of the Son of Heaven* by Roy Whitecross

Of life and death

Stan Arneil kept a diary of the entire period of his imprisonment from the fall of Singapore in February 1942, through the infamous camps on the Thai–Burma Railway on which he worked between May–December 1943, until the end of the war with Japan. In these entries he describes the horror of tropical ulcers, the incessant itch caused by body lice, amputations, the constant presence of death, as well as his desperate yearning for home.

21 September 1943
I feel a little depressed today. It must be the constant rain or the depressing local conditions. Our Unit alone has lost nineteen men in this camp and the death roll here today reached a total of 156.

I walked through the hospital today: the stench in the ulcer ward would turn the strongest stomach. The ulcer cases cannot get up to wash and they, like the whole camp, are infested with horrible grey body lice. Ninety per cent of the troops are affected with an itch and as I write this I frequently stop to scratch myself.

Only *one* officer has died in this camp, they are *all* well, have neither ulcers nor itch and are all well shod. But Burns said! The lice have no class distinctions.

23 September 1943
I have been intensely depressed all day by a couple of visits to the horrible ulcer ward and cannot shake off the feeling of hopelessness it has given me. Men are dying for want of simple things such as milk and butter. The pain of their ulcers seems to put them off eating our plain rice fare.

Doug is now looking after me but I am very worried about a couple of nasty patches on my feet, which may turn into ulcers. My job in the orderly room helps me but I still muddy my feet of course every time I poke my nose out of the door.

24 September 1943

Two of the best men of our unit have died in the last few days. Men are dying at the rate of five to ten per day and the total death (160) in the camp is rising rapidly.

This horrible itch kept me awake half the night and I think I am fighting a losing battle against two would-be ulcers on my right foot.

Nobody seems to know when we will move and Col. Kappe, the GOC, has been away for about six days. Unless we shift from this country shortly I can see those few who do eventually get out being half blind, half demented cripples.

Please heaven let the war finish soon. Surely we do not deserve this. Nineteen months POWs. Give us hot baths and clean skins again instead of dirt and scabby bodies. Give us peace of mind and cleanliness instead of worry and dirt.

25 September 1943

The sun deigned to shine today so that is a point in our favour. Poor Steve Porter died at No. 1 camp so all our hopes of our great holiday have died with him. Capt Taylor arrived from No. 1 camp and everybody is glad about *that*. We now have a doctor who will take an interest in us. Smallpox has broken out among the coolies. They have twenty-eight cases so far today and their hut is only thirty feet from us separated by a bamboo fence. Phil Schofield attacked my feet with a penknife and cleaned all my promising ulcers. They have begun to amputate limbs because of ulcers: so I want to clear mine up before they go too far. Today a chap lay on a bamboo stretcher under a primitive shelter of attap leaves and had his arm amputated. The open latrines were twenty yards away and two orderlies had to keep waving branches to shoo the flies away. That is enough news for one day surely.

N.B. The saw used in the amputation was the sole saw in the camp used primarily to cut wood for the kitchen fires. It was sterilised in boiling water before being used for amputations.

26 September 1943
Ulcers on my feet are now becoming very promising as to colour and size and it worries me a lot, particularly when I saw a young chap with ulcers on the feet having his leg amputated.

The sun has shone again all day and official opinion now thinks we may shift within a month. We were vaccinated against smallpox today, but this dreadful itch is driving me crazy.

All of the officers have been issued with a measure of gula malacca, sugar substitute. Tell me, is it an officer's privilege to think of the men first or of themselves?

27 September 1943
I severely kicked my ulcered toe last night in front of Capt Taylor and as a result I am on 'no duties' and, a special boon, am allowed to remain in the lines instead of going to the dreadful ulcer ward. My feet are now so bad that it is difficult for me to walk at all.

Last night we received the tremendously thrilling news that within a fortnight we will move back by train to Changi in eastern Singapore. It is so good that we can scarcely realise it and last night Doug, Len Payne, old John Gaden and I made a quiet celebration with a bottle of native whisky. Don't ask me where it came from, I don't know, but it cost us five dollars.

28 September 1943
Am just able to put my feet to the ground and this morning when I took off the bandages, I almost wept to see the horrible matter which had come away during the night.

The itch has me in its grip and has left me red raw in the crutch. It is a practical impossibility to refrain from scratching. It is very depressing and discouraging and I had a hard job today to prevent myself being whizzed into hospital.

Anyway there should not be too long to wait up here now, less than a couple of weeks should see us out of it.

29 September 1943
Feet just about the same but to my great joy I struck a medical orderly cobber of mine who dressed my feet, supplied me with treatment and will see me again tomorrow. It is a weight off my mind and I now feel much happier.

We are supposed to receive five dollars pay per head, and on the road the pressure is now right off. Reveille is now 7.30am instead of 5.30am. What is the largest-size bath towel one can buy in Australia? I intend to use snow white bath towels, five feet by seven when I return and nothing less than Johnson's Baby Soap, which is the best soap I know of.

Home seems very close now, because of the projected move and if I can remain alive for a further six months I should see you all again. The Last Post just played, up the hill, for a batch of chaps, two of our Unit among them, making about twenty-three of the 30th to die in this camp.

30 September 1943
Feet worse, one ulcer on the toe is down to the bone. Great pain to walk at all now so I have hot water brought to my bed and bathe my feet there. Last night we had a half-pint issue of sweet coffee. It was delicious.

Three 30th died today, making 104 deaths this month in this camp. It has been an unlucky month for me but still they are taking legs off every day and chaps are dying, so perhaps I am well off after all. The proposed move should see us all back in Changi by the end of October.

1 October 1943
My feet are worse today and are not calculated to cheer a man up at all. The itch is also just about driving me off my head. We lost Joe Carew, one of the Unit personalities today, with cardiac beri beri.

2 October 1943
Sitting here very quietly in the lines my thoughts fly back to home and to you people. Lovely thoughts, the setting sun over the river as

we return to the club after a regatta. Mass at St Mary's, proudly taking Daisy Belle to an evening in town, the quietness of Penrith from the evening train. Sydney Harbour and the lights of the city at dusk. What a goal to live for. It is a torch shining before me as I sit here bedridden with tropical ulcers, wondering if I will be alright or suffer like someone does here every day and lose a foot or a leg over the damn things. The war must finish or we are finished. Over 2000 have died of the total force of 7000 and seventy-five per cent out of the balance are in hospital, hundreds of those dangerously ill.

I must get home to the peace and quietness of you people whom I love. It is all I live for.

from *One Man's War* by Stan Arneil

Cholera

Cholera is a disease that flourishes in areas where there is poor sanitation, and so it was a common cause of death in the POW camps controlled by the Japanese. The following scene takes place in July 1943 in Kanyu Camp, near the Thai–Burma Railway.

Cholera is a disgustingly horrible disease, incredibly painful for the victim and distressing for the helper or onlooker. The symptoms are frequently violent, fluid of greyish-white colour being ejected forcefully in vomiting and diarrhoea as if the kidneys are trying to rid the body of invasive poisons. The result is rapid dehydration with accompanying muscular cramps of such intensity that muscle fibres can tear apart as the body writhes and twists in wrenching spasms. The pale colouring of the fluid is due to the mucous lining of the whole intestinal system disintegrating into tiny shreds and particles that are scoured away and flushed out, leaving the inner surfaces raw and unprotected.

The first signs of infection are sunken eyes in a pinched and drawn face, unnaturally cold breath from abnormally low body temperature, and cold and clammy skin with the fingertips wrinkled and purple as the kidneys draw fluids from the extremities to try to repair damage to the vital organs. If a man shows these signs there can be no doubt that the violent ordeal will follow – sometimes mercifully brief and sometimes drawn out. The only treatment is replacement of lost body fluids, and if the infection is moderate the patient can be given tea, which helps if he can hold it down. For several weeks our MO has been planning for just such an emergency, and has put together a crude but effective water distillation plant for intravenous salines – the difficulty here is in inserting a sharpened bamboo needle into collapsed veins. But his apparatus saves lives, quite miraculously. Their thickened blood is like dark treacle.

There is no more petrol after the first can, and massive quantities of firewood are needed for cremations. By the third day we have over 200 cases, and hygienic disposal of the bodies is critical, for flies can carry and distribute infected matter all over the place, such is the rate of infection.

We are warned not to touch our mouths with our fingers, and at meal times every man dips his mess tin and spoon (we have no use for knives or forks) into a kwali of rapidly boiling water before moving on to the serving point. The cookhouse is responsible for bringing rice to us in covered containers, and we must be especially careful not to allow flies to settle as we eat.

The Nips stop work on the railway for two days while we do our best to cope with the emergency. We have sent some of our tents to the cholera compound to accommodate the terrible increase in victims, and crowd ourselves even more tightly into the others, but nobody complains.

On the third day, it is announced that railway work will resume tomorrow, but some of the sick will be allowed to stay in camp for the 'light work' of cremation and grave-digging! Not surprisingly, nobody wants to report himself as sick – the gruesome work in camp doesn't appeal at all! But disposal of the dead is obviously beyond the resources of those marvellous men who have volunteered to work in the cholera compound. They have far too much on their hands, and help is absolutely necessary. So the so-called 'light duties' are allocated on a rota basis – everyone will have to take a turn.

The whole camp quickly settles into an ordered and disciplined routine, the success of which must owe a lot to our background of comradeship within the army framework, supplemented by our deepening hatred of the Nips, which binds us solidly together in our determination to *survive* and see them punished as they deserve, when we have won the war. We all have to rely on each other, and we must have full confidence that every man will pull his weight at all times.

from *One Fourteenth of an Elephant* by Ian Denys Peek

A hospital ward in Changi, Singapore, showing members of the 8th Division released from the Changi POW camp. All were suffering from malnutrition.

Over the wire

Over in Germany away from the harsh jungle terrain surrounding the Japanese camps, at least POWs could contemplate making a break for freedom. Here Lieutenant Jack Champ of the 2nd/6th Australian Infantry Battalion remembers his first escape attempt from Oflag VIB at Warburg:

We blackened our faces with soot from the stove, and pulled balaclava helmets over our heads. We ended up a strange-looking lot; like actors waiting for a play to begin, we wandered back and forth, making minute adjustments to our clothing and our packs. There was some desultory conversation, but generally the chaps were quiet; no doubt each was absorbed in his own thoughts. Even Rex was quiet – he sat like a statue on the end of a bench picking microscopic bits of fluff from the legs of his trousers. The minutes ticked slowly by.

The pit of my stomach was cold, and there was a peculiar emptiness – not the emptiness of hunger, but an inert hollowness that was an insidious by-product of tension. I was restless, uneasy and curiously cold. I looked across at Albert Arkwright, who was team leader on Number Two ladder. He was like myself – movements jerky and clockwork, his eyes continually flicking around the room, always ending up on the silent sentinel gazing steadfastly out into the compound. Albert reached down and re-tied his shoelaces.

I tried to think of home – that small, wondrous part of the vast continent of Australia that I knew so well. I closed my eyes and a dark image of Corio Bay danced into my mind. The scene lightened, and the water turned an azure blue as the image spread before me.

There, that was it – the colours were right, and I could even feel a slight swaying as I gently swung the small yacht into a sweet breeze, which swept lightly over me. The bright sun flashed gaily across the vivid surface, breaking and sparkling at each tiny convolution of the water. Gentle waves slapped laughingly at the bow, and overhead I could hear the strident cawcawing of a lone seagull wheeling above the lance of my mast.

Someone in the hut suddenly spluttered into a suppressed coughing fit, and the picture in my mind greyed over and disappeared. But it had given me a new peace, and evoked a determination to enjoy such earthly pleasures again. Some of the emptiness had left me, I felt warmer and more relaxed, and my resolve hardened. I clenched my fists and waited.

Nine fifteen passed, then 9.25. Rex and I, Tom and Dick moved over to the assembly, and assumed our positions by the ladders. The other six stood behind us. The room was gripped in a tight cord of emotion as the time approached. Nine thirty clicked over on my non-luminous watch, and I became tense. We were now well and truly in the hands of the starter, and we were straining like coiled springs. Why weren't we going? What was the delay? Oh God, don't let it be called off now!

Suddenly the camp plunged into total darkness, and I was jumping out of my skin. We weren't being given the signal to go? What was wrong?

Captain Johnstone gave the signal from the compound, and our controller bellowed, 'Go!'

This was it! Forty black-faced escapees sprang into action instantaneously. Rex and I pushed the apparatus out of the window. Stallard and Page grabbed the front end as it shot out of the window and pulled it out. We grabbed the other end again on our way out of the hut, and raced towards our spot at the wire. We came to the trip-wire, which had been whitewashed earlier, and it stood out well enough to ensure we didn't run into it.

Having crossed the wire, Stallard and Page pushed their end up high and we rammed our end onto the ground beside the inner fence.

All around us bedlam had broken loose, and right around the camp the diversions were ensuring complete pandemonium for the guards. They had no idea what was going on in the darkness and they didn't know which way to go, although most of their attention was attracted to the noisier diversions – a long way from us. The two sentries in the closest towers were busy shouting down at the groups of men who had thrown up the dummy ladders, and who were now scurrying back to their quarters, having ordered the guards, in German, not to take their eyes off the ladders!

Rex leapt onto our ladder with the ends of the platform firmly grasped in his hands, and the three of us held him steady as he ascended a couple of steps. With his great strength he extended the brutally heavy platform upwards and outwards. As it clicked into place he was up and over like a flash. The platform effectively straddled the wire, and Rex swung deftly through the hole using the trapeze bar, hit the ground and was off.

I was all of 3 feet behind him getting onto the ladder. From a few yards away beside me someone blurted out a loud obscenity in a familiar Australian accent, indicating trouble with one of the ladders, but my training was paying off, and I did not hesitate for a second as I repeated Rex's smooth actions, crossing the wires, grasping the bar, and swinging to the ground on the other side of the outer wire. I began sprinting after Rex. Behind me the diversions were in full swing, and the wire twanged loudly as it was tweaked back and forth through the holes in the posts. The familiar, highpitched and hysterical shouts of the Germans indicated their complete confusion.

I was about 20 yards clear when the first shot rang out. Adrenalin coursed through my veins as the sharp crack punctuated the night air. I ran fast, crouching low, and soon caught up with Rex. I slowed to his pace as we charged through a field of turnips. The shooting and shouting behind us rose to a crescendo. We could hear the machine guns in the towers rattle into action as the excited sentries ripped away at the ant-like army racing pell-mell from the camp.

We sped on into the stooked hayfield, bullets occasionally whining overhead. They say it is always a good sign when you can hear them!

Now we slowed down a little, and began an easier canter, keeping about 10 yards apart. Rex charged on, a determined look on his face, and as I looked across at him, a surge of elation raced through me. We were free for the first time in eighteen months. Free from Warburg, and the shackles of imprisonment. I was exultant!

Any doubts and apprehensions I had been harbouring before we started had vanished, and our team had worked like the proverbial well-oiled machine. We strode on, and after the initial dash I had been automatically counting our paces. Now we were about 800 yards out, quite cool, and more than a little cocky at our success. Then 1000 yards out we slowed down to a fast jog, our breath coming easily. Our campaign for physical fitness was now paying dividends.

Then suddenly, out of the darkness, disaster struck!

'Halt! Halt! Or we fire!'

Ten hysterical Germans sprang from behind a stack of hay. We had run smack-dab into the middle of the bloody standing patrol. Hell and be damned!

In seconds the two of us were surrounded by our highly excited captors, caught inexorably in the trap we knew to exist. Rifles and pistols were jabbed into our backs and our stomachs, and our breath was choked with the exertion, the fear, and the frustration. We stood there gasping, and a few moments later two more escapers were thrust into the middle of our small circle.

The German sergeant was furious, and obviously confused by the rapid events of the past couple of minutes. This was no time for heroics, as they were all jumpy, and despite our disappointment we knew that we now had a job to do – we must hold them here, and give the others a better chance. Three minutes; it stretched before us like an eternity.

'How many have escaped?' screamed the sergeant. 'How many away?!'

We stalled, and he barked, 'Answer me, or you will be shot. Right now!'

Rex handled the precarious situation magnificently.

'Four men!' he blurted out. 'Four men is all. You have us all!'

'How did you get out?' yelled the sergeant, his face inches from Rex's. 'How did you get past the wire?'

'We jumped over it!' lied Rex, with complete composure. 'It was easy!'

'You lie!' spat the sergeant. 'You lie, you lie! It is impossible!'

We stood mute as he ranted on, but we had grim satisfaction in knowing that the precious three minutes had now slipped by, and all the patrol was still standing around us and not pursuing the others, despite the constant rustle of scampering feet as they disappeared into the darkness of the night. We were the unlucky ones, but in essence it was immediately clear that the scheme had worked.

from *The Diggers of Colditz* by Jack Champ and Colin Burgess

War at Sea

War at Sea

Before 1910, Australia's navy had been a part of the Royal Navy, and the naval squadron charged with the defence of the colony was composed of British ships crewed by Australians. That year, however, a distinctly Australian navy was formed by Admiral Creswell. It was organised along Royal Navy lines and was considered to be an additional fleet involved in the protection of the empire.

In World War I the battle cruiser *Australia* was the pride of the Royal Australian Navy's fleet, which consisted of twelve cruisers and destroyers as well as two submarines. In one sea battle, the cruiser *Sydney* engaged and sank the *Emden* off the Cocos Islands. This elusive German raider had been attacking British ships in the Indian Ocean and was being hunted by large naval forces. But during the war, both Australian submarines were lost, the *AE1* off New Guinea and the *AE2* in Turkish waters, where she would have taken part in the Gallipoli campaign.

In the interval between the world wars, the RAN had to reduce its naval force as a part of the general reduction of armaments agreed to by the major powers after 'the war to end all wars'. Even HMAS *Australia* was sacrificed. The Royal Navy took on much of the role of protecting British interests in Asia, with the Singapore naval base at the centre of British naval power; the role of the Australian fleet, as always, was to guard shipping lanes.

During the 1939–45 war, the RAN was expanded and served in every corner of the world. Three cruisers, three destroyers and a number of smaller ships were destroyed. One of these was the light cruiser HMAS

Perth, which was sunk during a naval battle with a superior Japanese invasion force in the Sunda Strait between Java and Sumatra. Although not part of the regular navy, the small ship *Krait* will be remembered as the means by which Australian commandos reached Singapore and destroyed enemy shipping at anchor in the harbour.

By the end of World War II, the ships of the RAN were known and respected for the courage and determination of their crews. They had earned their place in the fighting tradition of the Australian armed forces.

Down and down she went . . .

The Australian submarine *AE2* braved mines, Turkish action and powerful, unpredictable tidal flows to successfully traverse the Dardanelles Strait and enter the Sea of Marmara. Lieutenant-Commander Dacre Stoker, the sub's captain, intended to disrupt the shipping that was bringing Turkish reinforcements for the forces arrayed against the Anzacs, who had landed on Gallipoli in April 1915.

After a few days, however, the *AE2* was sighted and fired on by a Turkish torpedo boat, the *Sultanhisar*, commanded by Captain Riza. The result was that Stoker was forced to scuttle the *AE2* and surrendered to save his crew. They were all rescued by the Turks but were jailed for the rest of the war.

The *AE2* still lies where she was sunk in Turkish waters and exists as an almost forgotten relic of the Anzac legend. The submarine's final moments are detailed in the following extract:

Heading back to Constantinople on 30 April, Riza decided to divert to the area around Karanburun Point at the southern end of Marmara, just near the opening of the Dardanelles Strait, to have another look for the marauding submarine. He sighted a vessel afar and ordered 'the good quality British coal' to be used to gain maximum speed. But Stoker in the *AE2*, as indeed it was, had seen the smoke of the approaching torpedo boat and dived to avoid it.

'The submarine was diving easily and comfortably; not a suspicion of impending disaster lay in our minds,' said Stoker. Suddenly, all hell broke loose. For no apparent reason, the *AE2*, instead of diving, pointed sharply upwards and started rising in the water. Frantically

Stoker juggled the diving rudders, increased power and shifted water ballast. But nothing could change the *AE2*'s strange upward thrust.

As *AE2* broke the surface, Stoker saw the *Sultanhisar* only 90 metres off, firing hard. 'We must get under again at once,' said Stoker, ordering the forward tanks to be flooded.

Riza had sighted the periscope and started firing. 'The periscope was damaged, but the submarine disappeared,' he said.

As the *AE2* dived again, Stoker tried to level off at 15 metres. But now the diving rudders seemed powerless and the *AE2* continued a downward plunge. Stoker expelled water ballast as quickly as possible to halt the descent, but the *AE2* simply kept plunging, quickly descending beyond 30 metres, the limit of its gauges.

'When that depth was passed she was still sinking rapidly,' said Stoker. 'We could not tell to what depths she was reaching. I ordered full speed astern on the motors . . . In a few moments – moments in which death seemed close to every man – there came a cry from the coxswain: "She's coming up, sir!" and the needle seemed to jerk itself reluctantly away from the 100-feet mark, and then rise rapidly.'

With all her ballast expelled, the *AE2* literally jumped to the surface. Stoker and his crew had lost control of their boat. As Stoker was ordering reflooding of the tanks to regain the ability to dive, another officer looked through the periscope and reported that the *Sultanhisar* was firing as it circled, and a second Turkish gunboat was approaching.

Riza claims that as *AE2* dived again it fired a torpedo at *Sultanhisar*. 'With a quick turn, we avoided the torpedo,' he said. 'Now a ferocious fight had started between the submarine and us. We had two torpedoes and I ordered them to be prepared to be fired. The submarine had submerged again.'

No account from the *AE2* reports that it fired a torpedo. Indeed, the submarine's yo-yoing left it in no position to fire anything. At the time Riza says a torpedo was fired, *AE2* was desperately trying to dive to avoid being hit by Turkish fire. And as the *AE2* started to submerge, Stoker had a new crisis on his hands that would have quickly obliterated any thought of attacking the Turkish ships.

The *AE2* started a new and even steeper downward plunge, once again out of control. Stoker gives a spine-tingling account of the next few minutes:

> Down and down she went, faster than before, 60, 80 and 100 feet. The inclination down by the bows became more and more pronounced – she seemed to be trying to stand on her nose. Eggs, bread, food of all sorts, knives, forks, plates, came tumbling forward from the petty officers' mess. Everything that could fall over fell; men, slipping and struggling, grasped hold of valves, gauges, rods, anything to hold them up in position to their posts.
>
> Full speed astern again . . . a thousand years passed – well, this time we were gone for ever.
>
> In heaven's name, what depth were we at? . . . Why did not the sides of the boat cave in under the pressure and finish it?

The nosedive to dangerous depths and the chaos aboard must have been terrifying. Able Seaman Charles Suckling reported that everyone's eyes 'were on the sides of the boat waiting for it to cave in'.

AE2's needle suddenly began to jump back from its 30-metre limit mark. The submarine began to shoot back up again, quickly rising to the surface where *Sultanhisar* was firing.

'BANG! . . . a cloud of smoke in the engine-room,' said Stoker. 'We were hit and holed! And again in quick succession two more holes.'

Riza's account aboard *Sultanhisar* again differs markedly. Riza says that as the submarine resurfaced he saw another torpedo coming towards *Sultanhisar*. 'If we were hit, there was no hope of any of us surviving,' he wrote. 'I ordered full speed ahead to try to avoid the torpedo as much as possible and minimise the damage. *Sultanhisar* suddenly turned and the torpedo barely missed us.'

Stoker reports no such firing. Indeed, he was in dire straits simply trying to control the *AE2* without positioning it for a torpedo attack. Riza, meanwhile, tried to ready his own torpedoes for firing.

The first failed to ignite and fell overboard. Riza fired a second, which missed the *AE2*.

By now, the two craft were quite close. 'The 93-ton *Sultanhisar* paled by comparison to the 800-plus-ton *AE2*,' said Riza. 'I decided to attack the submarine at its weakest point, its tail rudder, and started going towards it full speed.' Riza says that as *AE2* was again submerging, *Sultanhisar* hit the sub headfirst.

'This could almost have cost us our lives,' he said. 'Suddenly *AE2* started resurfacing very close to our vessel. The waves it created while resurfacing were splashing onto our deck. If its head had been in the direction of our deck, it would certainly have pushed us up from underneath and caused us to capsize. We quickly started to pull away. While we pulled away, the submarine fully resurfaced. The British flag was pulled up the mast.'

While Riza was grappling with his version of the monster from the deep, aboard *AE2* things looked bleak. Holed three times the submarine could no longer dive. 'Finished! We were caught!' thought Stoker. 'It but remained to avoid useless sacrifice of life. All hands were ordered on deck and overboard.'

Lieutenant Haggard apparently disagreed. 'My father was not in favour of scuttling the boat and thought they should at least have tried to fight on,' relates Jenny Smyth, Lieutenant Haggard's daughter.

But the hard reality of their predicament quickly overruled any foolhardy actions. The *AE2* could not submerge. And what could the *AE2* have done to attack *Sultanhisar* or the approaching Turkish warships? It did not have a deck gun, and was in no position to fire its last torpedo. Short of waving his revolver, Stoker and *AE2* had run out of options.

Stoker does not mention this difference with Haggard. Quite the contrary. In his official report to the British Admiralty he lists Haggard's assistance in flooding the tanks to scuttle the *AE2*. Stoker was very concerned not to allow *AE2* to fall into enemy hands. The submarine, little more than a year old, was state-of-the-art military technology. The Royal Navy had risked further losses to destroy

Brodie's *E15* after it had run aground in the Narrows only a fortnight before.

As the crew clambered out, led by Stoker's batman, Thomas Cheater, the third officer, Lieutenant John Cary, stood on the tiny bridge watching the water rise. His job was to tell Stoker and Haggard, then flooding the tanks, when they had to get out. Petty Officer Harry Kinder was one of the last crew to leave. He retrieved some of the *AE2*'s papers, a feat for which he was later mentioned in dispatches.

Cary shouted for them to hurry, but Stoker looked up through the conning tower and saw from the water level that there was still a minute or so to spare. He wrote later:

> I jumped down again and had a last look round – for, you see, I was fond of the *AE2*. What a sight! Pandemonium – I cannot attempt to describe it – food, clothing, flotsam and jetsam of the weirdest sorts floated up on the fast-entering water in the place which we had been so proud to keep neat and clean . . .
>
> An anxious shout from above, 'Hurry, sir, she's going down!'
>
> In the wardroom my eye was caught by my private dispatch case, which contained, I remembered, some money. That was bound to be useful – I ran and picked it up, and darted up the conning tower. As I reached the bridge the water was about two feet from the top of the conning tower, besides this only a small portion of the stern was out of the water. On it were clustered the last half dozen of the crew, the remainder were overboard.
>
> Curious incidents impress one at such times. As those last six men took to the water the neat dive of one of the engine-room ratings will remain pictured in my mind forever.

Other incidents impressed crew members. One recounted Stoker on the deck as the sub was sinking telling him, 'Come on then, it is no use stopping here.'

The *AE2* in Sydney.

Riza had another view of these last moments of the *AE2*. He watched as the *AE2* crew jumped into the water. 'Finally, there was only the captain left,' he said. 'He was refusing to leave his ship and was saluting the British flag. This demonstration of patriotism moved us immensely. We all saluted the British flag, which was by now floating in the water.'

As Stoker struggled in the water with his dispatch case, and together with his crew was hauled aboard *Sultanhisar*, the *AE2* slipped beneath the surface.

from *Stoker's Submarine* by Fred and Elizabeth Brenchley

Perth goes down

On 28 February 1942 the Australian light cruiser *Perth* and the American heavy cruiser *Houston*, both survivors of the Battle of the Java Sea, were sunk by a powerful Japanese naval force as they entered the Sunda Strait in an attempt to reach the Indian Ocean.

The text below concerns the men who plotted the *Perth*'s opening gunfire against the Japanese. They would also experience, with great bravery, the dreadful damage sustained in return.

Perth's bow swung to bring the broadside to bear on the enemy. Then at point-blank range, her 6-inch guns spewed shells and orange flame.

In the plot below the bridge, Supply Assistant Ronald Clohesy kicked Tiger Lyons on the shin.

'It's on,' he said. He might have been announcing lunch.

Lyons jerked upright and was just in time to hear the captain's order to the guns, and his words, 'One unknown.' That was Lyons's cue to break radio silence and report action to all shore stations. He scribbled the code signal and handed it to Clohesy, who ran to the radio-room behind the plot as the guns opened up.

And only Darwin, away to the south-east, ever acknowledged that signal that the Battle of Sunda Strait had begun.

Fear now was in Lyons's guts, fear cold and hard like a chunk of ice lodged between his solar plexus and his navel. Fear stayed with him for minutes, urgent and degrading, and in those minutes he felt physically dirty and hated himself. Then his panic ebbed as a shell hissed under the ship – hissed deep under the racing keel with the sound a soda siphon makes when it spits into a glass of whisky.

Now *Perth*'s guns were crashing like houses falling down, and through the speaking tube he heard someone on the bridge above say, 'There are four to starboard', and another voice, 'There are five in our port side'; and then a surprised, 'By God, they're all around us', he recognised as Allen McDonough, the Royal Australian Air Force flying officer with the ship.

Lyons heard the captain order divided control to the guns, and soon after independent control so that each gun could pick its own target. There were plenty, too. His plot of the action already showed thirteen Japanese destroyers and two cruisers attacking them – and that was only part of the enemy force. He knew then he and his shipmates were in for a dirty night, but his early panic never returned. His plot showed that the farthest Jap was only three miles away, the closest less than a mile. The Japanese cruisers were firing over and through their own destroyers, and he thought, 'I hope the bastards sink each other.' The Japanese and Australian and American gunners were almost looking down one another's guns.

As he plotted *Perth*'s zigzag course, Lyons, who in his steel room never saw one gun flash of that action, knew through his instruments that she was turning in a big circle with a diameter of about five miles. Waller's object, he could tell, was to circle and protect *Houston*'s blind stern and to manoeuvre against torpedo fire. The course changes were so frequent and violent as Waller, the ship's captain, swung his racing cruiser that Lyons jerked from one side of the plot to the other. It was like being in a car skidding badly on a slippery road. Mechanically, he recorded these course changes, watched his dials, jotted down times, speed, engine revolutions, enemy positions. He was not afraid – not even worried now. Instead, he felt a strange detachment – like being an onlooker watching the action from some independent vantage-point. But his shirt stuck to him like wallpaper, and sweat dripped down his fingers and down his pencil onto his pad.

At 11.26pm he noted down that *Perth* collected her first shell – in the forward funnel – with a burst of steam like a locomotive blowing off, and then another somewhere near the flag-deck at 11.32; and at 11.50 she got another, near the waterline, which burst in the ordinary seamen's mess. But she was still unharmed, although the Japanese had flung thousands of shells at her. Forty-four minutes after action started she was still fighting with every gun she had, except her useless machine-guns, and so was *Houston*.

Then, at 12.05am, a torpedo went into the forward engine-room on the starboard side, and Lyons felt *Perth* lift and hang as though she was actually floating in the air. He thought, 'When will she come down?' Then hundreds of ship identification photographs poured on top of him from pigeon-holes in a cabinet on the bulkhead above. They frightened him more than the torpedo. He cursed.

'Wouldn't it!' an assistant said. 'Now it's a bloody snowstorm.'

This was Fred Lasslett, one of his electrical mechanics, who was waiting in the plot for damage reports. Lasslett began to pick up the photographs, and David Griffiths, the other mechanic, helped him. They gathered them in bundles, sorted them into rough order, and stuffed them back into the pigeon-holes.

Then a second torpedo hit – and all the photographs poured out again. Lasslett shrugged and left them there. He took a slab of chocolate from his pocket and began to eat, gazing at the dials with their flickering needles. Shells howled over, but he didn't even look up.

'Do you reckon we'll make it?' Clohesy asked casually.

Lyons shook his head. 'Doesn't look like it.'

Clohesy opened a tin of biscuits scrounged from Tanjong and started munching. Lyons noticed with admiration how calm this thin-faced slender kid was. He showed no fear, no emotion except a sort of amused nonchalant detachment as though what was happening outside the plot was little concern of his. Lyons remembered then lying flat on the deck beside this youngster when the Jap bombers dropped a stick [bombs] across them at Tanjong before the Java Sea fight, and watching him, amazed, as he played noughts and crosses with a pencil stub on the deck as the bombs burst.

And watching him, eating biscuits now as though he was in his father's shop somewhere in Victoria, Lyons suddenly felt proud to be in action with a boy like this – and humble before such bravery.

from *Proud Echo* by Ronald McKie

The following extract concentrates on the actions and thoughts of the 'last man out of that ship alive' as *Perth* went down amidst scenes of turmoil:

'God, you know what's going to happen, I don't.' Gillan prayed as he followed Reece and Tuersley up the stokehold ladders. The ladders were almost horizontal now, and he realised with surprise mixed with a still sort of horror, that the ship was nearly on her side.

A stoker lost his grip and fell past Reece and Tuersley, but Gillan managed to grab the man's overalls and steady him till he could start climbing again. Then the fans stopped and the only sound Gillan heard was a silent singing sound deep in his ears, and the only thing he felt was the ship sliding away beneath his feet.

When the four men reached the airlock at the entrance to the stokehold, Gillan saw that they were standing on one wall of this pressure room, and that the steel door had now become the roof. The stoker was trying to open it.

'It won't move,' he yelled.

'Let's all push,' Gillan said.

They heaved at the thick door and it began to move – up, up, until it fell aside with a crash and they pulled themselves up and through into the alleyway. Gillan now saw that the true floor of the alley had become a wall, and that they were standing on the opposite wall which had become the floor, so that the overhead lights were now burning beside them instead of above them. They all knew there was a manhole farther aft, which led into the enclosed torpedo space below the 4-inch gun-deck. They hurried along the alley, and ahead saw the other stokers climbing through. And then they stopped and looked blankly at each other.

'Hell,' Reece said in alarm.

With the ship on her side, an across-ship alleyway had now become a deep well five feet wide between them and the escape manhole.

'We'll have to jump across,' Gillan said.

The lights flickered, but stayed on.

The stoker he had saved in the stokehold was first. The man jumped, but his boots slipped as he was taking off and he fell screaming into the well. The other three looked down into the awful blackness and yelled. There was no answer.

'Oh, God,' Reece said.

Reece and Tuersley jumped and ran forward. As Gillan followed he saw water start coming through the manhole, and saw Reece and Tuersley get through, and then water came through the manhole in a spout like a thick green tube.

The lights went out.

For a split second Gillan could not move. Terror anchored him. Then, with the picture of the spouting manhole still before his eyes in the blackness, he dashed those last few yards, took a deep breath, and forced himself against the water and through the manhole.

Most other men would have panicked and drowned inside that ship which was at that moment nearly under water. But Gillan kept his head. In those few seconds after he had pushed through the manhole he reasoned this way: he knew that *Perth* had now turned almost turtle, and that he was not only inside her and under water, but virtually underneath her; he knew also that she must have been badly battered, that there would be wreckage about everywhere, and that if he struggled or tried to force himself anywhere he would get caught in ropes and twisted steel and drown; he knew the ship was sliding to the bottom bow first, that this forward movement would be displacing water, and that the displaced water would be flowing backward. He decided in those seconds, or split seconds of trapped underwater reasoning, that he had one chance, and only one, of living – to float free and unresisting, and to let the water itself wash him out of the ship.

He tucked himself into a ball, his knees and chin almost meeting, and let the backward-moving water roll him over and over inside that sinking ship; and as he rolled he thought, 'Thank God my Mae [life jacket] isn't fully inflated. I'd be up against the roof if it was and would never get out.' He brushed against ropes, bumped into wreckage, but rolled on.

At last he hit the ship's rail and knew he was out of the enclosed torpedo space and on the submerged deck. And then he nearly drowned. The cord of the miner's lamp he was wearing on his cap became tangled in the rail wires and floating ropes. But instead of panicking, he pulled off his cap, which the water had not dislodged, broke the cord which led to a battery in his hip pocket, pulled out the battery and dropped it, and wriggled through the rails.

There the current grabbed him, as though it had hands, turned him over and over, pushed him upward, and then pushed him downward. As he went down he thought, 'This is like being on the big dipper at Luna Park.' Then he was in a whirlpool, because he spun like a propeller, sometimes head down, sometimes feet down, and his heart was hammering and his ears were hammering and he saw scarlet, green and purple lights flicking on and off.

Suddenly, the hammering ceased and everything was still. He was still within himself, and around him was stillness, and everything was stillness, and he left peaceful and happy and never wanted to move again. And yet at that moment he thought, 'If I don't struggle now I'll drown.'

He began to fight his way upward, to claw his way upward, like trying to climb a ladder made of treacle. He dog-paddled upward, clutching and snatching and pulling down at the water, fighting to get away from this underwater world of incredible peace and quiet he got into where the stillness was like a charm, soft, beautiful and insidious, and where he wanted to lie back and rest and rest and rest forever.

And then, with a rush like falling upward, he catapulted up and broke surface through two inches of oil and saw a biscuit tin and grabbed it with both arms. And as he hung there on the surface of the water, gulping air, he saw, 30 yards away, the tip of one of *Perth*'s propeller blades sinking into the sea.

A long 18-inch plank bumped into him, and he crawled onto it and sat on it, and past him floated a white solar topee, bobbing up and down, up and down, as though someone was walking jauntily underneath it. He thought, 'The sun's going to be hot tomorrow – I'll need you,' so he grabbed the topee and put it on his oil-covered head, and it fitted.

Then he looked up at the stars, the brilliant clusters of stars, and spoke to them aloud.

'I'm the last man out of that ship alive,' he said. 'God, I thank you.'

from *Proud Echo* by Ronald McKie

Crew members of HMAS *Perth*.

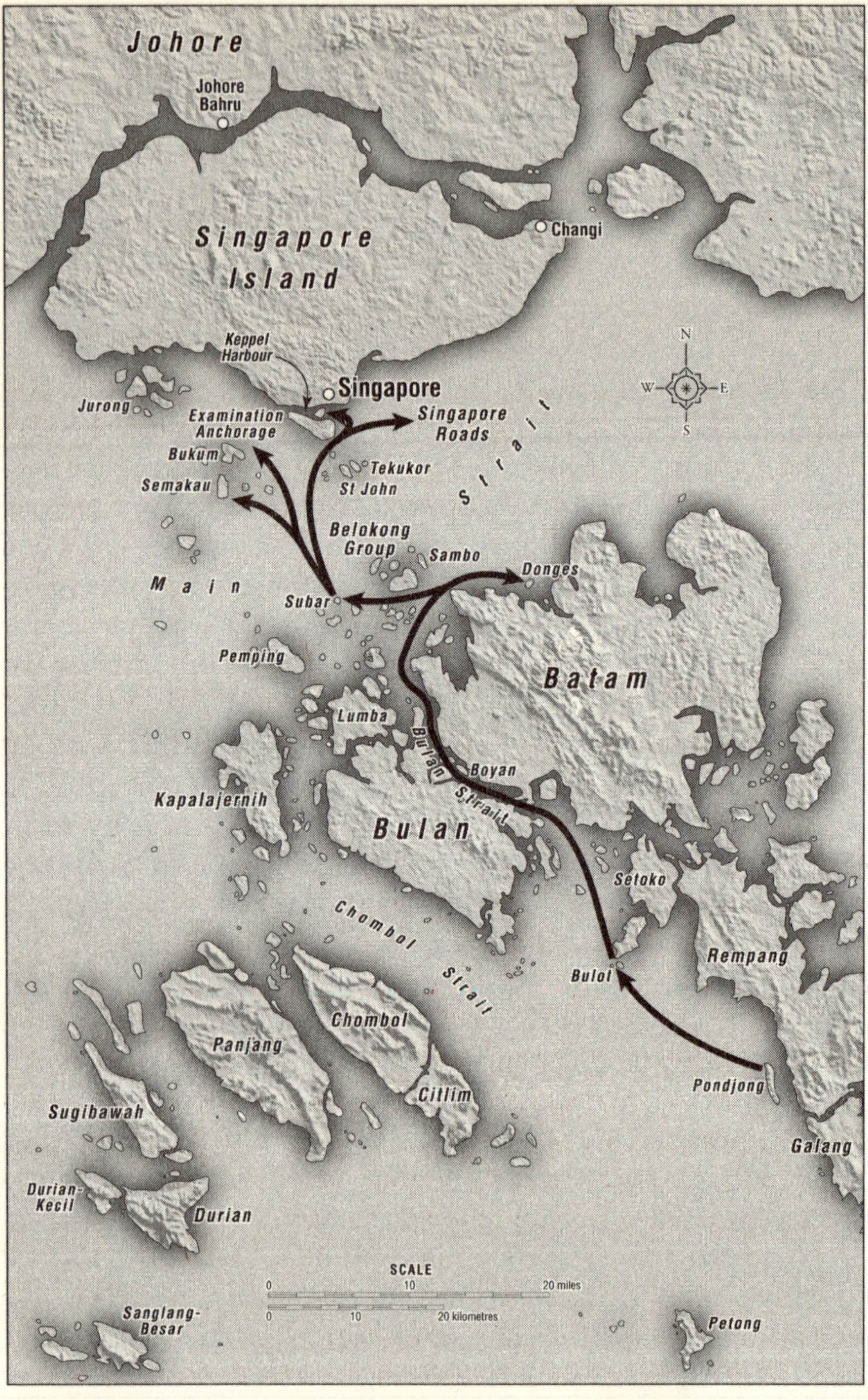

The *Krait*'s target, Singapore, behind its screen of islands.

Time to go

The *Krait* was the small ship that was used to transport a group of Australian commandos from Australia to the islands south of Singapore in 1943. Their aim was to strike at the Japanese enemy deep in the heartland of its power.

The commandos then prepared their canoes and supplies of limpet mines on a deserted island called Subar. The following piece takes up the story:

As the sun dropped towards the distant islands, towards far-off Sumatra, the withering heat of that day began to drain off Subar, though even at dusk Falls insisted the rocks were still hot enough to grill a steak, if anyone, as he said, was crazy enough to want to grill a steak on Subar. But with the easing of the heat, morale lifted and men, practically sleepless since the day before and now facing a night of action and days of paddling after that, started to prepare almost eagerly to leave their island hiding place. With their last tins of canned heat they boiled more billies of tea and ate their last meal of meat, limp chocolate and vitamin pills, and scratched holes for the empty tins among the still hot rocks. They had started packing their gear, just as the sun disappeared, when they heard a plane approaching and dropped where they were, faces to the earth, as a Japanese army transport – the only plane near Subar since daylight – spluttered over with engines throttling back, losing height as she made for one of the fields on Singapore Island.

'I'll bet anyone a quid they never even looked at us,' Page said, waving the razor he had begun to dry-shave with just before the plane appeared. 'If that Jap pilot was anything like ours, all he was thinking of was an iced tankard of saki.'

Lyon looked up from the bag he was packing. 'Anyone who mentions iced tankards again will go on a charge.'

In the quickening dusk they pulled on their black suits, slapped more brown stain on their faces and hair, and prepared to leave the little island. Down through the tumbled rocks, to the shingle on the eastern side, they first carried the heavy limpets and the emergency supplies and water, and then fetched the long canoes and put them into the sea and loaded them and rested.

Now that the attack was about to start, from inside the enemy harbour, within less than ten miles of Japanese headquarters itself, they were almost light-hearted as they waited restlessly for the first stars, not conscious any more that they needed sleep or that their bodies, after a journey of two thousand miles to achieve the 'impossible', to fulfil the 'wild idea' of one man, could not be driven much further.

'Time to go,' Davidson said at last, and in that moment, like a thin chill cry within, was fear, and then it was smothered by a muttered curse as someone slipped on a stone, the dull thump of a canoe bow on rock, a faint splash, the dark movement and never-to-be-forgotten finality of attack beginning.

Davidson and Falls, who had decided to leave earlier because they would have to paddle farther than the others during the night, got into their canoe, settled their legs and nervously checked their gear. Then, as hands fumbled for hands in the dark and faceless voices called good luck, paddles swirled and they were gone.

Twenty minutes later the two other teams pushed off from Subar and headed in across the black water under a moonless sky for the lights of Singapore.

'Down!' the leaders whispered as the searchlight beam splashed into the sea to port.

Way forward in their seats, their faces almost on the rubber decking, the two teams froze as the light played with the water, then edged towards them, yard by yard with awful logic as though it knew they were there.

Jones, in front of Page, sideways watched the creeping glare and saw the sea flowing across his vision like melted silver, and wanted to be sick. Nearer the light came, and Lyon, in the other canoe, his body folded into pain, his eyes watering with the strain, pleaded. 'Not now, not now,' over and over again in a monotonous voiceless chant.

The searchlight leapt skyward, up and up, then down, down to fall into the sea to starboard, and around them the water was acres of dazzling white light and in it they floated, black and motionless, like drifting logs.

Jones began to count, a gabble of sounds divorced from time: 'Eleven, twelve, thirteen' – like a bell in his brain – 'thirty-one, thirty-two' . . . on and on . . . 'sixty, sixty-one, sixty-two, sixty-three . . .'

The light went out.

Paddles snatched at the sea. The canoes slid forward, faster and faster . . . A hundred, two hundred yards, three hundred . . .

The light snapped on again, to fall where they had been, to follow the same inexorable pattern – down, forward, up in the air and over as though the men on the light had orders to jump some object, a ship perhaps, in the harbour. But this time the canoemen, drifting stilled in the twilight edge of the glare, knew they could not be seen.

Subar was five miles and two hours away, back across the currents sweeping Main Strait, and now, at 10pm, and about a mile from their target areas, the two teams stopped again to prepare for their separate attacks. As the black canoes lay together the teams arranged their limpets in their groups of three and set the fuses for explosion at five o'clock the next morning – a seven-hour delay. Each limpet also had a one-minute delay fuse, and the agreement was to press this fuse, if discovered fixing the limpets, and to paddle at top speed away from the ship before the charge or charges exploded. This fuse, for use only in extreme emergency, was designed to give the attacker at least a chance to get away and to be a warning signal to the others.

When the teams were ready they gripped hands across the water and separated, Lyon and Huston moving on towards the Examination Anchorage, and Page and Jones swinging left and heading for Bukum Island.

The lights along Bukum wharves wallowed and glittered in the water as Page and Jones slowly approached the island and stopped. They were no longer in the dark, for the sea around them now glowed with reflected light like a polished floor.

'Aren't we a bit close?' Jones whispered.

'For God's sake keep your voice down . . . No, they're looking from light into dark.'

Even Page's whisper seemed dangerously loud to Jones, who realised then, and later, that the most difficult thing at night and when under tension is to whisper quietly.

Page signalled with his right hand, and silently the paddle dipped and feathered, dipped and feathered, the water slicing down their shaved edges as they moved parallel to the wharves.

Then they stopped again in the thick salty twilight, conscious of the sweat trickling out of their hair and the heat inside their suits and their sweat-sodden backsides on the hard seats.

Opposite, where the Arabic calligraphy of the numbered wharves was white on black, a 5000-ton freighter was high in the water and obviously empty, and next to her was a small coastal-type ship with a long barge moored under her stern, and farther along a big low-riding tanker with red markings like mah-jong symbols on her black stack.

As they watched, light spluttered, violet-blue, and illuminated one end of the barge and the wharf piles high above the barge.

'Welders,' Page said, and again Jones noticed how unnaturally loud the whisper sounded in the still air close to the water.

They moved closer, narrowing the gap between them and the wharves, so that they could now hear the cries of working men above the grumble of winches.

'Target, freighter,' Bob Page said, after another interval of watching. 'Make for the middle – the darkest part.'

Page aimed the canoe and they dipped together and headed in, from twilight to half-light into full glow, half-expecting any second to hear shouts of discovery, a rifle shot, the stutter of automatics. Then they were in the freighter's shadow, up against her bulging belly, and for a minute or more they held the canoe with their paddles against the tide while their eyes adjusted to the dark and they could see clearly the black wall of the ship beside them.

Now Jones felt between his knees for the metal holdfast and eased the small magnetized frame onto the side of the ship, being careful not to let the magnets clang as they gripped. Then, as he held the holdfast cord with one hand to keep the bow of the canoe close to the ship, he pushed against the side to force the canoe's stern away from the ship as Page fitted the broomstick into the hole in the top of the first limpet, put the limpet over the side, reached down and, four feet under the water, eased the magnetized limpet onto the freighter.

As Page worked the broomstick out of the attached limpet, Jones released the holdfast, grabbed his paddle lying on the canoe's decking, and controlled the backward drift of the canoe as Page fed out the white cordtex, attached to the limpet, until the next position was reached. There the long-practised routine was repeated, and with the second limpet attached they again drifted along the side, Page feeding out the cordtex until the third position was reached.

At last all three limpets were fixed – the first on the engine-room, the others on the two holds, and all linked by the white cordtex and set so that the combined thirty pounds of plastic explosive would explode at 5am.

As Jones released the holdfast for the third time he nearly dropped it into the sea, his hands were trembling so violently, and his mouth was so dry that his tongue seemed too big for his mouth and upholstered with hard scale. Yet he was astonished to realise how alert he was and how physically alive he felt at this moment, as though every nerve, every muscle, every blood-vessel was functioning with perfection.

Paddles out now, they moved the canoe along the ship and under the flare of her bows and hung onto the rusty anchor chain and rested there. They were in the shadow of the wharf and only ten feet from the barge on which men were working at the other end among an argument of escaping steam and the violet crackling from the welder's torch, and above on the wharf itself Japanese, Chinese and Indians gabbled and shouted as they trundled cargo.

Page and Jones, more confident now after successfully limpeting their first kill, were holding the canoe against the anchor chain and eating a well-earned supper of limp chocolate when some primitive sense of danger warned them simultaneously. Cautiously they lifted their eyes to the wharf glow above them and froze.

Directly above them, and standing almost on the edge, was a Japanese sentry with slung rifle, his face under his peaked cap bisected by shadow. He stood there for several minutes, like a photograph, looking out to sea, then he cleared his throat, searched deep for the phlegm, and spat. The gob slapped the water beside the canoe as he eased the weight of the rifle on his shoulder and turned and strolled along the wharf.

Page touched Jones with his paddle. In went the blades and soundlessly they glided out from the anchor chain, waiting in the shadow of the barge for the sentry to move well down the wharf before paddling across the lighted area and into the welcome dark as sparks from the welder, working at the stern of the small ship, sprayed like a bunger fuse on Guy Fawkes night.

'I'm glad we're out of that,' Page whispered.

'Me, too. I didn't feel a bit brave.'

Jones opened a packet of chewing gum and handed a pellet back, as they rested, deciding what next to do, drifting. Then, well away from the wharf, which held no other worthwhile targets except the tanker – and tankers are hard to sink with limpets because of their many compartments – they saw the lights of another ship to seaward and let the drift take the canoe towards her. They had spent more than an hour on the first attack. Now two more had to be completed.

The classic approach for a limpet attack is to drift with the tide towards a ship's bows so as to be masked by their height and flare, but as Page and Jones approached their second target in what they guessed was nearly a five-knot race the glare from the lights on Bukum was just sufficient to dully polish her port side, and they were about to head to starboard when they noticed what looked like some of her crew leaning on the starboard rail. They were not sure that the group was not part of her structure, but the burst of a cigarette confirmed their suspicion a few seconds later and the canoemen continued on and soon were alongside, where Page back-watered as Jones tried to clamp the holdfast, failed, and got it on at the second attempt.

Their target was a big modern ship with three sets of goal-post masts, engine aft, and so low in the water with cargo that the attackers felt certain she had moved only that afternoon from the Bukum wharf. But there was too much reflected light on her side and on her port water for safety, and the two Australians worked as quickly as they could in the dangerous glow.

The first limpet went on, with a soft water-muffled clang, in line with her bridge, and the other two limpets were fixed to her aft holds. Then Jones had the holdfast off and they slid aft with the tide and away from her to be caught in a new and slower rip flowing eastward which took them, almost before they realised it, towards another ship like a smudge across the faint outer glow from Bukum.

They soon saw, however, that the rip was swinging them away from her, and began to paddle hard across the current until they could let the canoe sweep under her stern. They came in so quickly that they bumped her rudder and hung on, panting, fearful that the noise had been heard, while the current gargled and the water heaped up along one side of the tilting canoe.

This ship was an ancient, heavily loaded tramp, and so rusty that when they got against her the holdfast magnets would not grip on the sheets of flaking rust. She stank of rotten weed and acid and salt as Jones tore off enough of the corrosion to get the holdfast to grip. But their problems had only just started, for Page had to reach deep into the water to tear at the ship's plates with his nails to clear spaces for the limpets, for even their magnets, which were more powerful than those on the holdfast, would not at first grip on the flaking surface. This was difficult and painful work, and dangerous, too, because the scratching against the ship's side might attract attention. But at last they were away, sliding down the dark with one of the lights of the limpeted tramp receding and disappearing like the tail-lamp of a departing train at the end of a long platform.

The glow from Bukum was a mile away when they stopped and Page bent forward and tapped his partner on the shoulder with his paddle.

'Thanks, Joe,' he said.

'Thanks, Bob.'

Jones lifted the holdfast overboard and let it go without a splash. He reached for the spare holdfast and dropped it over, too, as Page ditched the spare limpet, for there was no more need for them now. They were just extra weight now the attack was completed.

And then, slumped in their sweat, they were both so violently tired they never wanted to move again – a frightening, sick sort of weariness that seemed to drain their bodies of all energy and wrap their brains in heavy wet cloth.

For minutes, as the canoe drifted on the dark sea, they did not stir. Then almost imperceptibly they recovered and a cool singing elation swept their dragging weariness away.

'We've done it,' Page whispered hoarsely. 'Joe, we've done it.'

Slowly they began to paddle towards Dongas.

It was nearly 2am on 27 September.

And only when they were halfway back did Jones realise that two huge saltwater boils had developed on his right knee and that they were throbbing.

Lyon and Huston, after separating from Page and Jones a mile from Bukum Island, went on into the Examination Anchorage, where they thought they would have no difficulty locating and limpeting targets observed by Davidson that afternoon from Subar.

But they were soon disillusioned, for whereas the lights on Bukum had been both a danger and an advantage to Page's canoe, the blackness of the anchorage and the shoreline hills behind the western end of Keppel Harbour made their approach extremely confusing and difficult.

Ships were in the anchorage. They knew that. But from almost sea-level the attackers could not see them against the coast of Singapore Island, and they could not tell in the dark, with distances almost impossible to judge, whether lights they did observe were on ships or on the island itself.

Lyon and Huston paddled around, stopping every few minutes to observe and listen, but an hour passed and they had still failed to find a ship. They moved towards one light for nearly ten minutes before they realised that it did not seem to be getting any closer and that it must be on the island.

For nearly two hours they searched, disheartened and worried, before Lyon saw a red light in the direction of Blakang Mati Island, and guessed that it was one of the tankers seen from Subar.

He whispered, 'Red four-five. If it's a tanker we'll put all the limpets on her and make sure.'

'Right, sir.'

They moved towards the red light and soon picked up the muddy silhouette of a tanker against the soft glow of the city behind Blakang Mati. Slowly they circled, noting with excitement how low she was in the water, then edged forward and came in under her stern where, covered even from the starlight, they were in almost total darkness.

Working cautiously along her port side, for they could hear voices, and even distinct words, on deck, they put their final set of three limpets on her engine-room plates. Then they moved astern, slung another set of three around her propeller and Lyon was about to put on the last of the third set of three on the starboard side of the engine-room when he felt that he was being watched, and looked up.

Not ten feet above them a man, his head out of a porthole was looking down on them, the lighter patch of his face clear against the blackness of the ship's side and the night sky.

Huston, who was gripping the holdfast cord and holding the canoe's stern away from the tanker so that Lyon could apply the last limpet, sensed from Lyon's sudden stillness that something was wrong and was about to whisper when the man above sniffed.

Not daring to move, hardly breathing, they waited for a challenge, for the general alarm that would inevitably follow, for the searchlights which would begin their thin cold probing. But for minutes all they heard was the soft slapping of the sea against the tanker's side, shrill voices high above them on deck, muffled sunken sounds deep inside the ship like far-off wind instruments.

The man above had a cold, for he sniffed wetly several times and cleared his throat, but he still didn't move and Lyon crouched almost in the sea, wondered if he would have time to fix the limpet, which he had in his lap, and to press the one-minute fuse if they were discovered. He was still wondering when the man withdrew his head and a few seconds later the raiders heard a faint click as a cabin light was switched on and a thin pipe of light came from the porthole. Now they waited for the man to return, for a torch to stab at them, for a shout in Japanese, and the muscles of Huston's neck were tight cords with waiting. Then, with new hope, he thought: he must be going to bed. Then he felt Lyon move as with infinite care the leader fitted the broomstick into the limpet, put the limpet overboard, and down into the water and slid it gently, without a sound, onto the tanker's plates.

Huston waited tensely as Lyon eased out the stick, then he released the holdfast and the current swept them along the tanker and away.

'Do you reckon he saw us?' Huston asked, when they were out of range.

'If he did he probably thought we were a fishing canoe.'

Huston wiped his face with his sleeve. 'I'm glad we've used all the limpets,' was all he said.

They turned seaward – for Dongas.

Davidson and Falls, who had left Subar before the other canoes, paddled hard across the tide and were past The Sisters and through between the islands of Tekukor and Blakang Mati by a little after 9pm.

They rested for five minutes, as a searchlight measured the sky, before diving deep among the shadows along Blakang Mati – where the barracks of the British fortress island were now lighted by the Japanese – and moving along the channel towards where the boom pylons at the Tanjong Pagar end of Keppel Harbour were visible against the city glare.

They were moving easily, almost enjoying the rhythmic thrust of the long thin bow, when Davidson, whose night vision was uncanny, saw a light and realised it was moving towards them. At first he could not guess its distance or speed, then with alarm he knew they were in danger of being run down.

'Go for you life,' he called, as he dug to swing the canoe, and together their paddles gripped the water to force her closer to the island. And then, as the light seemed to gather speed and rush at them, they worked frantically, and the light was on them and beside them as a big steam ferry thumped past not ten feet away and went on into the night trailing ribbons of sparks from her spatular funnel.

'My word,' Falls said, 'that was close.'

They seesawed in the wash, the water splashing over them, and then they were clear and paddling on to the boom.

Now they stopped at one of the rusting buoys and sat forward, tense and watchful, feeling for danger with their eyes, their ears, their skin, testing the air weighted with suspicion.

They could see no boom-defence vessel, no boom patrol of any kind. Crouched, still they let the canoe drift out so that the buoys were no longer close together like big onyx beads but strung in a long line, an etching of separated darkness on darkness. Now they could see that the boom gate was open, that the way was clear and apparently unguarded.

'Looks clear,' Davidson whispered.

But Falls heard the words so clearly that he hissed a warning.

'What's wrong?'

'Too loud.'

'Balls.'

Cautiously they moved back and then along the boom, like two black cats along a wall, yard by yard until they reached the entrance. They waited there, a minute, two, straining the dark. Then they turned the corner and drifted through – a long thin shadow.

They were inside Keppel Harbour, and then they heard singing, high, clear and close in the still night air, with shouts like inverted commas reaching above the voices.

'Our friends beating it up at the Yacht Club,' Davidson whispered.

The Yacht Club meant nothing to Falls – except that Japanese, enemies, were noisy, enjoying themselves, and dangerously close, and that he would much prefer to be thousands of miles away, safe at home.

The raiders moved across to the east wharf where there were two small ships not worth limpeting, and then went under the wharf so that they could examine the harbour in safety. But the decking dripped monotonously on their heads and down their necks, and the piles wallowing in the restless water trailed gardens of weeds which stank, and they came out again and went on, searching for targets.

The long main wharf was empty, but by keeping in its shadow they reached the entrance to the Empire Dock and saw ships inside and, the masts and funnels of others, and heard the nattering of winches, but the whole area was floodlit and active and Davidson decided they were wasting their time.

As they turned, an ocean-going tug came down harbour, so they waited before following her out, and as they paddled through the boom and headed for the Outer Roads the party at the Yacht Club had reached the shouting stage.

There were ships – plenty of them – in the Roads off the business heart of Singapore. Davidson and Falls could see their blurred shapes as they approached, though they also noticed that reflected light from the glowing city, over which the smoke from Chinatown was drifting like fog, made attack, except on the seaward side, dangerous. As they came closer a sampan went by, but the man paddling with a stern sweep did not see them, even though they were not a dozen yards away, and the lights of a car or truck crept along Collyer Quay past Clifford Pier and the brilliantly lighted Fullerton Building and disappeared as the vehicle swung to cross the bridge over the Singapore River.

A clock ashore chimed the quarter-hour – a chill and lonely sound to the men in the canoe – as they selected their first victim, a heavily laden freighter, and drifted under her bow and along the side to the engine-room.

Now it was almost slack water, and Falls had no trouble clamping the holdfast; but as he held the canoe steady and pushed against the side, he wondered why Davidson, generally so expert, took so long to fix the first limpet, and cursed at the delay when he knew that one glance from a sailor, having a final cigarette, might discover them. His impatience increased when he saw that, although the ship shielded them from the lights of the city, the Roads were not completely dark, and even in the seaward shadow of the ship, reflected light from the sky made the water like oiled copper.

The first limpet took so long to go on that Falls, who knew that speed under these conditions was vital, gave a sigh of relief when the signal came to release the holdfast and move to the second limpet position and then the third. But not until they had attacked their second ship and had reached the third did he know what had caused the long delay.

Ashore the Victoria Hall clock called 1am as they made a stern approach to their third victim, another engine-aft freighter, but this ship was showing so many strong lights aft that even under the gloom of her counter, the reflection from the water polished their faces like the light from a fire at night.

Two limpets were on and Davidson was about to fix the third when Falls glanced over his shoulder and nearly dropped the holdfast cord.

Davidson, his face glistening with sweat, his mouth like pliers as he pushed the broomstick into the top of the limpet, was wearing a monocle.

So that was the reason, Falls thought, as he gaped back at his companion.

And it was, for as Falls had waited, cursing, for Davidson to fix the first limpet on the first ship, Davidson, with a limpet resting on his knees, had fumbled in one of the zip breast pockets of his suit, and had crossed to search the other pocket until he found his monocle. Then he had screwed it into his eye, and had slipped its cord, made from finely plaited fishing line and blackened with boot polish, over his head. And only then was he ready to attack.

Now, as the holdfast came off the last ship and the tide took them along her side and away from her lights, Falls, who knew that Davidson's eyes were perfect – better than his own – and that he did not need glasses and never usually wore a monocle, didn't know whether to laugh or to hit Davidson over the head with his paddle.

First daylight was leaking into the sky that morning of 27 September when Page and Jones grounded on the bent beach of Dongas at 4.45am. After ten hours in the canoe their backs ached, their necks were stiff, their legs felt like plasticine so that when they got out they collapsed in the shallow water and had to drag themselves onto the sand with their hands.

Lyon and Huston, who had reached the hideout island half an hour before and who, though exhausted, had been able to recover a little from their all-night paddle, hobbled to their aid. They massaged their legs and backs and then, as they pulled up the canoe and unloaded her, pumped questions into the two men on the sand.

'How many did you get?' Lyon demanded.

'Three,' Page said, groaning at the pain in his back as he tried to ease cramped muscles.

'Good show. We put all ours on a tanker – couldn't find any others.'

'That should burn up some of their precious oil.'

As Page began to knead his leg muscles, feeling them tingle as the circulation slowly returned, Lyon asked, 'Did you hear an explosion – dull as if it was under water?'

'Yes – not long after we'd started back.' It was Jones, who had managed to stand, but who swayed on still numb legs.

'We thought someone had pushed the tit,' Huston said, rubbing Jones's legs. 'Gave me a touch of 'em.'

Page looked up. 'You don't think it was Donald?'

'I'm sure it wasn't.' Lyon said quickly. 'There was no alarm . . . If he got three we should have seven kills.'

'We'll soon know,' Jones said, and even his voice was tired. Page could stand now, though unsteadily. Slowly he exercised.

'What's the time?' he asked.

'Time those limpets were going off,' Lyon said. 'We'd better get up to the grandstand.'

They staggered to the camp with the canoe, and, still tottering, and snatching at vines for support, half-scrambled, half-pulled themselves up to the OP on the rise.

Although the light was growing, the lights on Sambo were still strong and the sky glow from Singapore like a false dawn. They waited, but only a few minutes, just time enough for the sea below the OP to push aside the gloom and emerge – like dark grey linoleum. Then from across the strait came a dull dry explosion like a distant bomb-burst as the combined flash of thirty pounds of plastic explosive smashed the plates of Jaywick's first victim.

'Thar she blows,' Page said, sitting up and wincing with the pain in his back.

Huston punched Jones. 'You beaut – you bloody beaut.'

Lyon shaded his torch and looked at his watch.

'Five fifteen . . . Not bad.'

They waited, staring into the half-light, waited five minutes, six minutes, before the second explosion, much louder than the first, seemed to roll across the water, reach them and roll on behind them across little Dongas and fall into the sea.

And as the sound was lost, the lights of both Singapore and nearby Sambo were blacked out, and in their place a ship's siren, faint and plaintive, began to wail like a bird in a fog.

'Two,' Lyon said.

'And now they're worried,' Page added.

In the next twenty minutes they heard five more explosions, two close together. But that was all.

'Seven,' Lyon said. 'What was your tonnage, Bob?'

'Hard to tell. Between fifteen and twenty thousand.'

'With our ten-thousand-ton tanker that gives us, perhaps, thirty thousand, and with another twenty thousand from Donald we should have fifty thousand.'

'And that's a lot of ships and cargo the Nips can kiss their arses to,' said Huston.'

Jones yawned and rubbed his eyes.
'What I'd call a decent night's work.'
He yawned again. 'I could sleep for a month.'

from *The Heroes* by Ronald McKie

War In The Air

War In The Air

The attraction of flying had always proved irresistible to Australians during the twentieth century, and in times of war there was no shortage of applicants flocking to fly for their country. It all began in 1915, when Australia created its own air force – the Australian Flying Corps (AFC). This had its origins in the military aviation base, the Central Flying School, which had been established with two flying instructors and five aircraft at Point Cook in 1914. While the AFC served within the Australian Imperial Force, it usually operated under the command of the British Royal Flying Corps. In 1921 the Australian Flying Corps was restructured to become the Royal Australian Air Force (RAAF).

After its arrival in Egypt in 1916, the Australian Flying Corps' No. 1 Squadron achieved prominence in the Middle East. During the Sinai campaign, flying in aircraft such as the BE-2C, which lacked manoeuvrability and performance, Australian pilots acquitted themselves ably against the German airmen in their superior Fokkers. When it was equipped with Bristol fighters at the end of 1917, No. 1 Squadron began to dominate aerial warfare in Palestine. Australia's only World War I air VC was awarded to the squadron's Lieutenant F.H. McNamara, for rescuing a downed Australian pilot from attacking Turkish cavalry.

Squadrons 2, 3 and 4 of the Australian Flying Corps served with great distinction on the Western Front between 1917 and 1918. Performing aerial reconnaissance, bombing and fighter duties, the Australian pilots flew planes such as Sopwith Camels, RE8 and DH5 reconnaissance aircraft, SE5a fighters and Handley Page bombers.

In World War II, Australian aircrew fought in the skies across the world, from the jungles of New Guinea and the Pacific to the sands of North Africa, from the beaches of Dunkirk to the icy waters of the Bay of Biscay. They flew in outmoded Wirraways against Japanese Zeroes, and in heavily laden Lancaster bombers against Messerschmitt ME-109 fighters. They flew Spitfires, Hurricanes, Kittyhawks, Tomahawks, Liberators, Lockheed Hudsons, Mosquitoes, Typhoons, Wellingtons, Beaufighters and even Sunderland flying boats. Most of them were unsung heroes.

Since 1945, the RAAF has provided air support for Australian troops in Korea, Vietnam, the Gulf War and Iraq. As technological advances took place, the RAAF equipped itself with the best aircraft available. In the Korean War of 1950–53, airmen of 77 Squadron had initially been equipped with propeller-driven P-51 Mustang fighters used towards the end of World War II. However, because of the superiority of the enemy's MiG-15 jet fighters, 77 Squadron switched to flying Meteor jets.

In Vietnam, Allied helicopter gunships and American B-52 bombers protected by fighters became familiar images of the war. Australian helicopters were used for moving troops quickly to battle zones, providing air cover and evacuating the wounded.

In 1973, after the Vietnam War, the first of the famous F111's was delivered to the RAAF. The F111 was often described as 'a swing-wing fighter' and it proved so successful that versions of it, together with the FA-18/Hornet, still form the basis of RAAF air power today.

Australian air corps hero

In March 1917, Lieutenant Frank McNamara became the first Australian airman to win a Victoria Cross. Alec Hepburn provides more on this outstanding Australian flyer:

The biggest problem faced by No. 1 Squadron in the desert war was not the Turks but their own aircraft, which were mostly woefully out of date. Some more advanced models of the ancient BE-2, as well as a few of the radically new Bristol F2B Fighters, were slowly arriving in the Middle East, but not in sufficient numbers to help the Australian airmen materially.

May 1917, Frank McNamara VC (on the left), is standing with other officers in front of a Martinsyde aircraft.

McNamara, when he had a chance to fly, usually went aloft in one of the single-seat Martinsyde 'Elephants', a machine full of flying eccentricities but having little better all-round performance than the lumbering 'Quirks', as the BE-2Cs were called by their pilots. Perhaps McNamara enjoyed the challenge to his flying skills that the clumsy Martinsyde provided.

With the first all-out attack on Gaza planned for 26 March 1917 the Australian Flying Corps stepped up its harassment of the enemy with numerous bombing sorties against their positions. During this period of intensive attacks the squadron commander, Major Williams, had a narrow escape from death or capture when the engine of his aircraft cut out over Tel el Sheria. Luckily, after frantically going through the restarting drill, Williams managed to get the powerplant going again after his aircraft had plunged to less than 150 metres above a battery of Turkish guns.

Blinding sandstorms grounded the squadron for several days but on 19 March the weather had cleared enough to allow a new series of raids to be launched against a wide variety of targets in the area between Junction Station and Tel el Sheria.

The same day also saw Ross Smith, later to gain fame as an England-to-Australia air pioneer, win a Military Cross. He was awarded his decoration for landing his aircraft behind the Turkish lines to rescue a downed British pilot – a feat that McNamara would repeat less than twenty-four hours later. Carried out under far more difficult circumstances, and with much greater danger than Smith's deed, McNamara's rescue won him the Victoria Cross.

On the evening of 19 March, Williams called McNamara and eight BE-2C pilots together for a briefing, outlining the mission for the coming dawn. The lumbering BE-2Cs, loaded with racks of conventional contact bombs, were to attack the vital Junction Station rail link at first light. McNamara in his Martinsyde was to have a dual role. Firstly, he was to provide the bombers with a token fighter cover on the flight to the target area, then act as a bomber himself – dropping five new-type time-shells. If these shells proved as successful as was hoped they might then be used to replace the normal contact bombs in future ground-attack missions against the Turks.

At first everything went strictly according to plan. The Australian aircraft took off just before dawn, were over Junction Station as the sun began to rise, and caught the sleepy Turkish defences completely by surprise.

Swooping in one after the other the BE-2Cs dropped their small bombloads right on target. Around the confused Turks, Junction Station erupted in flames, explosion after explosion rocking the area as the vital ammunition dumps caught fire and blew up. Smoke rose in thick, black clouds into the clear, desert air.

Their task completed, the little biplanes broke off their attack as quickly as it had begun. Now it was McNamara's turn to try out the experimental time-shells; however, this time the alerted Turkish defenders were ready, waiting, and very angry. The run into Junction Station would be the closest thing to suicide, but it had to be done.

Opening the throttle wide the lieutenant put the nose of his Martinsyde down into a barrage of anti-aircraft and machine-gun fire. A hail of bullets caught the biplane as it made its run in towards its target, ripping through the fabric of its wings and fuselage. However, nothing vital was hit as the stubby little biplane levelled out to complete its bombing run.

Seemingly immune to the sudden death exploding all around him McNamara concentrated all his thoughts on the job in hand. Swooping low over the heads of the defenders he dropped the first four bombs at regular intervals across Junction Station. Each of the special new missiles exploded just as planned, however, there was something wrong with time-shell number five – seconds after it left the bomb rack it exploded prematurely, only metres below the belly of the Martinsyde.

The explosion tossed the tiny biplane upwards and a large piece of shrapnel sliced its way through the fabric of its underside and tore a deep wound in the pilot's leg. The force of the impact caused McNamara to involuntarily kick the right rudder pedal fully forward, causing the Martinsyde to fall into a spin. In searing pain and with blood pouring from the gash the Australian pilot fought off waves of faintness as he managed to recover control over his madly spinning machine and bring it back on to an even keel, heading back towards base just 120 kilometres away.

It was then that he saw he was not the only pilot in trouble that morning: a BE-2C flown by Captain D.W. Rutherford, its engine spluttering on the edge of total failure, was gliding down to make a forced landing on the desert deep inside enemy-held territory.

Shaking his head violently from side to side in an effort to fight off nausea and faintness that threatened to overwhelm him at any second, McNamara watched his comrade go down. He also saw a Turkish cavalry unit galloping out across the desert to intercept the crippled BE-2C.

Despite the terrible pain and loss of blood from his gaping wound McNamara could not bring himself to abandon the downed Australian pilot. Fighting to stay conscious he rammed the nose of the damaged Martinsyde down into a dive and did not level out until he was only a matter of metres from the ground. Then he dragged back on the joystick, hit the earth hard, and slewed the scout to a stop just metres from the downed BE-2C.

The next instant Rutherford scrambled from his aircraft, dashed across the gap between the two machines, and threw himself onto the wing of the Martinsyde. The advancing cavalry, seeing that their would-be prisoner might be snatched from their fingers, began firing from the saddle as they galloped across the ever-narrowing strip of desert between themselves and the Australian airmen.

With Rutherford clinging on to the lower wing McNamara opened his throttle wide and the overloaded Martinsyde jumped forward, bouncing across the hard, stony earth as he attempted to take off again. However, things were not going to be that easy.

The young lieutenant found it very difficult to keep his machine trimmed with Rutherford's weight on its wing, also his injured leg was causing him agony. Then it happened: his blood-soaked boot slipped off the rudder-bar, the overloaded Martinsyde slewed violently, and crashed headlong into a wadi, a complete write-off.

Now the stricken BE-2C was the airmen's only slim hope of escape. Climbing from his blood-spattered cockpit McNamara began hobbling back towards the other machine. Each step sent pain shooting through his body but he dared not falter. Rutherford lingered at the wrecked Martinsyde just long enough to smash a petrol pipe and set the aircraft on fire.

Joining McNamara at the BE-2C the captain feverishly began to work on its engine as the lieutenant clambered into its rear cockpit. All the time the Turkish cavalry was getting nearer and nearer, their bullets thudding into the sand all around the downed aircraft.

McNamara attempted to sight the BE-2C's machine-gun on the advancing line of horsemen but its firing arc was too restricted; instead he tried to answer the Turkish fire with his service revolver.

As McNamara emptied the last chamber of his handgun in the general direction of the Turks, Rutherford shouted for contact and attempted to swing the heavy, wooden, four-bladed propeller. The airmen could hardly believe their luck as the 90-hp, eight-cylinder RAF 1a engine fired at the first swing – they were back in business again.

Rutherford leapt onto the wing as McNamara opened the throttle wide. The little BE-2C surged forward across the sand and with the captain clinging desperately to its wing struts the biplane lifted clear off the ground, just ahead of the enraged cavalry which at that moment thundered onto the crash scene. Slowly the heavily laden BE-2C climbed back into the sky and, turning for home, flew through a renewed barrage of anti-aircraft fire as they crossed back over the Turkish lines. However, the airmen's incredible luck held and the enemy fortifications were soon left well astern.

Clear of the Turkish lines a relieved Rutherford was able to climb into the safety of the forward observer's seat. McNamara now had a new fight on his hands, battling against unconsciousness until he finally put the battered aircraft down safely at El Arish. There he finally collapsed and was carried on a stretcher from the BE-2C to a field hospital. However, his epic Victoria Cross–winning deed was now complete and the young Australian had earned his place in history.

His leg wound was serious enough for the pilot to be invalided back home to Australia. Now promoted to captain, and the first Australian flyer ever to win a Victoria Cross, McNamara received a hero's welcome when his ship docked at Melbourne on 28 September 1917.

McNamara resigned from the Australian Flying Corps soon afterwards but then changed his mind and in 1918 was reappointed with his former rank and seniority. Later he passed into the newly formed Royal Australian Air Force, which replaced the old wartime Australian Flying Corps.

Over the years McNamara rose to the rank of air vice-marshal and was awarded the CBE. He died in England on 2 November 1961 at the age of sixty-seven.

from *True Australian War Tales* by Alec Hepburn

Australian air ace

Nicky Barr became a fighter pilot in the RAAF in 1940. He flew first Tomahawks and then Kittyhawks in North Africa while fighting against Rommel's Afrika Korps. Within twelve months he had shot down over twelve enemy planes. Later he was seriously wounded and was made a prisoner of war when he himself was shot down. He managed to escape, however, and joined a resistance group in Italy. The following piece captures the thrill of one of his desert sorties:

The next day, Saturday 13 December 1941, started quietly as Nicky's squadron spent most of the morning on standby. Standby was often stressful, and entailed patiently waiting around, fully kitted and ready for combat, generally lounging on chairs outside the 'ops' tent. Mostly the men talked quietly to each other, some played cards, others joked, but always they kept one eye on their planes, lined up ready to fly, less than a stone's throw away. Even though they tried to relax, there was always a degree of tension as they waited either for an assignment or for a signal to 'scramble'.

Men found different ways to cope with the stress of standby. Ed Jackson would often sit by himself playing solo. Nicky could tell he wasn't concentrating on the card games though; his mind was always deep in thought, preparing for the action to come or some other compelling problem.

Eventually, at four in the afternoon, the squadron was ordered to carry out a patrol over the Derna–Martuba area. Jackson led the formation of ten Tomahawks and for this, Nicky's eighth operation, Bobby Gibbes was his section leader. Some minutes after becoming airborne they approached Derna from the sea, flying below a thick layer of cloud at about 5000 feet, heading south. As they crossed the coastline, in the ten o'clock position ahead (twelve o'clock is directly in front, six o'clock behind) they spotted a V-formation of eight Me-110 bombers heading towards Alexandria. They were fitted with special reconnaissance cameras and were escorted by seven Me-109 fighters.

The Tomahawks were sighted before they could close, and the

109s swung around in formation to confront them – a chilling sight. The low cloud base prevented the 109s from creating an advantage, by allowing them to use their superior performance at height and also negated their 'pick and zoom' tactics, although Nicky realised the cloud could assist both sides with evasive tactics. Either way, Nicky wasn't going to wait.

He broke formation and thrust the Tomahawk forward to meet the 109s, which by now had swung around to attack the Tomahawks from the left rear. Once again, the squadron split up as the sky erupted into a swirling mixture of fighter planes clawing at each other in individual dogfights.

In his direct vision, Nicky caught sight of a 109 sitting in a perfect quarter-stern position, posturing to fire at a Tomahawk. Nicky saw his chance. He violently wrenched his plane around, banked, then climbed upwards, quickly reaching a position above the 109. Within a few seconds, he pushed his plane into a dive, rapidly shortening his distance to within 350 metres from the Messerschmitt. Although Nicky's shooting record had been adequate at training, he hadn't convinced himself he was an accurate shooter, so he forced himself closer to the 109, watching the plane fill his sights. At about 250 metres, he pressed the trigger. He followed the tracers spurting from his gun and was sure he'd hit the plane, but cursed to himself as he couldn't see any obvious or immediate effect on the 109. However, he was relieved to see the Tomahawk, which had been in the 109's sights, suddenly dive and turn off to port, apparently untouched.

The 109 pulled off from his line of attack and headed for the temporary shelter of the cloud. Nicky followed in close pursuit. The enemy fighter banked and wheeled in a hair-raising attempt to escape, with Nicky matching every turn.

By now, the cordite smell from the cockpit guns was very strong and Nicky's concentration was generated by adrenalin. Once again, it was close and hot in the confined space of the cockpit, but Nicky's main focus was on the plane ahead. His eyes narrowed; the distance closed, he was in range. He pressed the trigger again.

The 109 shuddered and half rolled. As Nicky watched, the plane flicked into a spin, a wisp of smoke trailing in its wake. He followed it visually until it crashed in flames into the ground, close to the burning wreckage of another Messerschmitt. There was also a burning Tomahawk some distance away.

His adrenalin still pumping, Nicky quickly searched the now almost empty sky. In the distance, all he could see were three 109s, so he climbed up into the cloud and flew south-east towards where he knew Gazala would be. It made sense to use cloud cover whenever it was available. Air fighting is not like land fighting, where it may be possible to find even some small cover. There are no trenches or shields on a plane, just a thin skin of metal and glass. The real risk is that no one knows who is in the cloud, there is no visibility and one needs to be reasonably good at instrument flying.

After some moments, he dived just below the cloud and realised he was south-west of the Gazala inlet, a clear milestone carved into the desert shale by the Mediterranean. The pressure was off a little now; there were no fighters in sight.

From Nicky's position high above the vastness of the Sahara, running parallel to the coastline was the black ribbon of the highway leading to Gazala. In the distance further along the road, Nicky noticed a swarm of Junkers Ju-88 twin-engined bombers attacking an Allied truck formation. Some of the vehicles had crashed into each other, and others were stranded in the clutching sand on the edge of the road. Some were stalled, and palls of black and blue smoke spiralled upwards, signalling their helplessness.

Nicky accelerated towards the marauding planes and stealthily moved inside the whirling formation. As he approached to within shooting distance, one Ju-88, after levelling out from an attacking sweep, swung around full into Nicky's air space and raced directly towards him. For a milli-second, Nicky flew right through the German's gun sights. Horrified, he waited for a spray of bullets to come at him. Luckily he was through before the pilot could react.

Instinctively, Nicky now violently manoeuvred his Tomahawk to a position setting himself in line for a front-to-quarter attack. The

German pilot would have seen him, but too late, he'd missed his chance. The side of the German's plane was perfectly exposed and presented a clear target. Nicky's bullets ripped along the plane's fuselage, cutting holes into it like a can-opener.

As the Junkers roared past him, Nicky slipped around behind the tail, and swung into a position below the plane and prepared for a second shot. He fired again at close range and saw his bullets bite into the left wing. Immediately, the wing dropped away and tumbled into space, leaving jagged edges of metal protruding from the fuselage. Now, unbalanced and out of control, the Junkers rocked and then dived sharply, rotated, then quickly generated into a flat spin.

The action was all over in a few seconds – sudden and violent. However, Nicky realised there was no time to consider the victory, or even savour it, as he knew others in the swarm would quickly react and then concentrate on this infiltrator – a viper in the nest. Without waiting to witness the Junkers' final death dive, Nicky quickly shot up into the protective cover of the clouds again.

With some degree of security and satisfaction, he settled himself on instruments then, a few minutes later, dived below the cloud cover again for a quick look. North-west of where the bombed trucks were now recovering and assessing their damage, Nicky could see a black pall of smoke pouring from a crumpled plane fiercely burning on the ground; almost certainly the Ju-88.

from *Nicky Barr, an Australian Air Ace* by Peter Dornan

'Night fighter on our tail'

In July 1940, after Dunkirk, British Prime Minister Winston Churchill wrote to his minister of Aircraft Production, Lord Beaverbrook, declaring that the best way of destroying the German war machine was by 'an absolutely devastating, exterminating attack by very heavy bombers from this country upon the Nazi homeland'. As a result, the production of bombers was increased and many more young men from Britain, Australia and other dominions were trained to become bomber crews. In 1942, Air Marshal Arthur Harris (who became known as 'Bomber' Harris) was placed in charge of Bomber Command. The bombing of German cities began in earnest.

Over 10,000 Australians flew bombing raids over Europe during World War II. It was an extremely hazardous occupation because of the German fighters and the flak. Many bombers were also destroyed through accidental collision or stray Allied bombs. Nearly 3500 Australians lost their lives in Bomber Command. Writer Peter Firkins' description of the destruction of a Wellington bomber attacking Hamburg and the crew's subsequent bale-out is presented through the personal thoughts and feelings of the Australian second pilot, Alex Kerr:

On 27 April 1940, four days after his nineteenth birthday, Kerr reported for duty as one of the intake of eager young men on No. 1 Course, Empire Air Training Scheme. Three months later he sailed to Canada to complete his flying training, and by early November 1940 he had won his coveted wings and been promoted to sergeant

Australians of the RAAF and RAF Bomber Command – World War II.

pilot. He joined 115 Squadron, RAF Bomber Command, as a second pilot flying Wellington bombers.

At 9pm on the night of 10–11 May 1941, he and his crew took off on their fourth operation together, as one of a force of 119 bombers briefed to attack Hamburg. The changeable European weather proved to be unusually kind, and their outward flight was uneventful. But, as Alex Kerr and his five companions began the always tense and dangerous bombing run into the target, everything was about to change. They dropped their bombs and turned for home, and Kerr still remembers with extraordinary clarity the puffs of grey flak smoke from the explosions close to the Wellington and the streams of white tracer curving over one another in graceful arcs. On previous raids he had remarked on the beauty of the colourful streams of tracer, forming a colourful display like some gala night in peacetime. So far the aircraft had never been hit by flak, and although he had felt some apprehension and his heart missed a beat occasionally when a flak shell burst nearby and buffeted the Wellington, he had not known real fear.

He stood in the astro-dome position, watching the flak and the searchlight beams and keeping a sharp eye open for night fighters, and suddenly heard Dave the rear-gunner exclaim, 'My turret's on fire, Andy!' ('Andy' was the skipper of the Wellington.)

Kerr recalls:

> There was no panic in his voice, only urgency. I didn't turn to look at the rear turret but kept my eye on the searchlights, three of which had picked us up and held us, due no doubt to the fire in the rear. Five seconds later the ground became a blaze of light as a large cone of approximately twenty searchlights sprang into life and focused on the unfortunate visitor. As I relayed this information to Andy I felt Bill, the navigator, brush past me, extinguisher in hand to assist Dave. Almost as soon as Andy acknowledged my message, Dave's voice rapped through the intercom once more: 'Night fighter on our tail!'
>
> My heart went into my throat as I became aware of the

> import of the statement – caught in the cone of searchlights, rear turret on fire, night fighter on our tail. I swung around. There it was – a dark shape hovering expectantly and moving into position on the starboard quarter.
>
> I was aware of a tingling sensation at the back of my neck as I realised that I might only have a few more minutes of life. There was no time to lose. I rapped instructions into a mike and felt the great plane starting to swing round to my instructions but it was too late.

Shells ripped through the fabric of the fuselage as the night fighter opened fire, and Kerr actually saw them flashing towards him before he was hit. He felt as though 'someone had punched me simultaneously all over my body' as the impact flung him back onto the canvas bed in the body of the aircraft. He did not know where he had been hit but he felt a combination of stark fear and indignation. He was furious that a German had actually shot him, and terrified because he could not move and a fire was raging only a couple of yards away. An incendiary shell had ignited one of the flares in the aircraft and it was burning fiercely. In his mind's eye, Kerr pictured the flames 'devouring my parachute harness, then my leather flying suit, then me'.

He lost consciousness, but:

> I came to my senses some way down the aircraft by the rear escape hatch. The flames were still there even more intense, lighting up the interior of the fuselage with a great yellow glare to the accompaniment of a loud crackling and hissing and the acrid smell of petrol and oil fumes. It was a huge grim bonfire. The fear that had first gripped me was gone now and in its place was a lulling lethargic calm, a slowness of movement that could well be fatal in an emergency.
>
> I was sitting on the deck with the large well-built form of Dave, the rear gunner, hovering behind me, parachute in hand. My own chute was clipped to my chest. My movements were

> almost mechanical, as if the stark realisation that at last I had been shot was numbing my brain and actions, and perhaps other members of the crew had been killed. As my brain became clearer, I ripped the cover off the escape hatch, checked my parachute, dangled my legs over the edge then looked around me . . . Perhaps the size of the flames were magnified in my eyes but it seemed to me that the entire forepart of the fuselage was afire. We were, I thought, a great flying torch!

Kerr's leather flying jacket was ripped open and stained with blood, and blood was oozing out of a tear in the left leg of his flying suit and trickling down his leg. His strange lethargy continued and he tried to talk to Dave the rear gunner, who was gesturing for him to jump, and to Bill the navigator, who had also been hit by the night fighter's bullets and was slumped by the astro hatch. The flames were roaring ferociously and 'every minute seemed like an hour', until Dave shoved him out of the hatch and the airflow whipped him backwards.

He pulled the rip cord . . .

> The rustling of the silk pilot chute, the sharp report of the big canopy opening, a hard jolt on my shoulders [told me] I was safe for the moment . . . The flaming body of our plane was descending, it seemed, at a terrifying rate. I have a dim recollection of seeing two other parachutes floating slowly downwards and was startled by the dark roaring shape of an aeroplane which flashed past uncomfortably close. I remember ripping off my flying helmet and goggles and flinging them away. Then all became quiet.

Probably Kerr was semi-conscious from loss of blood because he seemed to drift dreamily downwards and had almost dropped off to sleep, with blood trickling into the palm of his hand and down his leg, when he hit the earth. He heard voices, called feebly for help, and saw dark forms loom up as the parachute dragged him along the ground.

> I had no idea of the nature or the extent of my wounds but five minutes later, lying on a small wooden table in a small wooden hut lit by one feeble electric light bulb, I had an opportunity to take stock. I knew that I had been shot in the chest for the German soldier who had hoisted me on his back to carry me to the hut had brushed some blood from his hand as he removed my flying jacket. I thought it was a lung because I was finding it rather difficult to breathe. Then I caught sight of my arm. I could not make out the details of the wound but saw a bloody confused tangle of skin and leather. It didn't look too good, but probably didn't matter if I had been shot in the lung anyway.
>
> My breathing was becoming more laboured. It was as if someone was slowly but surely restricting my lung capacity. I had a terrible thirst. I was conscious of the whispered instructions being issued around me. I seemed to remember from first aid learnt in the past that if internal injury was suspected the patient should not be given anything to drink, but since I was beginning to think my hours were numbered I felt that if I were going to die I would sooner do so without a thirst. I called for water and took two greedy cupfuls. It was not water but coffee and it tasted good even though it was ersatz.

Kerr realised that another crew member, Bernie, was in the hut, and Dave was soon brought in. Bernie seemed to be in a trance, and Dave was 'shaken and very serious'. He stared at the bloody mess of Kerr's wounds while he was being questioned, and seemed to feel he was in the presence of imminent death. The Germans took the two flyers away, and soon gave Kerr a painful journey to hospital: 'It seemed to me, in later months, that the type of pain I had experienced then could not be compared with anything I had felt before or since. It was mental more than physical. My breath was coming in short, very short, gasps. I felt I had not very much longer to live. I had never been surer of anything in my life.'

Kerr was so sure he was dying that he tried to say the Lord's

Prayer, but discovered he had forgotten some of the words. Then, in mental and physical torment, he felt there was no point in trying to live and tried to end it all by holding his breath. After the third attempt he gave up, and he was still breathing in short gasps when the ambulance skidded to a halt outside Reserve Lazarette Stalag XA, a large hospital at Rendsburg on the Danish border. Dawn was just breaking, but he was in no mood to appreciate the crisp clear morning as he was hustled to the operating theatre.

> I surprised the doctors by living. I had not been wounded in the lungs as I thought. In fact it was but a small shallow wound almost directly over my heart but harmless enough anyhow. True, I had nearly died – but not from my wounds, rather from loss of blood. My tally to support this was ten wounds altogether, in the arm, leg and chest. An incision in the leg, two bullets in the liver and a six-inch incision on the stomach completed the score and advanced considerably my claims to the favour of mother luck, particularly since the doctors had taken from the small wound in my chest a complete bullet head which was twisted and misshapen. It had obviously ricocheted from somewhere inside the aircraft and was spent by the time it struck me over the heart.

Kerr's life hung in the balance, but constant care from a French surgeon attached to the hospital, Professor Rene Simon, who was one of Europe's leading pre-war surgeons, and a Polish doctor, enabled him to pull through.

from *Heroes Have Wings* by Peter Firkins

The rear gunner

The rear gunner – or 'tail-end Charlie' as he was often called – had a less than one-in-three chance of survival. His role was to protect the aircraft and fellow crew members when the plane was under attack from enemy fighters. As the following encounter shows, a rear gunner had to be courageous, determined and self-reliant:

They called them 'Press-on types' in the RAF; men who stayed at their allotted posts disdaining all attempts by the enemy to prevent them completing their given tasks. The official phrase was 'Devotion to duty', though such praise was usually loudly derided by the men concerned. Call it determination, obstinacy, or sheer bloody-mindedness if you will, but such men stayed to fight theoretically impossible odds against personal survival – and often won through. It was a trait found amongst all aircrew categories, yet particularly exemplified by the air gunners. Theirs was a double responsibility in a way. Primarily they were there for just that purpose – to ward off anything thrown at them by the enemy and thus protect their aircraft and crew. Any gunner leaving his post during action would automatically place the lives of his crew in jeopardy. Add to this direct responsibility a natural human desire to hit back when attacked, and one begins to comprehend the spirit which held such men in their seats when instinct and common sense dictated escape.

Norman Francis Williams would be the first to scoff at any suggestion of being a 'Press-on type'. An Australian from Leeton, New South Wales, in early 1943 he was a sergeant air gunner serving with 10 Squadron, flying in Halifax bombers from Melbourne, Yorkshire. The bombing offensive against Germany was at an intensive period, and in just two months of operations, Williams's skill and courage brought him the awards of a DFM and Bar – a rare medal combination. Volunteering for further operations with Don Bennett's elite Path Finder Force (PFF), he was transferred to 35 Squadron, another Halifax unit based, in June 1943, at Gravely, in Huntingdonshire. That same month Williams was in the rear turret of his Halifax bound for a raid on Dusseldorf. It was a bright moonlit night, though with thin haze distorting visibility, as he methodically quartered the sky searching for enemy nightfighters. Then, as his crew began their bombing run into the target, Williams saw the red winking flashes of a fighter's guns looming larger from the port quarter, slightly above him. Swinging his guns towards the attacker, Williams loosed several brief bursts – then 'the world fell on top of me'; a second fighter had curved in from below as the

Halifax began its evasion turn, raking the bomber with a stream of cannon shells and tracer bullets.

Williams was hit in the stomach by one cannon shell, and his legs and thighs riddled with bullets. Then a further burst, almost simultaneously, from the first fighter slashed through the port side of Williams's turret, knocking out one gun and rendering the turret temporarily out of action. Other damage to the bomber included wounding the mid-upper gunner in the head, and rupturing a main petrol tank. Burning fuel spilled along the wing, illuminating the Halifax as a perfect target for any German fighter within range. In great pain, and with his body paralysed below his waist, Williams continued to give his skipper evasion directions while keeping a lookout for the two fighters. Both Germans returned to the attack in a prolonged series of lightning assaults, and Williams continued directing his skipper; at the same time requesting the bomb aimer to take the place of the wounded mid-upper gunner. As the bomb aimer settled into the upper turret the pair of fighters bore in together from the port beam. Williams told the pilot to go into a steep bank, then as the nearest fighter came into his sight line, gave it a full burst from his guns. The fighter exploded in mid-air, and fell earthwards in a cascade of burning debris.

For the next few minutes the burning Halifax was unmolested so the bomb aimer climbed out of the mid-upper turret and went forward to complete his own job of releasing the bombload on target. Williams in his part-shattered rear turret began to regain feeling down one thigh and leg, when yet another fighter attack came roaring in from a variety of angles. Eventually the German lined up dead astern for its latest move, bringing it dead into Williams's sights. He waited coolly until the fighter filled his vision, then let it have a full burst. The German passed underneath the tail with Williams's fire following, then fell away shedding chunks of metal until it passed out of vision. At that point the Halifax had been subjected to a total of nearly 40 separate fighter attacks.

As the crew realised the danger had now passed – the wing fire had died down, so the pilot extinguished it in a short dive – they prepared for the return journey. Williams refused to leave his turret until they

Vickers Wellington rear gunner – Middle East, 1942.

were well out of enemy-occupied territorial skies, but when he finally agreed to be extricated, the turret doors were found to be jammed. Reaching base again the pilot brought the bomber in for a skilful crash-landing, and they had to chop Williams out of the shambles of his turret. Taken immediately to hospital, where he remained for the next two months, Norman Williams was later awarded a Conspicuous Gallantry Medal (CGM) to add to his DFM and Bar, making him Australia's most-decorated NCO airman of 1939–45.

from *Guns in the Sky* by Chaz Bowyer

Behind Enemy Lines

Behind Enemy Lines

Between the two world wars, Australians whose jobs saw them based on the New Guinean coastline and the islands to the north were formed into a loose-knit unit of observers by the Royal Australian Navy known as the Coastwatchers. In 1939, as fears of Japanese plans for expansion in the Pacific grew, the Coastwatchers organisation was expanded and its volunteers were given armed forces status.

Come the start of World War II and Japan's invasion of New Guinea, the Coastwatchers played a vital role in reporting enemy movements and concentrations of forces by radio to naval headquarters in Melbourne. They also co-ordinated native carrier lines to shift supplies and weapons dropped by Allied aircraft, and organised local resistance to Japanese patrols. The risk here was that native tribes, playing a desperate game for their own survival, would give information to both sides, often with tragic results.

Occasionally, however, soldiers behind enemy lines could be removed from a danger zone by a meeting with a submarine off the coast. In the Malayan jungle, wounded or lost Australian soldiers were sometimes able to survive by joining Chinese Communist guerrilla units also fighting the Japanese well behind enemy lines.

'Are there any Japanese about?'

Peter Ryan, a member of the New Guinea Volunteer Rifles, spent 1942 and 1943 observing the extent of the Japanese invasion of northern New Guinea and patrolling the mountains behind Lae. He usually operated with one or two companions and their mission was to spread news of

Australian soldier in New Guinea.

Japanese atrocities and the growing strength of Australian and American forces.

On patrol, they were faced with the rigours of jungle and mountainous travel – dense rainforest, swamps, malaria, rivers in flood, crocodiles, razor-sharp limestone crags. In addition, as Ryan and his team would discover to their cost, there was always the possibility of enemy ambushes after being betrayed by local natives.

By about three o'clock we had reached the large coconut-grove at the edge of the village, and looked up longingly at the cool green nuts. A crowd of Chivasing natives, with the tultul and doctor-boy, appeared suddenly at the other end of the grove and advanced to meet us. Some of them climbed the palms to get green coconuts for us to drink. We sat in the shade and let the cool fluid trickle down our dust-filled throats.

'Are there any Japanese about?' we asked at length, our inevitable question, which we hoped would be for the last time.

There was a silence. The steaming quietness of the Markham afternoon descended.

'Are there any Japanese about?' we repeated sharply.

'No-got, master! Me-fella no lookim some-fella belong Japan!' The answer came readily enough this time.

'Better make sure,' Les said. 'We'll send Arong into the village to have a look round.'

We called to Arong, who had had a drink, to move into the village. He was wearing no uniform, and there was nothing to mark him out from the Chivasing kanakas, so he would be safe enough even if there were Japanese there.

While he was away we tried to make conversation with the natives. They seemed strangely uneasy, but they said they had expected us and had the canoes all ready to take us down to Kirkland's. We wondered whether we imagined the tension in the atmosphere – whether the long strain now ending had made us over-suspicious. We were cheered when Arong came back a few minutes later with a smile on his face, to say that he had taken a look around the village and that all was as it should be. Then, Arong leading the way, and Les behind him, a few paces ahead of me, we walked into the village. Most of our boys stayed in the grove, still drinking coconut milk.

As we neared the clear space at the centre of the village there was a sudden burst of machine-gun fire and a volley of rifle-shots from one of the houses. Bullets kicked up the dirt all around us. We both made a dash for the creek that runs through the village, and as I jumped down into it there was another burst of fire from the house. Les gave a cry, fell, and lay still. Japanese – there seemed to be dozens of them – then jumped down from the houses and rushed over towards me. I lost my footing and fell into the water, got my clothes and Owen gun tangled in a submerged branch, and finally struggled across the creek and into the bush minus Owen gun and most of my shirt. Bullets were clipping the leaves all around me. I did not go far, but buried myself deep in the mud of a place where the pigs used to wallow, with only my nose showing, and stayed put.

For a few minutes all was quiet, but soon I heard the Japanese calling out to each other, and their feet sucking and squelching in the mud as they searched. I could not see, so I did not know exactly how close they were, but I could feel in my ears the pressure of their feet as they squeezed through the mud. It occurred to me that this was probably an occasion on which one might pray, and indeed was about to start a prayer. Then something stopped me. I said to myself so fiercely that I seemed to be shouting under the mud, 'To hell with God! If I get out of this bloody mess, I'll do it by myself!' It was no doubt a childish sort of pride, but I experienced a rather weary exhilaration that, terrified and abject, lying literally like a pig in the mud, I had not sufficiently abandoned personal integrity to pray for my skin to a God I didn't really believe in.

I lay there motionless, buried alive in mud and pig-filth, feeling, or imagining, creatures of unspeakable loathsomeness crawling over me in the slime. The voices became fainter and the squelching footsteps died away. I eased my face out, blinked the mud away from my eyes, and carefully pulled some leaves over my head in case the searchers returned.

For half an hour or so there was no sound. Then several natives walked around the outskirts of the village calling out to me. I heard their voices clearly, just a few yards away through the bushes:

'Master, you come! Japan all 'e go finish!'

I did not move. They continued to call out encouragingly for a quarter of an hour. Then one of them said, apparently to someone near by, ''Em 'e no hearim talk belong me-fella. I think 'em 'e go finish long bush.'

The Japanese started talking to each other again after that, having given up hope of capturing me, it seemed, now that the trick had failed.

I stayed in the same place until it was nearly dark. The mosquitoes were swarming on my head so thickly, and buzzing so loudly, that I thought they would give away my position. Then I crept out of the mud, wiped the mud off pistol and compass, and began to break bush, moving on a line south and west, which, as I remembered the map, should at last bring me to the bank of the Markham, some distance upstream from Chivasing, more or less opposite the mouth of the Watut River.

In a couple of years packed with bad journeys, that night's travel is the worst I can remember. Near the village it was essential to move with absolute quietness, no easy matter when the rows of hooked thorns on the vines caught at me continually and one hand was always occupied holding the compass. It was no use trying to free myself from the vines – as fast as one row of barbs was detached another took hold. It was easier, if more painful, to let them tear straight through the flesh. After the bush came the pit-pit – cane-grass eight or nine feet high, growing so thickly as to make a solid wall. It was impossible to part it and walk through it, and I was forced to push it over by leaning on it, and crawl over the top on all fours. It had leaves like razor-blades, which hurt terribly on bare legs; mine were soon dripping with blood from the cuts. Worse, the flattened grass left a trail a blind man could have followed. Though I had my compass handy the grass blocked all view of any object to sight on, and there were no stars, for it was a cloudy night. The two luminous points on the instrument danced and swung before my eyes. Sometimes I had to pause, close my eyes, and force my nerves to calmness before I could see properly. Every time I tried to march by sense alone, I found myself going wrong.

Hours later, during one of these pauses, I heard the dull swish of swiftly flowing water. The Markham! I had got there sooner than I expected. It would take every scrap of my energy to swim it, and I removed my clothes, such as they were, and buckled on again the belt which carried revolver, compass and sheath-knife. Then I stumbled forward, heading for the sound of the water. When I reached it I found it was nothing but a small creek flowing down to the river. I nearly cried with rage and disappointment, and decided to go no farther that night, but lay down naked where I was. The mosquitoes were terrible, settling all over my body in swarms, and their bites nearly closed both my eyes. Finally, to escape them, I dragged myself into a shallow puddle of mud at the edge of the stream, and slept there.

Shortly before daylight I moved on, weak and stumbling, my heart jumping in the frightening way I had noticed in the mountains. The last few miles were easier, for the pit-pit gave place to kunai, through which one could at least walk upright. At any moment I expected a volley of shots, for the country was flat, and if, after sunrise, the Japs had taken the trouble to post a few men in trees, they could not have failed to see me. I crossed one new track through the grass, which showed many enemy footprints, and reached the Markham about mid-morning. As I looked across its swift brown streams I knew that I was too tired to swim it before I had had a rest, so I crawled into a patch of bush and dozed until about midday. Then I swam as silently as possible from one island to the next, resting for a short while on each one. Every time I touched a log or floating piece of rubbish I was terrified it was a crocodile, and struck out with renewed vigour. I really believe it was this fear, coupled with the expectation of a burst of machine-gun fire from the north bank, that enabled me to make the distance.

On the south bank at last, I lay breathless in a patch of grass. Voices came from not far away. I eased my pistol out of its holster and peered through the grass. Two Chivasing natives, with their women, were walking straight towards me, chattering happily, quite unaware of any alien presence. As soon as they drew level I jumped from cover, shoving the pistol into the ribs of the nearest one. The men trembled, but made no sound, and the women moaned faintly. They were too terrified to shout – apparently they thought I was going to shoot them out of hand.

'You-fella got canoe? 'Em 'e stop where?'

They nodded, and pointed to a spot on the bank nearby. I made them lead me to it and ordered them to take me to Kirkland's. They were so terrified that I was afraid they would faint, but I jabbed them in the ribs with the pistol and forced them to get aboard.

Although I felt certain in my mind that Les was dead, I did not have positive evidence. I did not want to ask the Chivasing people directly, so I phrased the question in a way which did not reveal my ignorance.

'What are you going to do with the other white man?'

Their reply snuffed out the lingering spark of hope that Les might be alive.

'We will bury him in the cemetery at Chivasing,' one said in pidgin.

'We will see that he gets a proper funeral,' added the other man ingratiatingly, as if that would atone in some way for his people's treacherous share in Les's death.

The rapid muddy stream was sweeping us down towards Kirkland's, and I made the natives hug the south bank closely, to keep out of the range of Japanese who might be on the north side. When Kirkland's came in sight I stood up, waving my arms above my head and cooeeing, and I was shortly answered by a hail from the low kunai hill behind the camp. As the canoe nosed in under the foliage to touch at the landing-place, several Australian soldiers stepped out of the bushes and helped me ashore. Half carried, half supported, I made my way with them to the wretched little huts, and sat down in the mosquito-proof room while they brought me tea and some army biscuits.

Nobody said anything much, and I sat there dully, staring at the swamp. I had no sensation of joy or relief, though I knew in a remote and abstract way that I was now safe. I had no thoughts, no feelings whatsoever. I felt neither grief on account of Les nor anger at the Japanese or Chivasings. Nor did I feel any sense of warmth or companionship towards the soldiers who were now preparing water for me to wash, and giving me articles from their own scanty clothing to cover my nakedness. I was too spent, emotionally, to feel or think or care, and I know now that such a state is the nearest one can come to death – an emptiness of spirit much more deadly than a grievous wound.

After I had been sitting there for a little while, Kari, Watute, Dinkila, Pato, and all the other boys limped up to see me. They managed a salute, but I could see they felt as dispirited and weary as I did. They were cut about and tattered, and caked with grey Markham mud that cracked and dropped off in little flakes as the skin stretched beneath it. I shook hands with each one, and they shuffled back to the little hut, where they were crowded together. Kari and Watute remained for a few moments to talk. They had stayed across the river looking for me, they said, and when they found my tracks leading to the river, concluded I would be all right, and floated themselves down to Kirkland's on logs. Arong, the boy who had entered the village with Les and me, had been captured by the Japs and taken to Lae, Watute added.

Next day a horse was sent down for me, and I rode to Wampit. Here I had a proper hot shower, and willing helpers gathered around with needles and dug dozens of thorns out of my limbs and body. There was no skin at all on my legs, and my feet were so enormously swollen that I thought boots would never fit on them again. Months later, I was still digging out odd thorns that had been overlooked at Wampit.

The following morning I set out on horseback for Bulolo township, which had replaced Wau as the military headquarters of the area. The police and other natives followed on foot, and during the several days which for me were occupied in writing the long report of the patrol they straggled in by twos and threes, still very weary.

After a few days I went to the store to get new clothes. I was wearing a woollen shirt, a pair of ragged green shorts, and some old sand-shoes, but no hat or socks. All of these had been given me either at Kirkland's or Wampit.

'Where's your pay-book and your other papers?' demanded the quartermaster.

I explained the fate of my clothes and papers and other possessions.

'Good God, man, that's no excuse!' he snapped. 'Don't you realise it's a crime in the Army to lose your pay-book? You can't be issued with any equipment here without a pay-book.'

I didn't argue, but let the district officer arrange a new issue of clothing for me. But I started to wonder all over again if wars were really worth the trouble.

from *Fear Drive My Feet* by Peter Ryan

Rendezvous with a submarine

Captain Murray was one of the Australian Coastwatchers in New Guinea actively engaged behind enemy lines and radioing vital information back to headquarters. In the account that follows, he and his men have fought their way out of a Japanese ambush. Their next ordeal is to fight their way through the roaring surf to keep a difficult rendezvous with an American submarine:

With just enough light to see, they launched the rubber boat. Wind and rain lashed the island; the turbulent sea threw itself at the strip of sandy beach, catching the rubber craft and almost wrenching it from their grasp. As each man struggled to get aboard it became more difficult to keep the boat from being driven back on the sand.

In the fast fading light they cleared the beach and headed for the passage, the four Americans and two natives paddling, Murray acting as helmsman. The heavy surf and ground swells made the going tough; the passage was tricky and difficult to negotiate. A dozen times they nearly broached, the helmsman swinging the rudder just in time to straighten them out. There was barely enough light to get clear of the reef. The night had settled down to blow itself into a howling, boisterous gale.

Coastwatchers sending and receiving radio information.

Outside the reef the seas were mountainous, far higher than they had appeared from the shore. Paddling with all the energy their bodies could muster, the men desperately struggled to get the rubber boat away from the suction near the reef where the breakers dragged in across the coral. It took them half an hour – half an hour which seemed a lifetime.

One by one the four Americans and two natives succumbed to seasickness; Murray was more fortunate; he had never suffered from seasickness in his life, and even in this raging sea he was immune to it. The men retched their hearts out, but gamely kept the paddles going, urged on to greater effort by the helmsman, and by the compelling need to get clear of the island. The two natives lay prostrate in the bottom of the boat, not caring one way or the other. At the helm, Murray found his arms, chest and back aching unbearably with the strain of keeping the boat head-on to the seas. Time and again the small boat was tossed to the crest of a huge wave, then plunged down the deep depression between the following wave, shipping the water out as fast as it was shipped in; it was a miracle it remained afloat. Lieutenant Nirschel of the US Coast Guards, who had been associated with boats all his life, said he had never experienced a sea like it before – and fervently hoped he would never do so again.

The time passed slowly. A hundred times Murray checked his watch. Two hours to go . . . an hour and three-quarters . . . an hour and a half . . . Could they keep afloat till the rendezvous time? Would their strength hold out?

. . . It was half past nine – 21.30 hours – the time for their rendezvous with the submarine. Would it be there? Oh, God, they prayed, let it be there to get us out of this tempest.

Murray found his flashlight, and gave the signal. It was not until he switched on the light, however, that he discovered to his dismay that the red cover over the glass was missing.

'The red cover's gone from the flashlight,' he told the men. 'Has anyone got a torch with a red cover?'

'No,' they answered in unison. His own light, it appeared, had been the one and only torch carried by the whole team, and by some stroke of misfortune the red shield had fallen off somewhere in their getaway. He felt in his pockets, ran his hand around the bottom of the boat, and told the men to do the same, but it was not there.

The loss of the red cover for the torch now put them in a desperate position. The submarine commander would be expecting their signal in a red light, and would not acknowledge the signal from a white one. Seeing a white light signalling to him, he would naturally know that something was amiss; but even if he suspected it to be them, he would refrain from answering for fear of being led into a trap. He couldn't do anything else – the arrangements had been to signal with a red flashlight, and the ship under his command was far too valuable to risk answering a wrong signal. Murray realised their desperate position. He confided his worst fears to the men, who groaned in despair. The thought of the submarine being somewhere close at hand and not answering was the last straw.

'Red light or not, I'll keep signalling just the same, lads, so don't give up hope. They say you're never dead till they bury you – well we're not dead yet,' Murray assured them.

'If death is any worse than this, Cap'an, then I sure don't wanna die,' said one of the young lieutenants.

Every five minutes he gave another flash, hoping against hope that the submarine would realise it was them, and not the Japs trying to trap it . . . but no acknowledgment came. The time slipped past . . . slowly . . . ten o'clock . . . half past . . . eleven o'clock; it was an hour and a half past the time of rendezvous. Things looked hopeless. If the sub hadn't answered by this time, then it wouldn't do so at all. By now the men were completely exhausted; weakened from dry retching, and physically and mentally played out.

Quilici and Murray discussed their position; they decided that their best plan was to make for Malendok Island, stay hidden there during the day, and try to make contact with the submarine the following night. If they failed to make contact at all, then they would try to reach the east coast of New Ireland in the rubber boat and make for 'Place Mamboo', where Murray had left the wireless set, food, and a rifle hidden in the secret cache.

Their main problem at that moment, however, was how to locate Malendok Island. Which way would they head; to the left or right? How far were they from land? For all they knew they could have been washed miles out to sea, or they could be drifting in the channel between the two islands. Realising that it would be foolish to head either one way or the other for fear of landing back on Boang or heading out to sea, Murray decided that they would have to ride it out until dawn, then God willing, they might be lucky enough to get ashore on Malendok Island without being detected by the Japs.

This decided, Murray determined to make one last attempt to contact the sub.

'Try to hold her as steady as you can lads. I'm going to give one last flash, for luck,' he told them.

To give himself more height, he perilously clutched the helm tightly between his legs and stood up in the slippery rubber boat. He gave a prolonged flash, willing the submarine to answer.

All at once, out of the pitch-black, howling night, a single large F-L-A-S-H blinked back at them. A great cheer went up, a cheer mixed with laughter, tears and varied emotions.

'It's them! They've found us!'

'Where in Goddam hell they bin all this time, anyway?'

'Hail Mary, full of grace . . .' prayed one American.

'Yes sir, that's my baby!' yelled another with wild joy.

'You bloody beauty!' said Murray, aloud, but silently he thanked Almighty God with all his heart.

Seasickness, throbbing heads, aching bodies and limbs, were all forgotten as they began to paddle vigorously towards the spot where they imagined the submarine to be. No other flash came, but they didn't expect it. Murray gave a flash every minute or so to guide the sub to them. It took another three-quarters of an hour before the black shape of the submarine loomed up out of the darkness.

A voice sang out above the roaring wind: 'Is that you, Captain Murray?'

'Yes, sir! Is that you, Commander Nelson?'

'It is. Prepare to come aboard!'

'Nelson!' said Murray, in a state of utter relief. 'The best bloody seafaring name England ever had.'

'And the best one America ever had too, sir!' replied one of the Americans, with heart-felt sentiment.

In seas that were twenty-five feet from crest to trough, it was no easy matter to board the submarine, which rose and fell in the huge waves; one minute more than twenty feet above them, the next in a trough below.

'Prepare to come aboard! Prepare to come aboard!' The order passed among the crew, and was called out to the waiting men in the rubber boat. The formal naval order appealed to Murray's sense of humour and he laughed; the others laughed with him out of sheer relief. How the hell they were going to get aboard, he didn't know.

Repeated attempts were made to throw a line to them, but each time the wind or the sea carried it away. Finally, after what seemed an eternity, a rope was made fast as a guideline, but as the sub and boat rose and fell in a see-sawing fashion, the rope had to be slackened or tightened, for fear of pulling the rubber boat in too close to the suction of the submarine.

One by one the men waited for the right moment, then braving all the elements, grabbed the guideline and jumped for the deck of the sub. As they landed aboard, the crew grabbed them and pushed them through the hatchway at deck level.

As each man's weight left the boat it became more difficult to control, until at last Murray found himself alone in the boat with the bow tilted alarmingly upwards. Grimly he held on to the steer and the guideline, while the seas swept over him, almost washing him out. The boat was tossed high in the air, but always landed right side up. For the hundredth time the submarine disappeared yet again into the wallowing trough below him – but this time, when it came to the surface, the rubber boat, with Murray still at the helm, was sitting fair and square in the middle of the deck. By a miracle – by a chance in a million – the submarine came up directly under him, landing him on board without having to make the risky jump, and saving the boat and equipment as well.

Inside the warm, quiet, grey interior of the *Peto*, an officer escorted Murray to the conning-tower, where Commander Nelson was on duty. The two men shook hands warmly.

'I'm very glad to see you back, Captain. We thought you were gone,' said Nelson.

'We're very grateful to you, Commander, for answering our white signal. We had a few bad hours out there.'

'We've been watching your signals for hours. In the end I decided to risk it and answer. I'm very glad I did, Murray.'

At that moment the ship's general alarm sounded: Action stations! Actions stations! and the officers and crew moved at the double to their respective posts.

'They've found us, Murray!' said Commander Nelson. 'A boat

with a searchlight is heading straight for us. We'll have to make a run for it on the surface!'

In a matter of seconds the submarine was under way.

'Full speed ahead!' ordered the commander. 'Damn the reef, full speed ahead!'

The order was instantly obeyed, and the *Peto* moved through the sea gaining speed with every revolution of her powerful engines.

Through the intercommunication system came a steady, unruffled, voice:

'Boat giving chase, sir. Possibly five hundred yards off, sir.'

Then steadily the voice continued:

'Seven hundred and fifty yards, sir . . . One thousand yards, sir . . . One thousand five hundred yards, sir . . . Two thousand yards, sir.'

'We're leaving them behind. We'll soon lose them in this weather,' the commander said.

He was right. The weather, which had been the worst enemy of the team in the rubber boat, now proved the ally of the submarine. The *Peto* ploughed straight through the rough seas, and soon left the Japanese surface craft far astern.

The light of the searching enemy boat gradually grew smaller and smaller, and finally disappeared into the blackness of the sea.

Down below, Sergeant Dolby explained why the second boat hadn't managed to get ashore.

'We saw your signals just after eleven o'clock, but couldn't read them clearly in the rough conditions. What we did make out, appeared to read that you were warning us not to come. We stood by until after two o'clock, hoping that you could get back, but when you didn't show up, we thought you'd had it! I can tell you, Skipper, it's good to see you back. Everyone felt pretty badly about it.'

'We should have had a small wireless. Light signals on shore at water-level are not much use in rough weather,' said Murray wearily. 'However, all's well that ends well, so they say. Better luck next time, Bill.'

from *Hunted – A Coastwatcher's Story* by M. Murray

Left behind

Sergeant Arthur Shephard was part of the 600-strong force of Australian soldiers that confronted the Japanese invasion of Malaya during December 1941 and January 1942, facing 10,000 men of the elite Imperial Guards. Although they succeeded in halting the enemy's progress for a short time, their acts of heroism were no match for these fearsome odds. Soon enough, the decimated force was retreating to link up with the British troops at Singapore. All, that is, except for Arthur and three other seriously wounded Australians.

Rescued by Chinese Communist guerrillas, he survived the war and returned to Australia with the diaries that detail his epic struggle. The following extract describes that painful moment when the decision was made to leave him behind:

As dusk began to close in around the men of the 2/29th, in order to re-establish a 'night perimeter', they drew in on themselves somewhat, taking up previously prepared positions which, for the close conditions of the rubber plantation and darkness, represented a considerably tighter formation than had been adopted during the day. Although they had remained in a defensive posture for most of the time, they had been able to expand outwards slightly in some directions, depending on the conditions and the relative positions of the Japanese.

'I wonder if the little buggers'll try it on tonight?' Jim Kennedy's voice came out of the deepening gloom on Arthur's left. He was talking to Jack Roxburgh.

'They're not so bloody little, from what we've seen so far,' Bomber Wainright grunted from his position, also off to the left. 'And the bastards aren't all half-blind like they kept telling us back at Segamat.'

'No, but they can't see any better than us,' Arthur put in. 'They can't see in the bloody dark . . . at least I hope they can't.'

Almost as if the Japanese had heard him speaking and were out to prove him wrong, the night suddenly erupted into a cacophony of whistling mortar shells exploding in the battalion lines, mostly along the left-forward elements of C Company and their own Headquarters Company. There was the chatter of machine- and Bren-gun fire to the front from their own lines, and heavy small-arms fire, which indicated a Japanese attack. Everyone sank a little lower into their slit trenches, adjusted their steel helmets and peered into the night, concentrating and trying harder to see whatever there was to be seen. Within a few minutes, they again heard the distinctive sound of Samurai swords and bayonet scabbards, clinking against grenades and other webbing equipment, coming closer to them through the darkened corridors of rubber trees.

'They're comin' again,' Bomber called. 'Keep your eyes out.'

As he spoke, several grenades exploded close by and rifle fire erupted all around them. Several Australian voices, from Arthur's platoon although he couldn't recognise them, were heard shouting from further to the left. 'Here they come! Watch out, Charlie!', followed by more firing and yelling. Then, suddenly, there were figures amongst them in the dark. Bright flashes of fire from the rifles of both sides pierced the blackness for brief instants, leaving the area from which they originated even darker than before, and all accompanied by the sharp cracking of rifles and pistols and the stutter of submachine-gun fire, as well as frenzied yelling in both English and Japanese. For a few short minutes, the whole scene had an aura of madness, of a nightmare.

The Japanese had again charged with bayonets fixed, but although the darkness gave them the advantage of surprise and they had the initiative in being on the offensive, they also found the inability to see what they were attacking a serious hindrance. The Australians, too, had their bayonets fixed and were in a good situation to lunge quickly at the Japanese as they came by. After what seemed like an eternity, but was probably only five minutes or so, several loud whistles were heard, followed by much shouting in Japanese and then the attackers withdrew, disappearing into the trees as quickly as they had emerged.

For a few moments, there was silence as the Australians waited to see what might happen next, then voices began to chatter between the trees. 'Stopped the bastards again!' someone yelled. 'You bloody beauty!'

Australian infantry firing on the enemy.

'Have a look at this, will yer?' Bomber Wainright called out. A Japanese soldier had fallen dead near Bomber's slit trench, having been shot in mid-charge. 'He's got a bloody gasmask with him! Don't tell me the little bastards are going to try gas on us?' Bomber was acutely aware of how distasteful gas warfare could be, having survived two gas attacks in northern France in 1917.

It was soon discovered that all of the Japanese soldiers who had been killed during the attack had been carrying gas respirators and it was reasonably assumed that the others who had survived and retreated were also carrying them. The information, when passed on to Battalion Headquarters, surprised Major Olliff and he ordered Signaller Chris Nielson to pass it on immediately to Brigade. At Brigade Headquarters, the news was doubted. They just could not believe that the Japanese were about to initiate gas warfare – and yet they were clearly prepared for it, which was more than could be said for the Allied troops.

The attacks on the 2/29th during that evening of 18 January were conventional infantry attacks in which some one hundred and fifty Japanese had come into close combat with the Australians. Although the Australians realised they were still on the defensive, the fact that they had once again repulsed what they now knew to be an elite element of the Japanese army was a great boost to their morale. In addition, the almost mad fearlessness the Imperial Guards displayed in their charges and close-quarter fighting had not deterred the Australians on this occasion.

The experience of the previous evening and a growing understanding of the Japanese techniques had prepared the Australians somewhat. The Japanese clanking of their weapons and shouting as they came had been intended to frighten their adversaries, but once the Australians were aware of what the Japanese were doing, they used it to their own advantage. Waiting quietly in the dark, either in their shallow trenches, beside them, or behind a tree, they were able to use the Japanese shouting to pinpoint the target and to shoot or bayonet the attacking soldier with ease.

Each Japanese attack on various parts of the Australian lines had been thrown back with severe losses, which were increased when the Australians laid down heavy mortar barrage into the area through which the Japanese were retiring.

Although the 2/29th felt justifiable satisfaction in having turned the Japanese back on their heels once again, there was still the unpleasant sensation that the opposing forces were building up and that they now had a reasonably good idea of the layout of the Australian battalion and the positions and strength of the various platoons and companies. This was borne out during the night as the Japanese were able to direct a number of accurate mortar barrages of their own onto the Australians. The thick foliage of the rubber plantation provided some cover, but it was a mixed blessing. Some of the mortars exploded on contact with the branches of the trees and, while this sometimes dissipated the blast, in others it sent showers of shrapnel screaming down into the dugout positions, inflicting several casualties during the night.

Arthur Shephard and the rest of 1 Platoon, along with virtually everyone else in the battalion, had now been almost forty hours without proper sleep. Some, including Arthur, had managed to doze briefly during the afternoon, whenever there was a moment's respite. But now, in the pitch blackness of the rubber plantation, the desperate need to sleep crept over the men, even though they could not escape the feeling that their lives might depend on staying awake. There was a 'watch' system in operation whereby men would take turns in sleeping and standing watch during the night, but even those who dropped off to sleep legitimately found themselves shuddering awake with a start at the sound of machine-gun fire in the distance, an explosion or occasional ear-splitting yells from the Japanese in the jungle beyond their lines.

'Hey, Joe!' one of them would call in English. 'We coming to get you.' Or perhaps, 'Surrender now, or you die!' Or several of them might laugh, or produce a series of fiendish cackles which were simply designed to unnerve the Australians.

The tactics had their effect on some but, for the most part, the men of the 2/29th, after listening in surprised silence for a while, gave back as good as they received, although unfortunately not in Japanese.

'Pull yer flamin' head in, you little yellow bastards,' Bomber Wainright yelled back early in the night, much to the delight of those around him. 'If you step over here again, you'll end up with a bayonet up yer bum!'

Arthur managed a total of about four hours of intermittent sleep during the night, but by dawn he felt it had done him no good at all. His body was tingling with tiredness and, like the rest of his men, his brain felt numb with fatigue.

As dawn broke, the young Chinese man appeared in the lines again, begging the medical officer to help get his wife out. A small group of men, including a couple of stretcher bearers, was sent off with the man to bring the wounded woman and boy back. They quickly returned, carrying the woman to the aid post area where she and the boy were treated by Captain Brand, given a meal of bread and jam, and told they would be leaving before long in one of the ambulances that had got through to them during the night.

With the grey light of morning spreading through the rubber trees, and more movement in the battalion area, the men seemed to brighten up. Not that there was much to feel bright about. The situation around them was obviously deteriorating rapidly. It was now estimated that the strength of the Japanese forces surrounding the Australian unit, still one company short of battalion strength, was at least two infantry regiments: the Kunishi Pursuit Unit and the Iwaguro Pursuit Unit, as the Japanese called them. These were the 4th and 5th infantry regiments of the Imperial Guards – a total of almost four thousand men. Four thousand against the 2/29th's six hundred and the seven hundred of the 2/19th. And to make matters worse, a patrol had reported that the Japanese roadblock between the 2/29th and Bakri crossroads had been re-established at greater strength during the night, once again effectively isolating the 2/29th from any support from the Allied forces at Bakri and beyond. It was now impossible to get any more wounded out and there were no supplies or food coming in.

'We could probably fight our way out, sir,' the adjutant, Captain Morgan, said to Major Olliff as they discussed the situation in the morning. 'But we'd have to do it soon. The longer they are allowed to stay there, the more likely it is they'll be reinforced.'

'Right,' Olliff agreed, 'but we've got no orders for that. We have to wait. See if Captain Maher can spare a couple of platoons from B Company to go up there and assess the situation.' He paused a moment. 'If they can't clear it themselves, then they should get back here as quickly as possible with an estimate of what we're dealing with.'

Olliff radioed the news of the re-established roadblock, and his moves to deal with it, to Brigadier Duncan at 45 Brigade Headquarters. He told the brigadier, 'If you can keep the road open, we can stay here until hell freezes over.' Duncan, who was still working on the possibility of the combined counterattack, told Olliff to maintain his position, at least until the Jats [an Indian battalion] arrived, or until a decision had been made by higher command.

So, by the morning of 19 January, the 2/29th were facing a potentially disastrous situation. Brigadier Duncan knew it, as did General Gordon Bennett and General Percival. Percival had already directed the Australian 2/30th Battalion, still holding the Japanese at Gemas, to withdraw down the trunk road behind Segamat and to be ready for a further pullback to Yong Peng. It was now also patently clear that the forces in the Muar area, including the 2/29th and the 2/19th, should be withdrawn also, perhaps as far as Yong Peng. But no orders were given to this effect during the morning of the 19th.

At 45 Brigade Headquarters they were still waiting for the Indian Jats Battalion to come in from the jungle.

'Where the hell are they?' Colonel Anderson, CO of the 2/19th, fumed on several occasions during the morning as he waited for the Jats. He had been ordered to delay his planned mini-offensive until the Indian troops arrived. 'We can't do a damn thing until they turn up.'

'They've been in the jungle for three days now, sir,' his second-in-command, Major Vincent, said quietly. 'I don't think they'll be up to much even if they do come in.'

Shortly afterwards, Anderson held a brief field-telephone conversation with Brigadier Duncan and, in the absence of the Indian troops and the realisation that they would almost certainly not be able to make any worthwhile contribution to an offensive, Duncan now changed his plans and gave Anderson permission to mount an attack down the Muar road towards the embattled 2/29th position.

Anderson's plan was to send one company advancing down the Muar road to test the enemy strength and also, hopefully, to clear the area for the Jats' arrival through the jungle. If they were still coming, they should be very close by now, he reasoned. However, before his A Company, under Captain Beverly, could begin its advance, it had to wait for a British anti-tank gun unit which would support it. This did not arrive and, while waiting for it, the other companies of the 2/19th Battalion, which were spread out around the Bakri crossroads area, came under rear attack from a Japanese force which had been deployed from the Parit Jawa road eastward through the jungle.

Colonel Anderson responded quickly by sending two platoons from A Company, and all of B Company, to give the Japanese a taste of their own medicine by encircling them. The manoeuvre proved highly successful, catching the Japanese by surprise. They found themselves running around in circles, caught in vicious crossfire from the Australians, who then launched a bayonet charge against the scattering remnants of the Japanese force. At the end of the brief engagement, the ground was littered with corpses. One hundred and forty Japanese dead were counted against ten Australians killed and fifteen wounded.

Not long afterwards, at around 10am, a truckload of wounded from the 2/29th, one of the last few to get through from the battalion area during the night, prior to the Japanese re-establishing the roadblock, was preparing to leave 45 Brigade Headquarters on the thirty-mile drive to Yong Peng. Additional wounded from the just-completed action were being crowded into the back of the truck, which was parked under the cover of some rubber trees next to a small plantation bungalow that was being used as headquarters.

Inside the building, a group of officers, including Brigadier Duncan, stood huddled over a situation-map discussing a signal from Command Headquarters at Yong Peng.

Three Japanese 'Val' dive-bombers came screaming down on the area, strafing several vehicles, including a Bren-gun carrier and an armoured car in the road. Each of them released one 500-pound bomb as they passed. Two of the bombs fell harmlessly in an otherwise empty part of the rubber plantation, but the third came down through the trees, missing the truckload of wounded by hardly more than a dozen yards or so, to make a direct hit on the bungalow that was the Brigade Headquarters. Brigadier Duncan was hurled to the ground unconscious, while all of his staff, except two officers, were killed or seriously wounded.

The carnage was shocking. There were 'bodies lying everywhere', one of the wounded men in the truck, Lieutenant Ben Hackney, later wrote:

> Portions of men's stomachs hanging on limbs amongst the leaves of the trees . . . torn, bloodstained limbs scattered about with only a lump of bloody meat hanging from them to indicate the body from which they were torn. Just beside the road, a naked waist with two twisted legs lay about two yards away from a scarred, bleeding head with a neck, half a chest and one arm . . . there were some still alive, but bent over, and others crawling with every manner of injury.

Sergeant Clarrie Thornton, the anti-tank gun commander who was amongst the wounded, reported seeing the British brigade major rushing about in the chaotic aftermath of the explosion, giving orders for the wounded to be helped, while he himself was in a critical state, having had one of his arms blown off.

The bomb also destroyed all of the vital maps as well as the codes which the signallers needed for communicating with West Force Headquarters, and for some time they were unable to get through at all. When they finally did make contact and the news was passed to

General Gordon Bennett, he found the disaster almost impossible to believe.

When the extent of the blow was realised, the forces at the Bakri crossroads did what could be done to pull the situation together again. Colonel Anderson assumed command of the brigade. Brigadier Duncan was alive and not seriously wounded, but he was incapacitated by shock and concussion. Anderson decided that the 2/29th should be extracted from their perilous position as soon as possible, *if possible*, to join up with his own battalion somewhere behind Bakri crossroads. But the Indian Jats Battalion had still not shown up so, rather than totally abandon them, he opted to hold the 2/29th's attempt at withdrawal until the Jats arrived. The delay proved to be a costly one because, in waiting for the Indians, all of Anderson's own companies now came under renewed attack and heavy fire from the Japanese Iwaguro Regiment which were now pressing in increasing numbers up the road from Parit Jawa. At the same time, other enemy units, either from the Iwaguro Regiment, or the Ogaki – or both – had further infiltrated between the two Australian battalions to strengthen the roadblock on the Muar road and to slowly begin tightening their noose around the 2/29th.

Then, suddenly, around noon, the Jats began arriving through the rubber trees on the right flanks of the 2/29th's position. They were lucky not to have been shot up as they came, but after considerable yelling on their part to identify themselves, a ragged force of about two hundred were quickly allowed to enter the battalion area. The Indians had fought their way through other Japanese forces which had been seeking to extend their grip around the northern side of the 2/29th, but once they had managed to get by the Japanese, they were finally able to link up with the Australians after their long trek through the jungle.

They were in a deplorable condition. Not only were many of them young, insufficiently trained and frightened, but they were desperately tired, hungry and thirsty. Their first reaction upon their arrival in the Australian lines was to charge madly for the water truck which was standing in the trees near the battalion headquarters dugout.

'Stand back! Stand back!' Captain Brand shouted, jumping towards them. 'You'll all get a drink.' But they continued their wild dash for the truck and began to mill around, fighting for water. A shot rang out. Then another.

Captain Brand and Major Olliff, as well as one of the British officers commanding the Indian group, had all drawn their pistols and were aiming them at the soldiers at the taps.

'Back! Get back, unless you want to be shot,' Major Olliff yelled. 'Stand in line! You'll all get a drink. And keep down, under the trees, because if we don't shoot you, the Japs will.'

Fortunately, the wild scramble quietened down and within a short time all of the Jats had been given water. But while their thirst was slaked, their new situation with the 2/29th was hardly any better than it had been before. They were still well and truly trapped, as was the 2/29th.

Not long after the Jats' arrival, Major Olliff decided to launch an attack on the roadblock behind them to try to open up the way for the battalion's withdrawal. Until then, he had been unable to spare enough men to attempt an attack on the roadblock without seriously weakening the battalion's own defensive position in other areas. Now there was the opportunity of using some of the 2/29th and the newly arrived Jats in a joint effort to force a breakthrough.

But, because of their inexperience and also, perhaps, a combination of fatigue, disillusionment and fear, the Jats were not up to the task. They were cut to ribbons by the devastating firepower of the Japanese, who were now positioned at the roadblock in some strength as well as in the surrounding rubber plantations and on both sides of the road for some distance from the roadblock itself. The Jats broke and ran, but were mown down in numbers by heavy machine-gun fire.

The attempt to break the roadblock was called off and the Jats were regrouped into defensive positions at the battalion's rear. At the same time, although they did not know it then, other remnants of the Jats battalion were making a wider circle through the jungle, slightly further to the north, missing the 2/29th's position entirely, to meet up with Colonel Anderson's battalion at Bakri crossroads.

As the day wore on, the 2/29th's position worsened. With no supplies coming in, water and food were running low and the lack of ammunition would soon become critical. And to make matters worse, they now came under heavy bombardment from Japanese artillery; 5.9-inch shells began bursting all around them. They heard, one soldier later recalled, 'the faint reports of the guns firing in the distance, then the crescendo scream of the shells and the ear-splitting crash of the burst'. Everyone took what cover they could. The Jats, who had not dug any slit trenches, were panic-stricken and, despite calls to lie down, ran around hysterically, sustaining even more casualties.

In the meantime, Captain Brand and a couple of assistants continued their herculean task of trying to treat the wounded. Brand was amputating the remains of a soldier's foot with a pair of scissors when given the news that one of the stretcher bearers, Private 'Kanga' Boyd, had been killed while trying to bring other wounded soldiers to the Aid Post. Private Jack Dorward, the other stretcher bearer, had been severely wounded.

When the barrage finished, Brand rushed to the road, where he had been told there were several more wounded. He found one man lying with his thigh terribly smashed and near death, though conscious and in great pain. Brand administered almost a gram of morphia to the man and passed on to another, an Indian who pointed piteously at his legs, one of which was badly torn and broken. Telling the man to put his arms around his neck, Brand struggled to get him up the embankment. Unable to go any further, he called for help and, after another soldier left his slit trench to crawl to the edge of the cutting, the two were able to lift the Indian into the cover of the rubber trees.

Others now came to the aid station in a flood. Some were affected by 'metal splash', the result of exploding shells and shrapnel. One man, Sergeant Wedlick, had been sprayed by metal splinters across his face and neck, while another showed a line of large metal splinters across his back. But these casualties, as bad as they might have been under normal circumstances, were for the most part sent away, as Captain Brand was almost totally occupied with other, more seriously wounded: those with legs or arms blown off, or serious internal injuries which were life-threatening. One man came up to the aid post with a wound caused by a bullet passing right through his mouth, and out one cheek, tearing half his tongue off on the way. He took one look at the other men being treated by the medical officer and turned away.

At Bakri crossroads, meanwhile, Colonel Anderson, now in charge of what was left of 45 Brigade, was confronted with the news that his own line of retreat was now also cut. A Japanese force had breached the road behind the 2/19th's position and established a second major roadblock between Bakri and Parit Sulong. The Allied forces were being divided up piecemeal. A section of Bren-gun carriers was sent to attempt to force its way through, but was unable to, so heavy was the opposing fire.

Anderson now felt that the only course was to get the withdrawal of the 2/29th and the rest of 45 Brigade under way as soon as possible. But the 2/29th's position looked almost hopeless. The only way they could be given any significant help in their pullback would be to lay down a concentrated, timed barrage of artillery fire which would start close to their own position and move backwards through the Japanese roadblock as the men of the 2/29th followed it back towards Bakri.

The strategy behind this kind of tactic is the same for withdrawal as for an advance – the artillery fire is meant to keep the enemy's heads down until one's own troops are right upon them and in a position to fight their way through. The danger in the strategy is that it requires great accuracy on the part of the gunners, precise timing on the part of the friendly forces on the 'receiving' end, and good communications between the two. It would be difficult, if not impossible, to satisfy all of these conditions under the circumstances, but they had no choice but to try.

Radio signals of the escape plan got through to Major Olliff, but there would have to be a delay of some hours before the artillery barrage, from many miles to the rear, could be arranged. This meant that the withdrawal could not start before 6pm and, all the while, the Japanese attacks on the battalion were building up.

A force of Japanese machine-gunners, swinging around on the 2/29th's right flank through the rubber trees, launched an attack in mid-afternoon but was beaten off by the Australians who, leaving their foxholes and moving from tree to tree, advanced on the Japanese, forcing them to retreat. Similarly, on the left flank shortly afterwards, a Japanese attack and an Australian counterattack resulted in the Japanese force retiring. But with the weight of numbers building up behind them, the Australians knew that these were only temporary retirements. Just before 5.30pm, Major Olliff gave the order that word be passed on through the dugouts of the different platoons that the 2/29th was at last to move out, in an attempt to link up with the 2/19th Battalion.

'We're pulling back,' Lieutenant Sheldon told Arthur. 'Make sure everybody's ready. We're moving in exactly thirty minutes.'

'We're all bloody ready, sir,' Bomber said from one side. 'Don't worry about that.' He laughed softly. 'We've been bloody ready for three days!'

Some hours later after Arthur has been badly wounded . . . 'We have some badly wounded men,' Captain Morgan said. 'Could they make it?' He knew the answer before he asked the question.

'Show me,' the old man said.

He was taken to where Arthur and the others lay stretched out on the grass. The woodcutter turned away and spoke softly to the adjutant and they walked back towards his shack together.

Shortly afterwards, another of the officers came back to where the wounded were lying. It was Lieutenant Bill McCure, the commander of the battery of anti-tank guns which had been with the 2/29th on the Muar road. McCure sat down beside Arthur, clearly embarrassed and upset. He was a tall, thin man in his late twenties with curly, sandy hair and a pointed nose.

'Look, er, Sergeant Shephard . . .' He glanced across at the semi-comatose forms of Brown and Boyle. He began slowly, then spoke in rapid bursts. 'This Chinese bloke says he can get us through to

Parit Sulong. He knows a track through the jungle, but it's pretty rough. It'll be tough going, he says, and . . .'

'He doesn't think we'll make it,' Bomber Wainright put in.

'Well, no. That's right. He says he can get you through later, at your own pace, but not now, with the rest of them.'

'So what's going to happen?' Arthur asked. 'We're to stay here?'

'Yes, that's right. There'll be the four of you – yourself, Wainright, Brown and Boyle. We'll leave as much food as we can and he says he'll be able to feed and hide you until you're rested up enough to make the trip, perhaps in a day or two.'

None of the four men concerned spoke. Neither of the men with head wounds were well enough to say anything at all, and both Bomber and Arthur felt so weary as to be almost unaware of the implications. It was almost a relief not to have a face the prospect of struggling on any more, although in the back of their minds there lingered the dread feeling that this was the end of the road.

The extra supplies were brought to them, almost like offerings to be included in some sacrifice being left for the dragon. Several men came to say goodbye including, of course, Jim Kennedy and Jack Roxburgh who had stuck by Bomber and Arthur since the swamp. But now there was a terrible air of embarrassment about their parting. Of the two hundred men, these four were to be left alone, to survive as best they could. Although Captain Morgan and the others who were going on could rationalise the move on the basis that the four wounded men *had* to be left behind for the good of the majority, it was not a pleasant taste that was left in the mouths of the men as they moved off once again. Several of them glanced back and waved at the four who remained seated underneath two rubber trees. 'Goodbye, Shep . . . goodbye, Bomber,' Jim Kennedy called as the last of the men trooped off through the trees. 'We'll see you in Parit Sulong, mate.'

But each of them knew – the departing and the departed from – that there was little chance they would ever see each other alive again. Arthur continued leaning back against the trunk of the tree as he watched the last man in the group disappear through the lines of rubber trees. For a few more minutes, he and his three companions could still hear the sounds of the party moving away. Then there was silence, complete silence. He looked around at Bomber and the other two lonely figures, also each leaning against a tree and facing in the direction taken by the departing men. Here we are, Arthur thought, four wounded men, sitting on the ground alone in a rubber plantation, surrounded on all sides by bloody Nips and eight thousand miles from home. Fat bloody chance we've got!

from *Savage Jungle* by Iain Finlay

Korea

Korea

War came to Korea in June 1950 and was to last for three years. The roots of the conflict date back to just after World War II, when the Korean Peninsula was divided along the 38th parallel into North and South Korea. The North under Russian influence became Communist, while the South was a Democratic Republic established by the United Nations.

When Communist forces successfully invaded South Korea, UN forces under the command of General Douglas Macarthur pushed the Communists back across the 38th parallel. Australian Prime Minister Robert Menzies committed troops, aircraft and ships to support the UN effort and, in 1950, Australian forces formed part of the UN advance towards the Manchurian border in North Korea. However, the advance was checked and turned into a retreat, to the south of Seoul, when many Chinese volunteers poured into the North.

In 1951, at Kapyong near the North–South border, Australian diggers, together with other UN forces, battled Chinese troops in an heroic confrontation that earned members of the 3rd Australian Battalion a US citation for bravery. Later in that year, during a period of peace negotiations, Australian troops of the 3rd Battalion also distinguished themselves when they crossed the Imjin River over the border to reinforce other UN forces and influence the peace talks. Later, the 1st and 2nd battalions joined the 3rd Battalion.

Australian troops were supported in Korea by the RAAF's 77 Squadron, at first with Mustang fighters and then with Meteor jets. They were opposed by Russian MiG jets, which Australian pilots considered to be superior military aircraft. At sea, RAN ships blockaded and bombarded Communist troops and supply lines on the west coast of Korea. Battles at close range occurred between Australian ships and Communist shore defences. HMAS *Murchison*, for example, took part in close encounters with the enemy in the Han River estuary, part of the Imjin River area.

The Korean War ended in 1953. Over 300 Australian volunteers were casualties in a war in which neither the Communists nor the United Nations could claim victory. Korea was still left divided between North and South.

Sniper

Ian 'Robbie' Robertson was a born marksman who passionately wanted to join the army and even tried to enlist when he was only sixteen. Although he was too young for World War II, he was accepted for army service in Korea in 1950. Ian Robertson was no ordinary soldier – he was a sniper. His army service in Korea consisted of stalking and 'switching off' Chinese soldiers with deadly accuracy.

In Japan, Robertson had been working as the battalion photographer, but with war looming he was made a sniper because he was one of the 10 best marksman among the battalion's 600 troops. It was like being picked for the school sports, but more dangerous.

He went to Korea in the autumn of 1950. Days were crisp but nights freezing, a taste of the cruel winter ahead. If an enemy bomb or bullet didn't kill you, the standard-issue Australian uniform might: it was hopeless for northern winters. To survive, diggers had to beg, barter or steal extra gear – woollen caps, gauntlets, mittens, waterproofs – from the Americans, who had plenty of everything.

Snipers were issued with a modified version of the venerable Lee-Enfield .303 rifle used by British Empire troops since the Boer War half a century before. The sniper model had a small telescopic sight and a heavy barrel, but otherwise was little different from a million others lugged by Allied infantry in two world wars.

Robertson could group 15 rounds in a space smaller than his fist at 300 metres, hit a target the size of man's head at 600 metres, and

Private Ian 'Robbie' Robertson, Sniper.

was confident of hitting a man from 800 to 1000 metres if conditions were right. Not that long-range marksmanship helped much in his first engagement.

It was their first week in Korea. Robertson and his first sniper partner, a South Australian called Lance Gully, were escorting their commanding officers on reconnaissance – driving ahead in a Jeep to 'clear the ground'. It meant they would draw enemy fire first, protecting the officers.

They stopped their Jeep and split up to scout on foot. Minutes later, Gully surprised 30 or more enemy soldiers hiding in a ditch. They showered him with hand grenades. He jumped in the ditch with them to avoid the blasts, then backed out of it, firing as he went. If he missed he was dead. After nine shots for nine hits, a grenade burst wounded him.

When he heard firing, Robbie ran to help. He saw a flap of his mate's bloodied scalp hanging off his head and a crazy thought struck him: 'Lance looks sharp with that Mohawk haircut.' The wounded man screamed: 'There's a million of them in there, and they're all yours.'

Years before, an old digger had told him how to survive superior numbers at close range: *Keep both eyes open, point and snap-shoot, count the shots and reload after six. And be aggressive: give them time to think and they'll kill you . . .*

He ran up to the ditch, shooting anyone who opposed him, squeezed off six shots then ran back, jammed in another clip and ran at the ditch again. He did it six times, until no one was left alive.

Gully had shot nine. The rest of the jumble of bodies were down to Robertson. He could hardly believe he was alive, unhurt apart from a furrow across his wrist left by a machine-gun bullet. It was a miracle.

Officially, it was a 'skirmish' at the start of what historians call the Battle of the Apple Orchard. Lance Gully returned to the line later, but the shrapnel in his body made him too sick to stay.

So the boy from Preston got a new sniping partner, a reputation and the first of a lifetime of recurring dreams.

★

It was late winter, early 1951. He followed the same routine he had dozens of times. At dawn he crawled into the open, forward and to one side of the Australian line. He found a depression away from any landmark or reference point – 'never get behind a tree or a big rock' – and fired an incendiary round across the valley so he could adjust his rifle sights to the distance, about 1000 metres. Then he inched to another spot nearby. He was filthy with mud, and blended in with rocks and patches of melted snow. He rested his rifle on his pack and waited his chance.

Through the telescopic sight he could see enemy soldiers with binoculars scanning his hillside. He aimed at one – putting the vertical 'post' of the sight on the point of the chin – but did not fire until they turned to talk to each other, in case they saw a movement or rifle flash that would give him away.

The rifle's recoil meant he didn't see a bullet strike, so he could not be dead certain he had hit a particular target. A near miss meant his quarry would duck and hide, anyway. He was never sure which bullet was fatal. He found this element of doubt oddly comforting.

At Hill 614, in between scouting sorties, he spent hours alone on the hillside, methodically picking off his marks, one by one. He called it 'switching them off'. After each shot he would work the bolt gently to lever in another round, then lie stock still.

The Chinese had a proverb: *Kill one man, terrorise a thousand.* It was true, and it meant that each day, with each death, his job grew more dangerous.

All snipers were hated, good ones were feared. The better he shot, the more desperate enemy officers would be to kill him to stop the loss of morale. This is the sniper's dilemma: the more enemies you hit, the more return fire you attract and the more likely you are to die. Call it a Catch .303.

His only chance was to melt into the landscape. To make sure his muzzle blast didn't disturb grass, leaves or dirt. To avoid any quick movement. To resist the temptation to hide among trees and rocks that would attract artillery fire designed to deafen or maim if it didn't kill outright. If you held your nerve, it was safer in the open.

Sometimes he wondered what they called him. Feared snipers were given names by the enemy . . .

At the end of a week, the Australians took the hill with a bayonet charge, led by a heroic figure called Len Opie, who took several strongholds single-handedly. Robertson ran up to the enemy position he'd been shooting at earlier that day, and saw something he never forgot. Where he had been firing, there were 30 bodies. One morning's bloody work.

'Just one morning,' he repeats, shaking his head. 'And I'd been there all week. I got a feeling of horror. I never did the arithmetic. I still don't want to.'

The Chinese did do the arithmetic. A few months later, in April 1951, a mortar opened fire with pinpoint precision at the spot where Robertson and his sniper partner were. It was obvious the mortar had worked out where the snipers should be in relation to their platoon.

First the explosions burst his eardrums, then shrapnel ripped through his right hand. By next day it was 'the size of a pumpkin'.

Before they shipped him to hospital in Japan two days later, he handed in his binoculars, compass, watch and rifle to the quartermaster. He would return to Korea much later, as a platoon sergeant, but his sniping days were over.

from *A Sniper's Tale* by Andrew Rule

'Anzac item – break left – tracers!'

Ron Guthrie was an Australian fighter pilot flying with the famous RAAF 77 Squadron in Korea, but had the misfortune of being the squadron's first MiG victim. On 29 August 1951 he was in one of two flights of Meteor jets that were surprised by an attack of Russian MiGs and although he managed to down one, his plane was destroyed by the explosive shells of another enemy fighter. Having survived the ordeal, as well as a period as a POW of the Communists, he would co-author the following account of the action:

Silver trails of vapour in the placid morning sky define the passage of eight Meteor jet fighters along a patrol line adjacent to the Yalu

Gloster Meteor jets, 77th squadron.

River. This infamous segment of North Korean airspace, so frequently the playground of predatory Russian fighters, has earned the title of 'MiG Alley'. In two flights of four, the RAAF fighters, well-spaced in battle formation, cruise at a steady 39,000 feet. Each pilot's head swivels urgently as he seeks to cover his companions against intruders. The peaceful Korean sky endures its torment from the strident banshee wailings of sixteen Derwent jet engines whilst the contrasting quiet of the cockpits is broken only by occasional business-like commands from the leader.

Five thousand feet below, the second flight of eight Meteors executes a parallel path against a background of deceptively peaceful Korean and Manchurian landscape – sweeping endlessly away to the north. Presiding watchfully over this orderly scenario, the sun's fiery orb glows in high elevation. Suddenly this great orange mass, as though conspiring against the Australian pilots, assumes a sinister visage. Disgorging form its massive furnace there slides an avalanche of silver spears, in pairs, belching 37mm and 23mm cannon shells with menacing accuracy.

A fateful date emblazoned forever on Ron Guthrie's memory is 29 August 1951!

Suddenly I am startled by white-hot tracers streaming over and under my left wing like glowing ping-pong balls. I throw my Meteor into a hard left-hand turn and press the 'mike' button to call a 'break' to the others in my flight. Too late! I have been hit behind the cockpit and my radio is useless. I am only talking to myself as I call 'Anzac Item – break left – tracers!'

Now, two Russian MiG-15 jet fighters shoot past my nose and I instinctively turn back sharply to the right hoping to get one of them in my sights. Through the illuminated graticule of the gunsight, I can see a red star on a silver fuselage and the pilot's head in the cockpit. I quickly adjust the gunsight control to correct for a retreating target as my finger curls over the trigger of my four 20mm cannons. The guns rattle. I am gratified and excited as pieces fly off the enemy aircraft which now rolls to the inverted position and dives out of sight.

At this very instant I feel as though a load of bricks has fallen onto the rear end of my aircraft, which now shakes convulsively. Explosive shells from another MiG have destroyed my Meteor's tail. My aircraft – at this stage merely an uncontrollable mass of 'MiG meat' – begins to snap roll repeatedly. In shock, I prepare to make my first exit in a Martin Baker ejection-seat – at this great height and over enemy territory! I realise my guns are still firing and release the trigger.

The vibrating instrument panel catches my attention and two facts remain in my memory. The clock is reading six minutes past ten and the Mach meter – my gauge of speed – registers 0.84. As the speed of the dive increases beyond eighty-four per cent of the speed of sound, the aircraft begins to shudder in compressibility. It continues to roll.

Ron urgently grasped and pulled the canopy jettison handle. In an instant, a gigantic roar announced that his private cocoon had become part of the frigid swirling air mass into which he was about to plunge. Taking a two-handed grip on the ejection-seat loop handle above his head, he waited for the aircraft to finish its roll and on reaching the upright position pulled firmly on the control in order to fire himself out of the cockpit. Nothing happened! Distressing thoughts added their burden to the alarming cacophony of the 600 miles per hour air blast as he awaited the completion of another rotation. Surely the ejection-seat firing mechanism was not going to malfunction in this moment of desperate need. He repeated the process and was shocked as the mechanism failed once again! Then he discovered that his arms were being obstructed in their downward motion by the pistol holster under his right elbow and a Red Cross pack on his left side. Obviously this had to explain the dilemma. The third time around, with arms spread wide he made a final frantic effort. The altimeter needles were unwinding below 39,000 feet as a startling explosion produced an immense upward thrust out of the cockpit. The experience seemed momentary as he now lost consciousness.

My awareness returned some seconds later but I had a light-headed feeling that this was not really happening. Perhaps it was lack of oxygen or maybe it was shock, however it all seemed quite unreal, as in a half-dream. I tumbled and swayed until eventually the ejection-seat's little drogue parachute in full deployment steadied the descent. I could not breathe! This situation was quickly fixed by repositioning the goggles away from my mouth and lifting the oxygen mask from where it had slipped to my throat. I was relieved to feel the portable oxygen puffing onto my face.

The sensation was odd as he just sat there strapped to the ejection-seat, feeling quite stationary and quite detached, secured to his mechanical throne in space with no apparent means of support and no indications of motion. He was in a New World that was only half-real. The complete lack of noise was quite uncanny in its contrast with the clamour which had so recently conditioned his senses. Gone were the sounds of combat, followed so rapidly by the ejection-seat explosion intermingled with the overwhelming roar of a 600mph slipstream. Ron's personal segment of Korean sky, so recently a noisy battleground, was now a quiet and peaceful arena bereft of aircraft, friend and foe.

The silent, almost motionless experience seemed to invite the frigid atmosphere to ravage and assault his body and mind. Ron knew the temperature would be approximately –56°C but surprisingly he was not unduly disturbed by the cold in spite of being lightly dressed in nothing more than a normal cotton flying suit on top of summer underwear.

Gradually beginning to think and take stock, he was forced to confront the shocking reality of this new situation. He had been suddenly re-born as a pilot without a plane – a man without a home – a human without his friends. The perils of this situation became more obvious with each minute. The only option acceptable to Ron, on first consideration, was the avoidance of capture by the North Koreans. He had learned too much from the intelligence officers – anything but that! From this great height he could possibly drift seawards during the long descent and survive for some time in his dinghy thereby creating the opportunity for a recovery effort by the Air/Sea Rescue aircraft. With this plan in mind he unlocked the ejection-seat harness and kicked. The seat and its small drogue chute fell away. Then a sharp pull on the ripcord handle produced a welcome jerk as the beautiful Irvin parachute, blossoming out above, stabilised Ron in a quiet and peaceful descent.

It then became apparent that the immensely forceful airflow as I left the cockpit had ripped the chamois gloves from my hands and the knee pockets off my flying suit. Missing contents included spare socks and pistol ammunition. Obviously I had been lucky with regard to the oxygen-mask and goggles, which had merely been displaced. No doubt this was one of the benefits of the ejection-seat head-protection blind which had been drawn down in front of my face during propulsion into that violent airflow.

Looking down between my legs I was surprised to see another parachute. For a moment it seemed I had company – perhaps another unfortunate member of my flight, or hopefully a MiG pilot. Then it became apparent this was my own ejection-seat, still under the control of its small drogue 'chute.

Endeavouring to guide himself towards an ocean landing, Ron pulled down on one side of the canopy shrouds in the hope of producing some directional control. This had the unexpected and quite alarming effect of spilling the 'chute into a collapsed and ineffectual condition. Suddenly he was in a sickening descent with the parachute flapping above. Some anxious moments passed before the 'umbrella' restored its shape and its life-preserving function. Vowing he would not try that again, Ron became resigned to abandoning the possibility of a sea voyage in the little inflatable rubber raft, now quite useless in its attachment to his harness. There would be no encounter with 'Dumbo' – the USAF Air/Sea Rescue amphibian aircraft. Perhaps this had been a futile hope anyway, as he had no signalling beacon. The elements would decree the 'where and when' of touchdown on enemy soil.

Descending through the air seven miles above the countryside, my thoughts now turn to home. How will my mother bear the shocking news? Since her divorce she does not even have the support of a husband, and the loss of my only sister Cecile during her honeymoon on the Lane Cove River in Sydney in 1945 will now come back to haunt my poor mother!

I hope my squadron mates are all returning safely to Kimpo. There had been a lot of MiGs spearing through our formation during that sudden attack.

The Korean countryside far below looks more hostile with every minute of the descent. What will be waiting for me down there? I am probably too far north for any chance of a helicopter rescue.

The thought of falling into the hands of North Koreans fills me with anxiety. Our intelligence briefings have been most discouraging in this regard. The Geneva Convention will mean nothing. Harsh treatment will be guaranteed. The possibility of being shot on sight by their military forces is a big worry.

There is some momentary distraction in gazing overhead at the great silken canopy of the Irvin parachute and then casting eyes around the horizon. This unique experience, in spite of its hazards, is still able to offer some magnificent impressions to occupy the senses of this Meteor pilot during these last minutes of freedom. On this cloudless morning, the extreme visual clarity presents the observer with panoramic views of a curved earth, bound by exquisitely rounded horizons vanishing away to infinity in all directions. His eyes, at a glance, can take in the full 150-mile width of North Korea as well as the Sea of Japan shimmering and fading in its eastern extremities. The snaking pathway of the Yalu River in its entirety winds its way into the mountains of Manchuria. To the west, the Yellow Sea beckons, but due to the slight eastward drift of Ron's parachute, the sanctuary of this tantalisingly close expanse of ocean seems unattainable. He is dropping inevitably towards the countryside and almost certain capture.

Ron permitted himself a few minutes of resentful consideration of the futile operational undertaking which had placed him in this predicament. Formidable aircraft though the Meteor had been when first in service, it was no competitor for the new Russian jets they were required to oppose. The MiG-15s had most of the advantages, being specialised high-altitude, swept-wing fighters with higher speed and much greater rate of climb. Additionally, the enemy pilots were able to climb to heights above Meteor operational capability whilst over neutral Manchuria before diving into the legitimate combat zone and pouncing from above.

Having the experience of being the first 77 Squadron MiG victim was a dubious honour but Ron was to subsequently meet others in the POW camps who had been similarly afflicted. They all had a healthy respect for the capabilities of the sneaky little Russian and wished they had been flying the North American Sabre, now being so successfully operated by the USAF. These bitter thoughts, so obviously unproductive, soon gave way to more practical apprehensions regarding his imminent encounter with enemy soldiers, an experience for which most airmen were ill prepared.

The emergency oxygen supply lasted to probably about 20,000 feet, below which height the ambient air was adequate. By now the topography was becoming clearer, with mountains, rivers and townships increasingly in focus. Ron would normally have experienced some pleasure at this unique experience, however the visual titillation was severely overshadowed by a sense of foreboding. Descending through the lower levels, such apprehension was reinforced by a terrible realisation.

I could hear strange sounds like 'fitttt-fitttt' and looked up at the canopy. Holes were appearing! Enemy troops were shooting and the bullets were zipping past very close! This was what we had been warned about at our briefings. In alarm, I attempted evasive action by pulling on the cords in order to swing myself from side to side. Again I spilt the 'chute and had to stop pulling. This was a frightening experience as I was so near the ground but fortunately my parachute quickly re-erected.

At very low levels the descent seemed to accelerate and the last couple of hundred feet slipped by rapidly. Descending towards a paddy field, for a moment it seemed I was going to land on top of two women bending over their work. In fact, my feet planted in the soft ground squarely between the two girls. I remained upright. The two ladies leaped into the air in fright and ran a short distance, then stopped as they saw there was no threat. I was still standing securely, with the spongy soil up to my ankles. As I unstrapped, the smiling girls each took one of my hands and one said 'Russki da?' Thinking quickly I repeated 'Russki da!' They began to lead me away.

Then bullets started to fly! Ron's guardians absconded in fright. Seeking shelter by crawling behind a paddy wall he drew his 0.38 revolver. Conscious of the fact that this weapon had been supplied for such occasions, it seemed a natural action to expend those six bullets in his personal defence. Perhaps he was not thinking clearly, but merely reacting instinctively. Ron had certainly been programmed by the intelligence officers to anticipate extreme and probably fatal belligerence from the North Korean military.

I can see three separate army patrols approaching my position. This frightening situation is brought home to me as the nearest soldier begins shooting from the hip as he runs. I flinch at the chatter of the 'burp' gun as bullets hit the ground nearby. They are obviously out to kill me! Perhaps I can take one of them with me! I reply with two revolver shots and the one who has been firing drops to his knees – bleeding profusely. Before there is any time for further firing I am seized from behind, the pistol is torn from my grasp and the teenage soldier runs around firing my gun into the air. All other shooting stops. I rise to my feet – surrounded!

Little interest or attention was displayed towards the soldier lying in the paddy a few yards away. They were all quite absorbed with their novel catch. A large number of excited North Korean troops crowded around and proceeded to strip Ron of his Mae West and flying suit. Fortunately the excellent combat boots did not appeal and remained on his feet. Perhaps the muddy condition of these most essential items saved them from the souvenir hunters. His RAAF watch disappeared along with a signet ring – a gift from his mother. His last glance at the watch showed the time to be ten to eleven. There was a party atmosphere amongst the soldiers as they bargained with each other over the distribution of spoils.

When stripped down to his underclothes, Ron's arms were firmly wired behind his back with a length of telephone cable. In the custody of a diligent escort of six triumphant members of the North Korean Peoples Army the bewildered captive was promptly marched off into a very uncertain but most inauspicious future.

from *Escape from North Korea* by Col King and Ron Guthrie

Open fire!

The frigate HMAS *Murchison* was one of a number of UN small ships harassing Communist troops and installations on the west coast of Korea. The ship's tour of duty lasted for 60 days, during which the *Murchison* continually sailed the Han River estuary and engaged the enemy in a bombardment at the furthest point of its patrol. Various names such as

Sickle, Fork, Piccadilly and Pall Mall were given to features along the river's banks, from which Communist gunfire was a constant threat.

The difficulties involved in these patrols, as well as the skill and bravery of Commander Allen Dollard and his Australian crew, are clearly demonstrated in the following extract:

In Korea's Siberian winter the Han is a highway of ice almost along the 38th parallel. In summer it moves, swift and black – a dirty evil river – through a hot dry countryside to the Yellow Sea.

But the Han does not merge with the sea as a river should. It loses itself in a spiderweb estuary of narrow channels, low islands and tidal mud banks. At high water – and high it is for the tide in the Han lifts 28 feet – the estuary is five miles across, but at low tide the water flows meanly among a wasteland of temporary islands and stinking mud.

The Han estuary is no place for ships, even baby ones, to move and manoeuvre, but in Korea, where many concepts of war had to be discarded, the Han became a mobile stage for some of the most unconventional and gallant actions in naval warfare.

The battles of 'Operation Han' were unconventional because the ships which fought them ceased to be ships and became more like amphibious tanks than anything else. And the battles were brave because men fought at point-blank range against land armament which ranged from 75mm guns and heavy mortars down to light machine guns and small arms.

'Operation Han' was no war of broadsides at ten miles. It was a Little Ship affair which began in July 1951, and went on for many months. It began when the Chinese pulled back beyond the line of the Imjin River and the Allied Naval Command decided to send their frigates into the black Han, if they could get them there, to play hide and seek among the creeks and mud banks while bombarding across part of the Communist Yellow Sea flank.

Dollard took *Murchison* along Lambeth to Knife and finally anchored at Knife Edge, seven miles west of Fork, where Frank Smith, who already knew his targets, swung his two twin four-inch and waited.

At last Dollard gave the order.

'Stand by bombardment starboard.'

'Ready to open fire, sir,' reported Woc Roberts, the Principal Control Officer.

'Open fire.'

The guns cracked and the shells went away – over the paddy fields, over the foothills, to burst on the railway yards at Yonan, five miles from the river. Smith could see the tall buildings of the town among the hills, but he could not see the fall of his shells. Then, from their naval spotting plane, came the word that he was right on the target, and after that he wasted no time. He put fifty-two shells into Yonan before Dollard lifted the anchor and headed back along Lambeth.

One of the problems in the erratic Han was that all patrol and bombardment trips along the channels had to be made on the rising tide and all return trips had to be completed before high water. This

The frigate HMAS *Murchison* in Korean waters.

meant that on the average a frigate had only an hour and a half, or a little more, to do a round-trip operation. Speed was therefore very important.

Back at Fork, Dollard swung north up Piccadilly and then made for Pall Mall along Sickle, bombarding into the foothills beyond Paekchon as he steamed at fourteen knots. He was nearing the mouth of the Yesong River, just north of Pall Mall, when aft and bridge lookouts reported:

'Gun flashes on the port bow.'

'Action port,' Dollard called. 'All positions engage.'

As he spoke, enemy shells burst black in the mud of the river bank, then beat the black water into white columns as the Communist gunners found the range. And, with the shells, came long bursts from machine guns back from the river and bullets from riflemen, dug in along the bank, hammered the ship or ricocheted and whined away.

Murchison's four-inch and Bofors were pumping out shells as the frigate reached the mouth of the Yesong, anchored, swung to the anchor, and moved back along Sickle at fifteen knots. An enemy mortar bomb exploded near the stern and another alongside. Then a burst from a machine gun rattled the ship's side with the noise of a street drill, and rifle bullets scarred the deck and sprayed the bridge and Director Tower.

Fifteen hundred yards from the river enemy gun flashes were little scarlet stabs of colour across the flat paddy green. The guns were inside farmhouses and covered from the air. The muzzles pointed through broken walls. The shells came in and Dollard thought, 'Thank God they're going over.' And they did. Then more shells hit the bank and shrapnel cried above the bridge like kittens in a basket. *Murchison* put a broadside into one of the houses and an umbrella of greyish smoke opened above the roof. This was a direct hit on a 75. Then another of her broadsides exploded in a trench, so South Korean guerrillas reported later, and the forty soldiers in it never knew what hit them.

While this was going on, the Bofors, coughing like noisy old men, were concentrating on the Chinese riflemen along the bank. Some were dug in, some lay in the grass. With glasses you could see the faces of some of them as they fired. One man came out of his hole and began to run, but he had moved only a few yards when a shell blew him to pieces. Then another soldier made for a patch of long grass but two Bofors fired at him and he disintegrated among the bursts.

As *Murchison* went along Sickle, enemy fire seemed to hesitate. Then it came on again in one final burst, which filled the air with lead and metal, before the ship moved out of range.

There was only one Australian casualty that afternoon. This was Able Seaman Chandler, on one of the Bofors, who was hit in the arm with a rifle bullet. His friends, however, wouldn't believe it. They said nothing could hit him because he was so thin he had to stand twice to even throw a shadow.

But the Chinese were still not finished with the Australian frigate.

During this Friday's action the English frigate *St Brides Bay*, anchored at Fork, had been bombarding at extreme range over *Murchison*. But the New Zealand frigate *Rotoiti* relieved *St Brides Bay* on the Saturday and Dollard, who was to take *Murchison* out of the Han on the Monday, agreed to show the channels to the Kiwi captain, Lieutenant-Commander Brian Turner.

On Sunday 30 September, *Murchison* again went up Piccadilly and along Sickle. The afternoon was fine and steamy, with cloud banks, like dirty crumpled handkerchiefs, down river above the Yellow Sea. The hills seemed very close and above and beyond them, far inland, were specks that were planes. On one of the Bofors sailors were singing, with the irony of sailors, 'Sailing down the river on a Sunday afternoon', but the singing suddenly stopped as the body of a Chinese soldier, in bleached khaki, his face paper white, his cropped hair very black, rocked gently in the wash and was left astern. 'Poor bastard,' one of the bridge lookouts said.

Dollard reached the Yesong, turned and gave the order to bombard as he began his run back along Sickle. But as the four-inch fired, the Chinese replied with everything they owned – 75s, 50mm anti-tank guns, mortars, machine guns and the rest. It was a repetition of Friday's battle, but enemy fire was much heavier and more accurate. An anti-tank shell went into *Murchison* but nobody heard it above the clamour of the armament. A 75 exploded in the engine room but did no vital damage. To Frank Smith, the shrapnel and bullets hitting his Director Tower was like someone belting nails into an iron roof. Then a shell – he swears it was 120mm – went through the radar aerials a foot above his head with a fluttering roar. Once he yelled for binoculars from the bridge and, as he swung his turret, he put his hand behind him to receive them. Instead, Woc Roberts put a lump of shrapnel in his hand. It weighed four pounds, it was jagged, it was still hot.

Part of the way down Sickle the enemy fire weakened and faded. Then Dollard had to reduce speed and almost stop as a stray rain squall came in from the sea across the river and spread grey drapes over the vital navigational buoys. For fifteen seconds *Murchison* was lost in the mist. Then the squall passed, the sunlight polished the wet ship, and Dollard was able to go on.

Murchison was nearing the western end of Sickle when, suddenly, the Chinese began again from a new cluster of guns, the nearest only 600 yards away. But as shells and bullets hit the frigate, Dollard was too busy with his navigation to notice them, although he knew that one shell in his steering gear and he would be aground and being pounded to pieces. Like a native medicine man he kept up his monotonous chant:

'Steer one seven zero.'

'Steer one seven one.'

'Port fifteen.'

'Steady.'

'Steer one six zero.'

Once he noticed that the two leadsmen, abreast of the wings of the bridge, had ignored the enemy fire and were still calmly swinging and calling, although none could hear their reports above the gunfire.

'Lay in the lead and take cover,' he yelled.

Then he resumed his chant.

Once he glanced up and saw enemy tracer shells, like flaming onions, rising incredibly slowly it seemed and in a high curve, and heard Turner, the New Zealand captain, call, 'This lot's coming right on the bridge.' But the shells went over, and behind and above in the Director Tower Jock Chalmers yelled 'Mortars' to Smith and pointed. Four mortar bombs were dropping towards the ship and four more had just been fired. The four-inch swung. They fired. The two men watched the four tracer shells go out from the muzzles towards the land and explode, and in the black explosion stained with orange and grey, four bodies jerked into the air and seemed to lie there before they slowly fell. And as the soldiers fell and disappeared from view white darts rose from the ground behind them and came swiftly towards the ship, and as they moved they got higher and whiter and Smith watched them coming and said to himself, 'Bazookas'.

During that Sunday afternoon run one sailor was seriously wounded and two were slightly wounded, and *Murchison* had seven shell holes in her, shrapnel and bullet scars all over her, and one of her Bofors damaged and out of action. In return she destroyed a 75, mortars and machine guns.

Later, when the New Zealander Brian Turner wrote his official report of that action he left no doubt what he thought of Dollard or his crew. In one part he said: 'Dollard set an admirable example of coolness and concentration at a time when divided attention might have spelled disaster.' In another part he had this to say: 'Dollard's handling of his ship and general direction of the armament was faultless and imperturbable. The range was barely 600 yards, which reduced the accuracy of the four-inch armament even when it could bear . . . The guns' crews and the control parties were admirable and this spirit . . . was right throughout the ship down to the engine room in which a shell exploded after having neatly drilled the ship's side and the reinforced corner of the watertight door . . .'

No one was surprised when later Dollard and his Navigator, Lieutenant 'Ned' Kelly, were awarded Distinguished Service Crosses.

There are many stories from the Han, but one of the best, largely because it gives a clear picture of Dollard the man, concerns *Murchison*'s 'Guns', Frank Smith. On one of many trips to Knife Edge, when only a few shots were fired against them, Smith saw an ox cart, which the Chinese used to carry ammunition and food, making for a village about 1000 yards from the river. He fired the four-inch and missed, and as the shells kicked up the mud of a paddy field just ahead of the cart Smith could see the owner belting the ox with a stick. As the ox began to canter and then gallop he fired and missed again – and missed with every shot after that before his target reached the village. Twenty minutes later, on their way back from Knife Edge, Smith saw what looked like the same ox cart coming out from the other end of the village.

'I'll get the bastard this time,' he yelped, still furious with his poor shooting.

But from the Compass Platform, Dollard called: 'No, Guns. You've wasted enough bloody ammunition. Let him go.'

To Dollard, however, the most memorable day of the sixty he spent up the river was 31 January 1952. On that day the tall and elegant Rear Admiral Scott-Moncrieff, whom the Australians admired tremendously, moved his flag from the cruiser *Belfast* to *Murchison* when the Little Ship made her final tour among the channels of the Han, and fired her final broadsides at the game Chinese. And when that day was over and *Murchison* was once more outside in the Yellow Sea, Scott-Moncrieff wined and dined Allen Dollard and his officers and later sent two farewell signals which Dollard has never forgotten.

The first read:

'I dislike the thought of continuing the war without *Murchison* but I will have to accept it now as a fact. You have been a tower of strength and your good name will always be associated with the infamous Han. No ship could have done better. For fine seamanship and steadiness under fire you have proved yourselves beyond reproach. Good luck in all your sailings and a happy home coming to you all.'

The second was:

'For your long tenancy of the Han, for mastery of all insidious and doubtful delights, and for insecurity of tenure I think you should be created Baron Murchison of the Han, Lord Fork and Viscount Spoon.'

from 'Baron Murchison of Han' by Ronald McKie,
in *With the Australians in Korea* by Norman Bartlett (ed.)

The Vietnam War

The Vietnam War

The Vietnam War was for the most part a guerrilla war fought in the jungle by two sides with diametrically opposed ideologies. On one side, the Viet Cong (Vietnamese Communist) guerrillas and the North Vietnamese army believed that they were fighting to keep their country free from an aggressive, foreign superpower – the United States; on the other, America and other western powers, supporting the South, feared that unless communism was stopped in Vietnam, then the rest of Asia would soon be overwhelmed.

The seeds of the bitter war that officially lasted from 1959 to 1975 were sown in the previous decade, when imperialist France was expelled from the country following the Battle of Dien Bien Phu in 1954. As a result of France's catastrophic defeat, the Geneva Convention that year saw Vietnam divided into two nations: North Vietnam and South Vietnam. The North was to be governed by France's vanquishers, the Viet Minh, led by Ho Chi Min, while South Vietnam came under the leadership of General Ngo Dinh Diem, whose sympathies lay with the United States. Diem's government proved to be a corrupt, totalitarian regime and soon lost the support of the South Vietnamese people. In addition, there was violent resistance from the Viet Cong – those members of the Viet Minh who had either stayed in the South or returned from North Vietnam in the years following the division. In desperation, General Diem appealed to the United States for military aid and the first US military advisers arrived in 1961. During the next seven years, until Richard Nixon became president, America's involvement rapidly increased with the instability of South Vietnamese governments and the increased military offensives of the Viet Cong. The result was a war that was very different from the traditional idea of armed conflict. There were no massed armies attacking each other over open terrain, in fact, it was often impossible for the Allies to distinguish the enemy from the civilians. The villagers appeared placid, but many of the South Vietnamese peasants were sympathetic to the Viet Cong. The main policy of the American and Australian ground forces was to employ 'search-and-destroy' missions against the VC but the thick vegetation impeded mobility and reduced visibility. The Viet Cong were an elusive enemy, experts in hiding themselves in underground bunkers and caves. They used the familiar terrain to considerable advantage in creating ambushes and booby traps.

To overcome these tactics, the Americans exercised a massive deployment of air power. The US Army was quickly able to despatch waves of helicopter gunships, followed by large troop-carrying helicopters to the aid of its troops in the jungle, whose positions were in danger of being overrun by the Viet Cong. In the bombing of North Vietnam, the Americans used B-52 bombers, protected by fighters. Despite the impressive array of military technology available to the Allies, the VC had already shown France and the rest of the world that they were masters of guerrilla warfare, and a stalemate ensued.

In Australia, Prime Minister Menzies had long subscribed to the 'domino theory' of communism in the region, and had pledged Australia's support for its American ally. Consequently in August 1962, 30 Australian army instructors were despatched to help train the Army of the Republic of Vietnam, and as the United States increased its military forces, so did Australia. In June 1965, Australia's first combat troops, the 1st Battalion Royal Australian Regiment, arrived in South Vietnam and were entrusted with the task of securing Bien Hoa, a large American air base. By September that year, 1350 Australian soldiers were based at Bien Hoa.

The 1st Battalion were highly professional soldiers, some of whom had fought in Korea and Malaya, and they showed themselves to be experts in jungle warfare. They employed very different tactics from those of the Americans. Whereas the American troops would call for heavy air strikes and make concentrated attacks, the Australians preferred to operate stealthily in small patrols, which, when one was attacked, could be co-ordinated to close in rapidly and attack the enemy from a number of

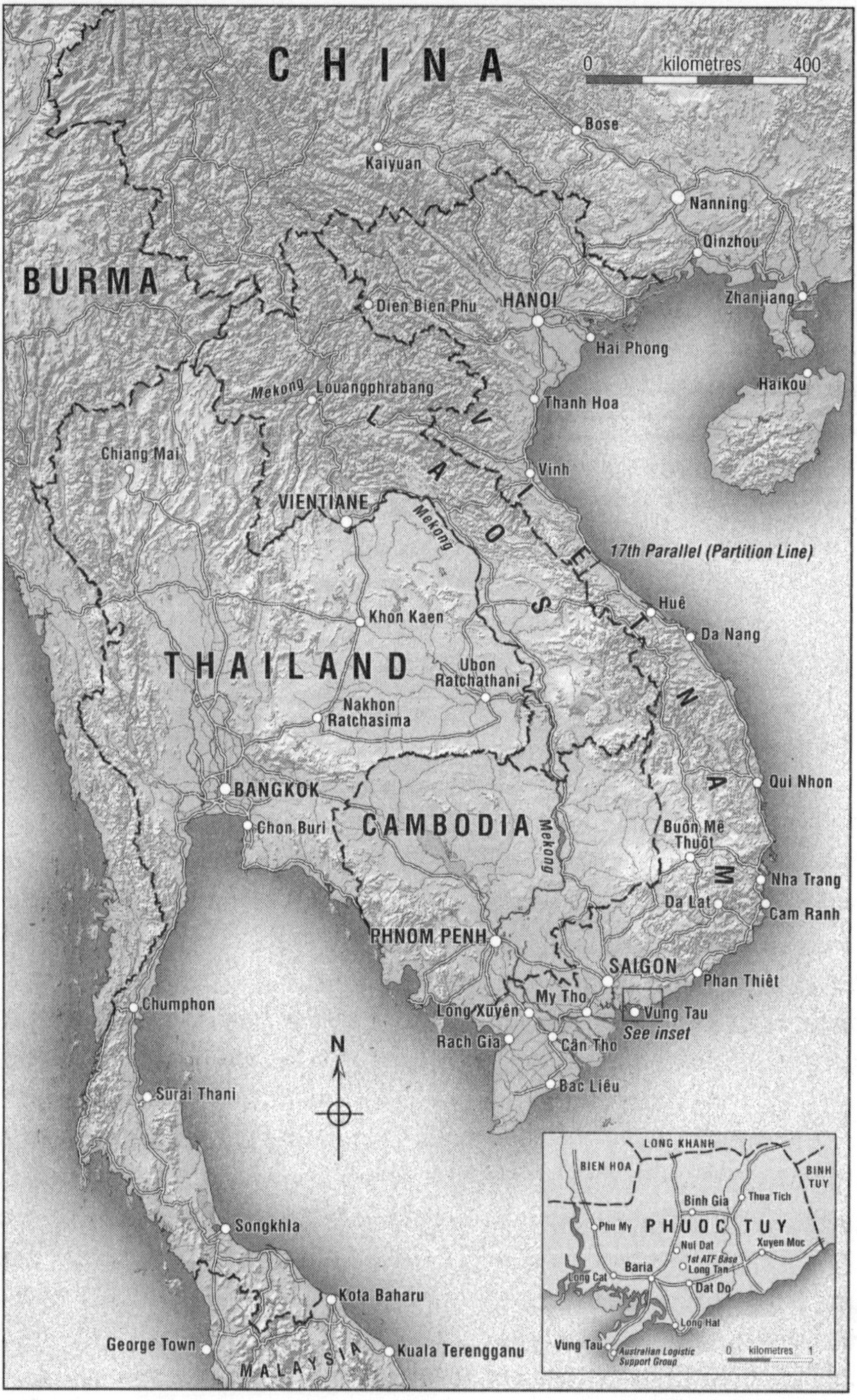

Southeast Asia, 1965.

directions. Using these tactics, the Australians showed that they were superior to the Viet Cong in battles in January and March 1966.

With the introduction of conscription and the expanded participation of Australian troops, the Australian forces were given the responsibility for the protection of the province of Phuoc Tuy. The task force duly set up its new base at Nui Dat in mid 1966. That August, they won a decisive battle at nearby Long Tan, thanks in part to the New Zealand battery's precision artillery fire. In light of the vastly superior numbers of Viet Cong involved, it was a stunning victory for the Australians. As the full horrors of the Vietnam War were televised throughout Australia and America, the anti-war movement escalated in both countries. By February 1968, when the North launched its Tet Offensive, it was clear to the shocked viewers that the Communists were far from defeated. Bowing to the resultant political pressure, President Nixon initiated the 'phased withdrawal' of US troops from 1969 onwards, and Australia followed suit two years later.

The Australian soldiers involved in the conflict had fought with courage and distinction. Not only had they gained a reputation from the enemy for their determination and professionalism, but they had shown that they were the equal of their famous forebears.

Jungle warfare

Dennis Cole was an infantry officer in Vietnam in 1969. The incident he describes shows how extremely perilous it was patrolling the jungle there:

In the jungle I think it was as much good luck as judgment if you turned up at the right place. You'd get a map with three creeks on it and you'd have crossed five creeks before you got to the first one on the map. It was just so inaccurate. Plus you couldn't take a bearing on anything. You'd hit a clump of bamboo and you'd have to go right around it, plus you've got a guy whose job it is to count every step and you've got to translate steps into yards, which depends on the territory. Normally I think it was one hundred and twenty steps to one hundred yards in open going, but you get into jungle and you're stepping over rocks and roots and tree stumps and you just have to take an educated guess. It was bloody near impossible. We lost one or two platoon commanders early in the piece by walking back into harbours from the wrong direction and being brassed up.

I think it was pretty heavily timbered country. It was very flat. We came across a rise in the ground, crawled up, and there was a creek at the bottom and then across the other side there were all these trees, about seven foot tall, very heavily leafed all the way down to the ground. It didn't look natural. It was a strange sort of setting.

The creek was only eight or nine foot wide, not deep, and the order came down for me to take a section across and clear the other side, which we did, but it was very hairy because you couldn't see anyone next to you, the foliage was that thick. They were a very strange sort of tree. I don't really know how to describe them. We cleared it as much as we could, probably fifty yards, and came back and the whole company went over and then they found a fish trap where the creek swung around.

Bob Carr had hurt his ankle so I took over his section and the platoon commander grabbed my section and set off up one side of the track. By the time I'd got hold of Bob's section and moved off I was probably level with the last man on the other side. We got about three-quarters of the way up level with them, moving around a left-hand bend when the claymore [mine] went off.

I just happened to look across to the right as it went off and a piece of shrapnel went through my ear and round the back of my skull. It was like someone had hit me across the head with a cricket bat and the next thing I knew I was on the ground. My head was ringing like a church bell and I didn't have much idea what was going on. I didn't even hear the gunfire. I sort of scrambled off the track, but then I could hear Johnny Higgins calling out. He was rat-shit. I thought he'd been hit by something, but he just couldn't move, he just lay there in the middle of the track. I was shit scared, but I went back and dragged him off the track into the bamboo. He was just lying there saying, 'I can't move, I can't move.'

I could hear the screams from the guys up in front. Two of my best mates were killed, another one lost both his legs and another fellow lost his mind.

Heavily laden with his equipment and ammunition, Sergent Peter Buckney of the 8th Battalion, Royal Australian Regiment, moves along a jungle trail in Southern Long Khanh Province.

I moved up with the medic and all I could see were my mates littered all over the place, bits and pieces of them. One guy I could see was stone dead, George Neagle. He was just lying there with his eyes open, virtually unmarked, but as white as a bloody ghost. Then I saw Johnny Hallam. He'd lost his legs.

Somehow or other we got a hoochie underneath him and sort of carted him back. I thought he was gone. One leg was completely gone and the other leg was just hanging by a shred of skin and he was sort of in shock. I thought he wouldn't even see out the helicopter ride, wherever he's going.

They carried Midge back. He looked okay. He was laying there having a smoke and they said he'd just been wounded in the stomach and he looked okay. He died within an hour or so. We'd been hoochie mates for nine months. Apparently he'd got one through the throat as well which you couldn't see and he was dead before they hit the hospital. He'd only had a baby three months before he came overseas and when his wife found out she put her head in the oven and killed herself. That was probably a bigger shock than anything, really, when we heard that. You know, it was bad enough believing that he was killed.

Jimmy came back. Half his head seemed to be missing. They were carrying him, but you could see half his head was shot away. I don't think I'll ever forget the sight, or the way I felt. I couldn't believe it could happen to us.

They took the first chopper out with the badly wounded guys then they put me and Johnny Higgins and George Neagle, the dead bloke, on the second or third chopper. He had a poncho over him and his boots were sticking out the bottom and you knew who it was and knew he was dead.

We'd been in-country less than a month.

from *Ashes of Vietnam* by Stuart Rintoul

Choppers

The Vietnam War was the war of 'the chopper'. It was characterised by the heavy, repetitive throb of the approaching helicopter. The RAAF and RAN used the American HU-1 Iroquois or 'Huey', as they were affectionately known. The choppers were used for every conceivable task: they deployed troops on search and destroy missions, provided firepower against the attacking enemy, and transported the wounded in the midst of battle to immediate hospital care.

Bob Stephens was a helicopter crewman in Vietnam in 1970–71. Here he remembers the destruction of the helicopter and his emotional reaction to the horrifying experience:

It was late in the afternoon and we were called up into the Long Hais, a treacherous part of the province. We had to pick up some wounded, some South Vietnamese troops with some Australian advisers.

We came into the position. They threw us smoke so we knew where they were but couldn't land because of the rough terrain.

We went in, hovering about twenty feet above the ground, everything was going all right, and I sent a winch down. I could see wounded and bodies lying there. The first bloke they put into the litter was a fellow that had both legs blown off at the knees, a South Vietnamese, and I remember he had a piece of bone about three or four inches protruding from one knee.

I'd just started to winch this guy up when we were shot down by automatic weapons fire. You could hear the rounds hitting the aircraft and they must have hit the engine because the next thing there was no noise.

We hit the rocks, the aircraft rolled over onto its right side. As it was rolling I was looking out the door and I could see the fellow in the litter, who thought that the aircraft was rolling onto him. He didn't scream, but just the look of despair on his face . . .

I dived in behind the back of the pilot's seat for safety and the aircraft shook itself to pieces until the rotor broke itself off and the aircraft stopped. Straightaway there was a lot of smoke, there was screaming. The aircraft was on its side and I was standing in the opening on the ground realising that I was still alive. The gunner and then the co-pilot brushed past me and went up through the opening.

I watched the co-pilot slide to the ground alongside the aircraft and I watched him rolling down the hill. Then the Army medic, who had taken my machine gun while I was on the winch, yelled out 'Help me, I'm stuck, I'm stuck.' Something had rolled forward onto the back of his legs and he was sort of kneeling. I put my arms under his armpits to lift him out but I couldn't move him.

I could hear screams coming from the front somewhere and I didn't know whether it was the pilot or some of the men who had been underneath the aircraft when we crashed. I thought I would get out and smash the windscreen in but I couldn't climb out and I thought, 'I'm caught, I'm going to be the next one.' Then I realised that I still had on my safety harness, which stops you from falling out of the aircraft. I got outside and I was about to knock the windscreen in when the aircraft captain, who had already got out, yelled to me to get away before it blew up. He was down behind a large boulder.

I started to run to where he was and I saw the body of one of the Australian advisers who had been assisting in putting that wounded fellow in the litter. He was killed.

It wasn't long after that you could hear the aircraft burning and the ammunition was going off. Once I heard that I knew that I couldn't have gone back even if I had wanted to.

A helicopter came in to get us out just on dusk. There was a wounded South Vietnamese fellow who had taken shrapnel wounds to the head. He was bandaged up, but he was standing underneath the aircraft to be winched up and the downwash from the rotor blades was just swirling his blood everywhere. You could see it going against all the rocks and everything.

When I got on, there was wounded and dead everywhere. Normally they probably would have had a couple of aircraft to remove that many people, but it was right on dark and I suppose if they didn't get us out then they wouldn't have been able to get us out.

I went around and I sat next to the gunner and I just broke down and cried. I was relieved to be getting out of that place and I thought of what had happened and I just broke down and cried. The gunner put his arm around my shoulders and tried to comfort me. I just felt

Troops of 1st Australian Task Force wait for a US Chinook helicopter to leave the ground before returning to their base at Nui Dat.

exhausted, as though all my strength and energy had been drained right out of me.

We landed on the pad at the hospital at Vung Tau and the place was all packed with people ready to tend the wounded and the dead, and I just stepped straight off and sort of ambled over. I still had my pistol at that stage and I was trying to get the magazine out and an Army fellow quickly snatched that off me in case something happened there. I was just sort of lost. I felt I was nowhere.

from *Ashes of Vietnam* by Stuart Rintoul

Landmines and tunnels

In the Vietnam War, almost half the Australian casualties were caused by landmines, some of which the Viet Cong had extracted from Allied minefields. Another weapon the VC used to great effect was tunnel complexes that enabled them to literally disappear from sight. In time, these tunnels became storage areas for food and ammunition, sleeping chambers, kitchens and aid stations for the wounded.

Ted Cowell was a field engineer in Vietnam. Understandably distraught, he witnessed two horrifying incidents, one involving a landmine and the other a deadly tunnel complex:

When Jose got his foot blown off and we couldn't do nothing about it, I actually cried that time. He stood on one of them chicom jumpers, the type that would punch straight up once you let the pressure off; once you hear the click you know you've had it.

I tried to get a bayonet under his boot and hold the pin down while he pissed off, but it wouldn't work. I wouldn't have been able to hold the pressure on. The blokes were busy trying to fill up sandbags and packs and Christ knows what to try to hold the bayonet down and keep pressure on it, but it wouldn't have worked because once he lifted his foot the pressure-release spring would have been too great, it would have just punched up in the air.

So he just told us to piss off, get out of his way, you know. We sandbagged his foot so he wouldn't lose his families and then once we were out and behind trees he lifted it and it blew his foot off. It blew the front part of his foot off, but they didn't bring him home straightaway and gangrene set in, so they cut it off a bit higher and then flew him home. Now he's lost it up to his knee. The gangrene had set in and then come up the bone so they had to cut the whole bloody thing off. He had a lot of guts too, Jose. We were pretty close, real good mates.

The truth, I was swearing, I was cursing the world. See, he knew it and I knew it. I didn't want to accept it, but he already had because he'd stood on it. I couldn't accept it. I told all the blokes, every bastard, I said I'll shoot any bastard who ever says anything about any of this, I'll kill you on the spot. Jesus, I was wild, I was wild with the world. I threw the anger at them.

Shorty was something else. Shorty and I had formed a hell of a relationship, the way a lot of blokes do in a war when you're fighting and one life depends on the other. It's not just camaraderie; it's more, it goes deeper. Shorty and I were like brothers.

When we came back from our R&R in Taipei the boss said to me, 'Righto you pair of bastards, you've had a real good bludge, you're straight out in the paddock because there's an operation going on.' The crunchies had found a tunnel complex and instead of pissing off they wanted to investigate it. I don't know why they kept telling us about it. By that time I was worn out. I wouldn't admit it but I'd had it, I was a real nutso case. That was why they gave us the break. We were both going off our heads.

I had this funny feeling that if I went in I wouldn't come out. Call it a sixth sense, call it whatever you like, but I knew if I went in I'd be dead. Shorty could see I hesitated and he said, 'Piss off, this one's mine.' Well, I rolled it over a bit because I had already done the last three before that and left him seconds, so I said, 'Yeah, righto mate, take it easy, eh. I'll follow up.' And in he went.

I was talking to him on the radio for a while, listening to him, and then it went dead.

I ended up dragging him out by his feet because he got it, he was killed, and they done a good job of it too. That was the end of me. I went back in and I was down there for seventeen hours going through the complex, unhooking little booby traps and in general killing any bastard I got my hands on.

But it's a real slow job. It might take you anything up to an hour to move one foot, or if you're lucky two feet. Sometimes you know they're there, you sense it, and you're really keyed, you're hyped up. I think one of the worst things, more than even finding a track or a snake or anything like that, is to hear a bloke breathing; if you can hear a bastard breathing you know he's pretty close and you say, righto, you've got a fight on your hands and you're wondering whether he's doing it on purpose trying to lure you in.

In actual hand-to-hand combat I killed three in the complex, and then the next morning I got a bloke by the river.

from *Ashes of Vietnam* by Stuart Rintoul

The Battle of Long Tan

In August 1966, Australian forces became involved in a major battle with the Viet Cong in a rubber plantation near Long Tan, five kilometres from the Australian base at Nui Dat. The 108 Australians won a decisive victory over the 2500 attacking Viet Cong. At the crucial stage of the battle, in torrential rain, a relief force of armoured personnel carriers moved up on the Viet Cong and forced them to withdraw with heavy losses. At the end of the three-hour battle, 18 Australians had been killed and 24 wounded; 245 Viet Cong bodies were found after the engagement and an estimated 500 were wounded.

Lance Corporal Phil Buttitgieg, who served two tours of duty in South Vietnam, describes in graphic detail the Battle of Long Tan:

On the morning of 18 August, we farewelled the bulk of the company and set off towards the Long Tan rubber. About 6000–7000 metres along our route we discovered a mortar base plate position. We were mystified that it had not been hit by our own counter-mortar artillery bombardments, which were quite frequent in this area.

We pushed on to the Long Tan rubber itself and made a day harbour position on its western edge. From here two patrols were dispatched to investigate all of the fresh signs (tracks left by the enemy). One patrol, led by Spike Jones (later decorated with the Military Medal), went due south along a track through the rubber. The other patrol, led by Harry Kleen, went north-east into the rubber. Visibility was good under the foliage of the rubber plantation. We could see for several hundred metres as there was very little undergrowth.

Spike Jones' patrol soon reported finding hastily evacuated 57mm recoil-less rifle positions. They had been well covered by our artillery shells and there was evidence that many casualties had been inflicted. Fresh tracks showed that bodies were being moved on oxcarts. There was also a fresh trail made by large numbers of well-equipped troops, which led generally east, deep into the rubber plantation.

Harry Kleen's patrol reported finding freshly discarded US

ammunition containers not far from a rubber tapper's masonry hut (where the enemy later appeared in very large numbers). In time we realised that somewhere in this region there had been an enemy standing patrol observing our every action. The next day we found two parallel lines, several hundred metres long, of enemy fighting pits running in a north–south direction in the lower ground east of the hut.

Back at headquarters 6 RAR, it had become apparent that enemy numbers were too large for our depleted B Company, and so D Company was dispatched to the area. In the meantime our patrols had returned to our day harbour. We improved the security of our position and awaited the arrival of D Company led by Major Harry Smith.

It was about 1300 hours when D Company arrived from the south in single file. They passed to the east until we were central of them. They went to ground in a slightly more open formation and had lunch while the commanders conferred. Sometime later we left and moved back towards the Task Force base via the enemy mortar base plate position. We had no idea of the dramatic battle that was soon to unfold. Like a change between acts in a play – the scene suddenly changed.

The sky became overcast in readiness for the monsoonal drenching, which occurred almost on time every day at 1600 hours. Visibility shortened around us and the Long Tan rubber, now 1000 metres behind us, was shrouded in a sinister darkness.

Suddenly D Company had contact. We immediately cursed their luck until we heard the massive volume of fire. The radios told us D Company had chased a fleeing standing patrol, but now it sounded like they had been sucked into an ambush. We were still moving away from the rubber until Major Forde decided to hold our position on a small knoll. There we smoked and listened to the battle develop, anticipating a return to D Company to help. In fact the volume of fire was so massive I could not understand why we were not already on our way.

Eventually the order came. We were returning to assist D Company, whose position was becoming desperate. They were under attack on three sides. The enemy, having completely encircled them, were now between us and D Company's perimeter. Our problem was to get as close to the perimeter as we could before we exposed our presence. We knew that once we were discovered, it would become a dash under fire through the open rubber and maybe through the enemy assault groups to link up with D Company.

We were vastly outnumbered as we cautiously moved towards D Company, who were now about 400–500 metres away. It was teeming rain. Our jungle greens were so drenched they appeared black like the clothes of the enemy. Suddenly, over the radio, Major Smith called for immediate relief or D Company would fall. We stopped moving via our covered creek line approach and turned directly towards the main firing.

Major Forde withdrew his pistol and organised us into assault formation as we moved forward. We had no depth. It was three sections in line with Company HQ about central. We charged towards the desperate D Company somewhere to our front in the rapidly failing light. The tracer bullets painted 'blood shot' lines all around us as the enemy attacked the D Company position. We were assaulting up a low wide spur of ground. My section was on the right. Poor visibility posed a real problem for me. It was extremely difficult to watch for enemy groups and at the same time maintain a physical link with the fast-moving sections to our left.

As we crossed a wire fence line on our route, A Company appeared from the north mounted in armoured personnel carriers (APCs). They mistook us for assaulting enemy and began firing on us. The section beside mine took casualties – all of whom remained on duty. One was a machine gunner struck three times with bullets.

Somewhere here, B Company changed direction without my section! We did not know and so continued away from the remainder of our company who had turned north-east. My section continued moving east. The surrounding noises and poor visibility made the task of knowing which way to go near impossible. I halted and secured my section to do a quick appreciation. Bodies were now evident throughout the rubber – as some light got in through the large holes in the rubber canopy caused by our pounding artillery. We all had eyes like mad cats – trying to see without being seen. It looked like we would have to get through the night as a lone section, until I heard my name called out to our left.

Soon after, an APC section picked my section up and dropped us a couple of hundred metres to the north just short of D Company – and amongst the rest of my platoon. There was no time for explanations. Everything was still at a desperate pace. The firing was shifting further to the east as A Company pushed the enemy away from the crippled D Company and we set about establishing a new defensive perimeter around the Delta Company survivors. As I received my brief orders for the defence from John O'Halloran, a sniper's bullet struck a D Company machine gunner nearby. He fell over his gun like a shot kangaroo. Someone attended him. I raced back to the boys with fresh instructions.

The enemy mortars began falling 50 metres in front of us. We were expecting an attack. I ordered my section to dig shellscrapes. We had just *one* entrenching tool and our bayonets. God knows why no attack came. The mortars stopped. APC motors could be heard to our east and I figured that A Company with the APCs had pushed the enemy off. Sporadic firing still occurred well into the night from various directions – but mainly towards the east. Behind us the wounded were being collected by D Company. Burning cigarettes could be seen and the voices of many exhausted men could be heard chattering like excited monkeys.

I have no idea what time we moved from the battle site, but eventually B Company got orders to secure an LZ [landing zone] 400–500 metres away so the seriously wounded could be lifted out. An APC ambulance was set up for the injured, who would stay in the field until the next day. We moved in pitch darkness with compasses tied to our backs for aids. We held on to the man in front. It was a test of patience and nerves, stepping over fallen trees and bodies, expecting at any time to cop a burst of fire from the ground. After we had gone several hundred metres, I was called to the OC's position. Major

Forde told me to go alone on a bearing of 80 degrees until I located the CO's party and guide them back into our position. This was the longest 100 metres I have ever walked. On the way I expected to be shot by either a wounded enemy lying on the ground, by the CO's party or by B Company. When I heard the noise of the CO's party and the CO's familiar voice answering my challenge, I almost leapt into his arms with relief. The return to B Company was easy.

By about 0230 hours, we were defending the LZ aid post and the air evacuations had been completed. My section was exhausted – like everyone else. I decided to be part of the first sentry watch, which was interrupted when I woke up with John O'Halloran's rifle butt in my mouth. He was in a rage and threatened to ram the rifle butt up my bum if he ever caught me asleep again. I had never slept on sentry before and never did again in my remaining twenty years service. His rifle butt could so easily have been the enemy's.

At Long Tan, three years after the battle, Australian soldiers, including survivors of the fighting, hold a memorial service for those who were killed.

Next morning, D Company remnants led the battalion assault back over the battleground, closely supported by all of us in case a major contact occurred. The scene was rivetting. There were enemy bodies and absolute devastation everywhere, and the odd Australian body including one man, still alive, found sitting up against a tree.

We then dug graves for two days and buried 265 of the enemy. By then I had been in Vietnam for two months and couldn't help wondering how many more men I would bury in the remaining ten months of my tour.

from *Vietnam Fragments* by Gary McKay

Women at War

Women at War

In World War II, Australian women were involved in the war effort by working in essential services such as farming, industry, transport and hospital services. There were also women who went overseas to fight, and suffered in the front line against German and Japanese forces.

Nancy Wake, an Australian in occupied France, risked her life against German troops and even the dreaded Gestapo, whose Montluçon headquarters she helped to destroy.

Like Vivien Bullwinkel, Sister Betty Jeffrey survived when the ship evacuating Australian Army Nursing Service sisters from Singapore was bombed and sunk by Japanese planes. Betty floated in the sea for many hours until she and her companions were washed ashore. Somehow, Betty also made it through three-and-a-half years of cruel imprisonment under the Japanese.

As a war correspondent, Lorraine Stumm witnessed the terrible results of the dropping of the atomic bomb on Hiroshima on 6 August 1945. This event ended the war but destroyed a city and posed a long-term threat to the future of humankind.

La Maquisarde

Nancy Wake, who held the rank of ensign and spoke French fluently, was parachuted into France on 1 March 1944. Known variously as Gertie, Ducks and Andrée, she helped train the French resistance, the Maquis. With her Maquis comrades, she was involved in pitched battles with German troops and, at one time, destroyed the Gestapo headquarters in the town of

Nancy Wake.

Montluçon. On another occasion, Nancy's group sabotaged a factory producing machine parts vital to the Germans.

Throughout her tour of duty, Nancy radioed vital information back to London and gave details of drop zones for supplies and weapons to the Maquis from the air.

Her courage and bravery are made clear in the following account:

The seven thousand Maquis were being attacked in a determined attempt to wipe them out, by a huge encircling force of twenty-two thousand SS troops. The Germans were being supported by artillery, mortars, spotter aircraft and dive bombers. Steadily they closed in from all sides and then began their grey-crawling drive up towards the plateau itself. Confidently the Frenchmen awaited them.

Nancy, Hubert, Gaspard, Laurent and Fournier held a hurried conference at the village of Freydefont on the edge of the plateau. Nancy listened to the steady stream of battle orders that were dispatched to all points around the perimeter – listened to them and memorised them. Only Gaspard's orders displeased her. He and his men, he declared, would fight to the death.

Nancy knew that it was not the task of any of them to fight to the death. To fight, yes: but only fight to fight another day. There was a long war ahead of them yet and if all Gaspard's men died, the group couldn't possibly execute all the future tasks that would be assigned to them by London to hamper the Germans *after* D-Day, in the battles that had been planned to secure the liberation of both France and Europe.

'We'll get out tonight under cover of darkness,' each leader agreed, except Gaspard. Nothing Nancy could say would alter his decision. Furiously she went and found Denis.

'Got through to London yet, Den?'

'Yep, Gertie. They've given me a time to come back on the air. They'll be ready for me an hour from now.'

'Well, when you get through, tell them about this attack: tell them we're going to try to get away tonight: cancel today's parachutage and ask our people to *order* Gaspard to evacuate tonight. The idiot wants to stay here and fight it out.'

Carefully Denis began coding the long message. So far it had been a hellish morning. First of all the dawn flight from Chaudes-Aigues; then tapping furiously at his set for over an hour trying to attract London's attention at a time when London, not expecting him, wouldn't listen to his unscheduled transmission; now, less than fifty minutes in which to prepare all his message and start transmitting again. Shells began to crash down into the village. Nancy looked across at him and smiled.

'Gertie,' he muttered absently, 'I'm terrified.' But he kept on coding. Nancy kissed him affectionately from behind his chair. 'I'll go and collect last night's containers and see how the boys are doing,' she said.

First she drove alone to the scene of the previous night's parachutage. They had not had time to unpack any of the containers then. Now, with a battle on, all these supplies would be needed.

Single-handed she opened every container and loaded its contents on to a truck. For hours she worked, ignoring the occasional mortar bombs that exploded on the field, completely occupied with the physical effort of opening containers, lifting out their grease-packed arms, carrying them to her truck and loading them. But at last it was done.

She then drove to all the fortified vantage points on the plateau and at each one she found the Maquis blazing away happily and effectively. Wherever they were needed, she distributed more weapons or ammunition. For all their vast superiority in numbers and arms, she noted, the Germans were being pinned down and suffering heavy casualties among the mountain-side's volcanic rocks. Bazooka, when she met him, was furious that she travelled alone, but she told him to stay where he was.

'Keep your eye on their fire,' she told him. 'Make sure they aim low.'

'OK, OK,' he growled. 'But tonight when we pull out, I'm gonna make sure there's someone to look after you.'

'Bazooka,' she mocked, though secretly touched by his chivalry, 'I didn't know you cared!'

'Bah,' he shouted after her, 'scram!'

She continued her drive and noticed, a little absent-mindedly, that the shelling was becoming heavier. An observation plane circled maliciously around her car and directed artillery fire which pursued her into the village. The house trembled under a barrage of explosions as she entered it.

'Did you get through?' she asked Denis. He nodded.

'Parachutage cancelled?'

'It's all done, Gertie. Don't like this shelling much.'

'Why don't you get outside?'

'Waiting for the message about Gaspard.'

'Oh, yes. The idiot still says he won't budge. Well, there's nothing we can do till London comes through. I think I'll have forty winks.'

'In *this* lot, Ducks?'

'I could sleep anywhere,' she replied. 'Anyway, there's nothing else I can do. I might as well rest.' Retiring to her bed, with shells pounding the whole village, she took off her revolvers and her boots, loosened the belt on her trousers and went to sleep.

A frantic Fournier woke her up a little later.

'Andrée,' he shouted, 'you must not lie here. Already the house has been hit.'

'The Germans are still being held, aren't they?' she demanded.

'Yes.'

'Then I can sleep.' Again he shook her.

'You must not sleep here,' he persisted. Complaining bitterly she got up, put on her boots, did up her belt, collected her carbine, Sten gun and revolvers and walked outside. A shell exploded in the street and splinters of stone smacked against the wall behind her.

'Much worse out here,' she grumbled and dashed across the road. She found a convenient patch of cool shade under a tree and lay down. It was a fine hot day on the plateau.

'I will be here if anyone wants me,' she told her companion. Then she went to sleep again.

She was woken next time with the news that London had sent through a personal message for Gaspard. It ordered peremptorily that he evacuate under cover of darkness with the rest of the Maquis, and it was alleged to have been inspired by General König himself, König being the head of Free French Headquarters.

'London says König says Gaspard's got to withdraw with the rest of us,' Denis shouted.

'Thank God for that then.'

'Do you believe König really said it, or do you reckon London made it up?'

'I don't even care, Den. Just you write that message out again and this time *sign* it König.'

Delighted at such an unscrupulous order, Denis obeyed it at once.

Straightaway Nancy drove alone and under fire to Gaspard's position. She handed him the message. A grunt was the only indication he gave that it meant anything to him at all: but she now knew him well enough to be confident that this meant that he would do as he was told.

'See you later on,' she shouted in farewell. A small village about a hundred kilometres away, and close to Saint Santin, was their rendezvous when and if they escaped the German encirclement. Leaving Gaspard to repel a heavy attack, she drove off along the winding and exposed mountain-top road, heading back towards Fournier's group at 'Fridfront'.

Five planes flew overhead and machine-gunned Gaspard's position. Nancy careered along the difficult road and flung an apprehensive glance back over her shoulder to see where exactly the hated Henschels were. To her horror two of the planes at once broke sharply out of formation and headed wickedly down the road towards her.

There was a vicious clattering behind her, a roar overhead and the dusty spure of machine-gun bullets along the road in front – then both planes whipped away from her. In her rear vision mirror Nancy could see that the back of her car was riddled. She swore volubly in French and felt better.

But it was not yet over. Climbing sharply upwards the planes parted company. One whirled down towards Gaspard again: the second swung around sharply and then hurtled straight back at her car.

The car and the Henschel 126 arrowed towards one another. For one the road was straight and there was no cover. Instinctively, in her terror, Nancy slowed down. The bullets spat like chain-stitching into the road ahead and the burst ended twenty feet from the car's radiator. Her sudden change in speed had spoilt the pilot's aim. As he thundered low above her Nancy caught sight of goggles and helmet and muttered to herself: 'Good God, Old Nick himself.'

Twice more he attacked and twice she slowed and swerved to save herself. And she was still more than two miles from Freydefont, with the Henschel preparing for yet another onslaught, when a young Maquisard flung himself into the roadway and signalled her to halt.

'The village has been evacuated,' he gasped. 'Quick, follow me.'

They flung themselves into a ditch as the plane, chattering unpleasantly, returned. As soon as it had passed, the young Frenchman leapt to his feet and started running.

'Just a minute,' Nancy called after him. Puzzled he halted. She dashed back to the car and wrenched the door open. Already she could hear the snarl of Old Nick's approach as she rummaged along the bullet-torn back seat. Finally, she flung herself back into the ditch. Machine guns chattered: the car exploded in flames and, the second the plane had roared past her, she joined her companion behind a rock.

'Forgot these,' she explained. Proudly she displayed a small saucepan, a jar of face cream, a packet of tea and a red satin cushion. The Frenchman looked at her as if she were mad and then, shrugging, told her that Fournier's group were in the woods some distance away.

For a long time the presence of a Gestapo headquarters in Montluçon had irritated Tardivat. He discussed the matter with Nancy and they decided that life would be pleasanter if the Gestapo were to vanish.

The town was very thoroughly reconnoitred and the movements of its large German garrison carefully noted. Similar attention was paid to the habits of the officers in the Gestapo headquarters.

Finally it was agreed that the best time to deal with the problem was at twenty-five minutes past midday. At that time, invariably (for they were systematic creatures) all the Gestapo gentlemen would be sipping *apéritifs* just prior to taking their lunch at half-past twelve.

At noon, in four cars, Nancy and fourteen others, all dressed in make-shift uniform, drove into the town, a covering party having preceded them into Montluçon and scattered into various 'safe houses', where they had collected an impressive array of Bren and Sten guns.

Precisely at twelve twenty-five, it had been planned, Nancy, Tardivat and their small band of attackers would rush up to the Gestapo headquarters in cars. At the same moment, their cover-party would arrive, to provide any support necessary to their withdrawal after the attack.

The plan worked perfectly. To the second, the entire force was punctual, halting violently at the unguarded rear door of the building.

Nancy leapt out of her car, dashed through the back entrance, ran up the staircase, flung open the first door, deposited her hand grenade inside it and was halfway down the stairs again when it exploded. Every room in the building was similarly treated. Half a minute later they were into their cars and roaring away down the street, their cover-party following in their own vehicles.

Roused by a series of shattering explosions in the middle of the town, the locals came rushing out into the street. And, seeing a convoy of semi-uniformed Allies, they began to cheer and shout:

'*Les Alliés sont arrivés.*'

'My God,' screamed Nancy, 'stop them or soon they'll all be waving Union Jacks! They think we're liberating them!'

Frantically they persuaded the excited inhabitants to return indoors. Then they quit the town. Behind them they left a destroyed headquarters and, in it, thirty-eight dead Germans.

There was a factory producing machine parts vital to the Germans in Gaspard's area. Rather than allow it to contribute even more ball-bearings to Hitler's war effort, the Maquis decided to destroy it.

Contacts on the factory staff gave them all the details of vital installations and working shifts; reconnaissance revealed to them the enemy system of guarding the plant.

There were four gates into the factory – gates in a high wall. Each gate was guarded continuously by two German sentries who patrolled up a short stretch of the wall, each in an opposite direction, and then marched back again to the entrance.

The surrounding country was flat, with low scrub that reached to within ten yards of the wall. That ten yards had been completely cleared.

It was decided that the attack should be made in two waves against each entrance. The first wave was to silence all eight of the German sentries: the second was immediately to enter the factory through the unguarded gates, set its charges and then withdraw. Nancy was put in command of one of the groups in the first wave.

In the darkest part of the night they left their transport and crawled into the scrub. On their bellies they wormed their way forward. In half an hour, undetected, they had reached the cleared strip around the wall. Silently they edged their way down until they lay opposite their gate.

At this stage they must wait till the sentries met, about-turned and had taken their first few steps apart. Then they must run between them, overpower and silence both Germans simultaneously, and then wave off the second team.

Quite still, Nancy and her three men lay and watched. Twice the Germans walked past on their beat, met, turned and walked it again. On the third occasion, four or five paces after they had parted, Nancy gave the signal. Four dark figures sprang across the cleared strip towards the backs of the unsuspecting sentries. They must do their job swiftly, surely and silently. There must be no shots and no shouts to disturb the other gates.

Nancy and her companions were within six feet of their victim and still he seemed unaware of their presence. She was glad of this because it meant they need only knock him unconscious and he would suffer no more than a headache for his misfortune. But then he turned and saw her.

There was no time to think or to hesitate. Like a tiger she sprang and, as his mouth opened to shout, her forearm clamped under his jaw and snapped backwards. The dirty work she had always loathed in her training days had at last become not training but fact. There was a sharp click and the German slumped limply against her. Utterly revolted, she allowed the dead man to slide to the ground. At the same time she heard his colleague thud down. She waved on the demolition team and watched them sprint through the gateway, herself standing sickly against the wall.

She and her men guarded the gate against a surprise attack by the Germans whilst the others laid their bombs and explosives inside. Time after time she found herself wiping her hands on the side of her trousers, trying to remove the taint of violence. Her teeth were clenched so hard that they ached and her throat was dry. Then the demolition squad emerged and the whole party faded off into the night. They were halfway home to their camp when the factory blew up. Gaspard's men were triumphant, but Nancy could still feel only the suddenly lifeless weight of the sentry's body against hers, so that she was glad when she could leave them and return to her room at the château.

from *Nancy Wake* by Peter Fitzsimons

An Australian Army nursing sister

Betty Jeffrey wrote *White Coolies* in which she describes the anguish and torment of being a prisoner of the Japanese and tells how she survived to eventually return to Australia.

The following extract tells of the evacuation by sea of Australian Army Nursing Service sisters, members of the 8th Division AIF, shortly before the fall of Singapore to the victorious Japanese army. However, their ship, the *Vyner Brooke* was bombed and sunk. Betty Jeffrey was with one group of swimmers who drifted apart until she and another girl floated and swam ashore, reaching a Malay village where they were cared for.

They were persuaded to give themselves up to the Japanese and were jailed along with other survivors from the bombing at sea as well as hundred of civilians.

The last survivor to enter the jail was Sister Vivian Bullwinkel. She was the only one left alive after Japanese troops massacred 22 Australian Army Nurses in the surf.

Singapore seemed to be ablaze. There were fires burning everywhere behind and around us, and on the wharf hundreds of people trying to get away, long queues of civilian men and women, and a long grey line – us. Masts of sunken ships were sticking out of the water, but no ships were in sight other than forlorn-looking barges.

As we walked along the wharf we noticed that dozens of beautiful cars had been dumped in the water; some were smashed on top

A Singapore street showing bomb damage after a Japanese air attack.

of each other, others were visible only by a wheel or a small part of the engine sticking out of the water. Cars during the last week in Singapore were literally given away as people evacuated; these obviously were scuttled to prevent the Japanese from using them.

While we waited for our ships another air raid started. This time the ack-ack guns were alongside us – terribly noisy things which made the tin roofs of buildings near by rattle and rumble.

At last we were on the move – into a tug which took us down harbour to a small, sinister-looking dark-grey ship, *Vyner Brooke*, flying a naval flag – a white ensign, I think. Before the war she had been privately owned by Sir Charles Vyner Brooke, Rajah of Sarawak.

Much to my relief, we were told to live on the top deck – I loathe cabins and ships' insides! – and after a 'meal' of dry biscuits and bully-beef we were under way, just as darkness set in. It was a never-to-be-forgotten scene – huge fires were burning along the whole front of Singapore and the black smoke billowed higher and higher far behind the town.

We soon settled down to sleep on the decks with our coats over us and gas respirators for pillows. During the night at sea guns fired from ships and searchlights flashed; we must have been on the outskirts of a small naval battle. Next morning we learnt that we had lost our convoy during the night and got lost in the minefields – thank Heaven we didn't know that at the time!

This day, significantly, was Friday, 13 February. We spent it keeping our fingers crossed and hiding behind islands, stopping all the time. We all kept wishing we could get on with the journey we were supposed to be making towards Java. And the noise of battle rolled not so far away.

That night we anchored again. Progress was so slow that by 2pm next day we had travelled only 160 miles from Singapore. It seemed so futile. If we were evacuating Singapore, why spend days and nights anchoring alongside the most inviting beaches?

How Pat Blake and I longed for a swim as we stood leaning on the deck rail! We did not know just what a long one was in store for us before the day was out.

As food was short we decided not to have lunch, but to rest instead. At 2pm we were wakened by the ships' siren from the first decent sleep we had had for at least a week. Aircraft overhead. No doubting whose – those horrible red spots told the story. We had to don lifebelts, tin hats, etc., go down deck and lie on the floor of the lounge (right under the bridge) and wait, while the six planes collected themselves into formations of three and proceeded to bomb us.

We had a view – too horribly clear – of it all. First time they missed, but she was a very small ship and the near misses made her rattle. She zigzagged just in the same way as a ship we had seen being attacked off the Malacca Swimming Club two months before. On that occasion the ship was not hit.

I felt certain that the bombs would miss us, too. We were able to relax a little while the planes gathered themselves together to try again, but it was nerve-racking, really, waiting. And it was most uncomfortable on the floor. There were about two hundred people on board, far too many for so small a ship, which didn't leave much room for my long legs, and I always seemed to have a small child's feet under my tummy.

The poor little kid was wonderfully brave. She didn't utter a sound. Her mother had four small children with her and she calmly prayed aloud – the Lord's Prayer. Poor soul, if anyone needed help she did.

Back came the planes . . . and this time we were just about lifted out of the water. The little ship shuddered and rattled. There was a terrific bang, and after that she was still. No more zigzagging. A bomb hit the bridge. Another went straight down the funnel. For a minute the place was blacked out. We were told by an officer to 'stay put', so, moving Hazel's foot to another part of my tummy, I chatted with Sister Ennis about 'near misses'.

Down the planes came again, and what a crash! It felt as if the bomb had landed right in the room with us. Then shattering glass, tons of it, smoke, and the sounds of crashing walls.

We had been given instructions that morning on what the drill was to be if we were bombed or torpedoed. Different jobs were allotted to each nurse. Now everyone hurried about the decks doing the task assigned to her.

We were all carrying morphia, field-dressings, and extra dressings we had made on board. Sister Ennis and I made a bee-line for the bridge, being the last down into the lounge. Taking a child each with us, we were first out. We left the children with an Englishwoman and dashed towards the bridge, only to find it was an unregonisable mess and burning fiercely. I grabbed a Malay sailor and put my inadequate field-dressing on the worst part of burns on his leg. It was an emergency dressing I had brought all the way from Melbourne and carried around Malaya for nine months!

Even this critical time had its lighter moments. During the scramble to get up on deck and top the lifeboat stations a woman's high-pitched voice called out above the din, 'Everybody stand still!' It had an amazing effect. Immediately there was dead silence. Everybody stood unmoving. Then the same voice came again, 'My husband has dropped his glasses.' This eased the situation and there were gales of laughter – but the glasses were not found.

We had been told to see that every civilian person was off the ship before leaving it ourselves. Believe me, we didn't waste time getting them overboard! Nobody was anxious to linger on a burning and rapidly sinking ship.

But the planes had not finished with us. Over they came again and machine-gunned the deck and all the lifeboats – rather effectively. The ropes holding the three lifeboats on our side were severed. Two dropped into the sea. One filled and sank, the other turned upside down and floated away. The third was already manned by two Malay sailors and I'm sure they never anticipated such a quick trip down. I couldn't help laughing at the expressions on their faces as they hit the water and found that their boat had filled almost immediately and left them.

Beth Cuthbertson searched the ship when it was at a very odd angle to make sure all wounded people had been taken off and that nobody remained, while other nurses were busy getting people into the sea.

At this stage there were quite a few people in the water – including the ack-ack crew, who had been blown there with the first bombs – and the ship was listing heavily to starboard. The oldest people, the wounded, Matron Drummond and some of our girls with all the first-aid equipment, were put into the remaining lifeboats on the starboard side and lowered into the sea. Two boats got away safely. Greatcoats and rugs were thrown down into them and with bright calls of 'See you later!', they rowed away. The last I saw of them, some sisters were frantically bailing out water with their steel helmets.

The third boat was caught by the ship when she started to roll on her side and so had to be evacuated very smartly.

Matron Paschke set a superb example to us all by the calm way in which she organised the evacuation of the ship. As the Australian sisters went over the side, she said, 'We'll all meet on the shore, girls, and get teed up again.'

It was our turn. 'Take off your shoes and get over the side as quickly as you can!' came the order. Off came our shoes – I'll never do that again; I am still shoeless – and we all got busy getting over.

One sister thought the order silly. 'I'll drown anyway, as I can't swim' was her comment as she went over in her shoes. Sixteen hours later she landed – in her shoes, and she still has them.

It was wonderful to see the way those girls jumped over or crawled down rope ladders into the sea. They made no more fuss than if they had been jumping into the swimming pool at Malacca.

Land was just visible, a big hill jutting up out of the sea about ten miles away.

I had been so busy helping people over the side that I had to go in a very big hurry myself. Couldn't find a rope ladder so tried to be Tarzan and slip down a rope. Result, terribly burnt fingers, all skin missing from six fingers and both palms of my hands, they seemed quite raw. I landed with an awful thud and my tin hat landed on top of me.

What a glorious sensation! The coolness of the water was marvellous after the heat of the ship. We all swam away from her and grabbed anything that floated and hung on to it in small groups. We hopelessly watched the *Vyner Brooke* take her last roll and disappear under the waves. I looked at my watch – twenty to three. (Most of our watches are still twenty to three.) Then up came oil – that awful, horrible oil, ugh!

I was swimming from group to group looking for Matron Paschke, who that very morning had jokingly asked me to help her swim for it if we had to go over the side. Nobody had seen her leave the ship, so I went on searching wherever I saw groups of girls in grey uniform. I met Win Davis and Pat Gunther clinging to an upturned canvas stretcher and stayed with them for a while, then went on again through that revolting oil when I saw a raft packed with people and more grey uniforms. There was Matron, clinging to this crowded thing. She was terribly pleased with herself for having kept afloat for three hours, and as she was no swimmer I quite agreed with her. Never have I met such an amazing spirit in any person.

On this raft were two Malay sailors, one a bit burnt, who were ineffectively trying to paddle the thing, but had no idea how. Sister Ennis was holding two small children, a Chinese boy aged four and a little English girl about three years of age. There were four or five civilian women and Sisters Harper, Trennery and McDonald from the 13th AGH, Sister Dorsch from the 2/4th CCS, and Matron Paschke and Sisters Ennis, Clarke and myself from the 2/10th AGH. There seemed no hope of being picked up, so we tried to organise things a little better. Our oars were two small pieces of wood from a packing case and nobody seemed to be able to use them to effect, so more rearranging was done. Those who were able hung on to the sides of the raft, those who were hurt or ill sat on it, while Matron, Iole Harper and I rowed all night long in turn. Iole was wonderful – when not rowing she would get off, swim all around everybody, and collect those who got tired of hanging on, making them use their feet properly to assist in pushing the thing along.

We seemed to pass, or be passed by, many of the sisters in small groups on wreckage or rafts. Everybody appeared to be gradually making slow progress towards the shore, and every one of us felt quite sure she would eventually get in.

The last thing we saw before night fell was the smoke from at least five ships on the horizon and we thought we were saved. Surely this was the British navy? Later on we saw motor-boats searching for people in the darkness; we shouted to them, but they missed us. We eventually came in close to a long pier, but were carried out to sea again. We saw a fire on the shore and knew the lifeboats had made it, so we paddled furiously to get there. We gradually got nearer and nearer and saw the girls, even heard them talking, but they could neither hear nor see us because of a storm, which took us out to sea again. We tried again; it was a lighthouse this time, but once more we missed it by a narrow margin. We seemed helpless against those vile currents. A ship's officer floated past us sitting on a piece of wreckage; he told us where to go when we landed and wished us luck. We didn't see him again.

When daylight came we were all very tired and just as far out to sea as we were when bombed, but miles farther down the coast; beaches had disappeared and all we could see was a distant line of tree-tops and what looked like jungle. Behind us were about fifteen ships, some of them firing guns towards Muntok.

As we were not getting anywhere and the load was far too heavy, the two Malays, Iole Harper and I left the raft to swim alongside and so lighten the load. My hands were badly cut about now and too swollen to even cling to the ropes, also we were too tired to row any longer. Two other sisters took over and at last we made progress. We were all coming in well, we four swimming alongside and keeping up a bright conversation about what we'd do and drink when we got in – then suddenly the raft was once more caught in a current which missed us and carried them swiftly out to sea. They called to us, but we didn't have a hope of getting back to it; they were travelling too fast for us to catch them. And so we were left there.

We didn't see Matron Paschke and those sisters again. They were wonderful.

from *White Coolies* by Betty Jeffrey

The war correspondent

On 6 August 1945 an American bomber dropped the first atomic bomb on the Japanese city of Hiroshima totally destroying the city and immediately killing over 70,000 people. Many more later died from sicknesses spread from the radioactive fallout of the huge mushroom cloud that rose over the ruins.

Lorraine Stumm, a newspaper reporter in Singapore was another to escape from the city just before the Japanese captured it. She then became an Australian war correspondent covering the Pacific area for the London *Daily Mirror*. Although it was a journalistic scoop for her professionally, Lorraine was assigned the unenviable task of viewing the after effects of the atomic bomb on Hiroshima, and, later, the condition of the first known survivor, a Roman Catholic priest named Father Kleinsorge who spoke of his experiences both during the explosion and afterwards wandering around the devastated city.

Appropriately, Lorraine would later compile her war memories under the title *I Saw Too Much*:

I was the first Australian woman to see the devastation of Hiroshima after the dropping of the atomic bomb on 6 August 1945. I and a party of journalists were given permission to fly over Hiroshima six weeks after the bomb was dropped.

I will never forget what it was like. I had expected the rubble and the devastation, but nothing prepared me for the piles of bodies, clearly recognisable, and the bitter desolation of a once prosperous community.

The usual journalist's banter in the aircraft stopped as we neared the city. We were all so silent. This continued, even when the plane touched down. No one said a word.

A few days later I learned through a former professor at Tokyo University, George Caiger, who had returned home before the war's outbreak to become an Australian intelligence officer, that the first known survivor of Hiroshima, a Lutheran priest, could be found in a little hospital, eight miles out of Tokyo.

With Lachie Macdonald of London's *Daily Mail*, I scooped the

The ruins of Hiroshima caused by the world's first atomic bomb attack.

world with the story of Father Kleinsorge, the first known survivor of the atomic blast.

This is what I cabled to the *Daily Mirror* in London on 30 September 1945:

> One of the few victims of the first atomic bombing at Hiroshima, who is now recovering from his wounds received on August 6, told me what an atomic bomb impact is like. He is Father William Kleinsorge, a 39-year-old Jesuit priest from the Roman Catholic Church in Hiroshima. Emaciated, six foot, the father is recovering at Tokyo's Siebo Beoyan Hospital in the Western District. This was formerly a foreign maternity and general hospital.
>
> He is still weak and tremulous after three weeks of hospitalisation and constant care from mother directress, Mother Mary Haas, an English nun from Newport who has been superintendent and medical officer of this hospital for 14 years. Mother Haas is a fully qualified doctor.
>
> Father Kleinsorge described walking barefoot through devastated Hiroshima for hours after the bombing. 'I was in a presbytery 500 metres from where the bomb hit,' he said. 'I was lying on my bed on the second floor of the house, which was a strongly built European-style wooden building, erected by one of the brothers.
>
> 'An air raid alarm was lifted at 10 minutes to eight in the morning. The bomb fell at 8.15. I was wearing a shirt and shorts and I was reading a book in my attic room which had a very small window. I remember the flash. I didn't think it was a bomb because the alarm had been lifted.
>
> 'I don't remember hearing any explosion or how I came from the second floor to the ground floor, but when I did, I found that our house was the only one left standing as far as I could see. It was black as night. Six people, four brother priests, one student and one servant collected together and we dug out the wife and daughter of the caretaker from under the

wreckage. Fires had broken out all over Hiroshima. They raged at us from every direction.

'We all had small splinter-like wounds all over our bodies, but only one priest was seriously injured. We carried him and walked over the shattered roofs of houses to a park where we took shelter from the fires. That saved our lives.

'In the afternoon after the bombing, a whirlwind sprang up which made the sky pitch black and drove many people into the river, where they drowned. We saw the wife of the director of the Methodist Girls' College swept into the river with her daughter. The daughter was saved, but the mother was lost.

'People were wandering about with their whole faces one large blister from the searing effect of the bomb. Only 40 out of 600 school girls at the Methodist College survived. Three hundred little girls at the government school were killed instantly. Thousands of young soldiers in training at barracks were slaughtered. I walked for two hours and only saw 200 people alive.

'The Japanese shrugged and said, "There is no help [remedy] for it." I heard no hatred or hostility towards the Allies, although we all realised that this must have been a new and unusually destructive weapon.'

After four hours, Father Kleinsorge realised that his shoes had been blown from his feet and he found another pair. After the bombing he said he saw 30 Japanese soldiers, remnants of the garrison at Hiroshima, most of whom had their eyes burnt out.

Two days after the bombing Japanese military forces from outside entered Hiroshima and collected two hundred thousand bodies for cremation. In addition to those killed outright, many more died through lack of medical attention, as every hospital had been destroyed. Meanwhile the father and his party had been subsisting on rations retrieved from their air raid shelter, which was undamaged.

Four weeks after the bombing, Father Kleinsorge left

Hiroshima for Kobe where he was hospitalised with high fever and inflamed wounds. The Japanese were afraid to give him blood transfusions which he needed desperately, because they had discovered that Hiroshima bomb victims bled to death, if even a slight incision was made by a hypodermic needle. A blood count revealed that his white blood corpuscles were down to the dangerous level of 1300. He was brought to Siebo Beoyan Hospital where Mother Haas devoted all her energy and medical skill to saving his life.

'When he was brought in he swayed and tottered like a drunken man,' she said. 'His face was absolutely bloodless. I am convinced that if the victims stay in Hiroshima they will never recover.'

Father Kleinsorge, who celebrated his 39th birthday with his first press interview, had been in Japan for the past 10 years. He intends to remain and hopes to return to help reconstruct Hiroshima. His mother and three sisters live in Cologne in Germany, but he has not had word of them since 19 July 1944 and he fears that they are all dead.

Father Kleinsorge is the first Hiroshima bomb victim to give an exhaustive account of the bombing and medical treatment to the commission of the US Army and British medical officers now visiting Hiroshima and Nagasaski to investigate the effects of radio activity.

One of the doctors told me, 'Kleinsorge's symptoms are all the usual ones of radio-activation, but he is making a complete recovery and should suffer no after effects.'

History was to show that this was a very optimistic post-bomb appraisal.

from *I Saw Too Much* by Lorraine Stumm

The War Photographers – Images of War

The War Photographers – Images of War

It is not uncommon for war photographers and correspondents to be killed in action and this was especially so in World War II. Recording a war at first hand is a dangerous profession. Famous cameramen Damien Parer and Neil Davis met their death as they filmed under fire.

Some of the images of Parer, Davis and Frank Hurley have achieved icon status. All three of these photographers often risked their lives to capture on film the experiences of front-line troops. Damien Parer explained what he thought a good photograph should be: 'When I take pictures of men at the front, I like pictures of them as they are. Men who have been weeks in the jungle, flat on their bellies, waiting for a chance to shoot a Jap before he snipes at them, do not feel like smiling when asked to.' The following unforgettable images of Hurley, Parer and Davis show the terrible reality of war.

Frank Hurley – photographer of two wars

Frank Hurley was born in Glebe, Sydney, in 1895. At fifteen he bought his first camera and within a year had become an expert photographer. His first major opportunity came when Douglas Mawson appointed him official photographer to Australia's first Antarctic expedition.

In mid 1917, still in his early twenties, Hurley became official photographer to the Australian Imperial Forces and soon established himself as one of the finest photographers of World War I with his dramatic scenes of Ypres and the Australian Light Horse in Palestine in 1918. As his dairies often reveal, he constantly risked his life to achieve artistic perfection. 'Our

Frank Hurley in September 1917 standing besides a large German shell which had failed to explode on the Pozieres Road in France.

own position now was highly hazardous,' he wrote on 22 February 1918, in Jericho. 'We dodged from cover to cover amongst the sparse and stunted sage bush, evading the fusillade of rifle fire and sniping at 400 yards range.' Over twenty years later, he was back in the desert in the midst of danger with the Rats of Tobruk and at the Battle of Alamein, photographing 'the infantry advancing through the dust at dawn, tanks rumbling with them'.

Frank Hurley died in bed on 16 January 1962. He had lived life to the full. His doctor's words, 'The old warrior is gone!', provided a fitting tribute to Hurley's adventurous life.

The battle for Menin Road

The Menin Road led out of the ruined city of Ypres to the town of Menin 20 kilometres away, which was under German occupation. The road itself was ravaged by the constant shelling by German guns. In the following extract Frank Hurley conveys the horror of the endless slaughter of men and animals on the Menin Road in 1917:

20 September: I was up at 3.00am and by 4.00am we were on our way to Dranoutre where we arrived at 5.00am. It was necessary that we should make an early start, as the Boche generally sends over a barrage on the Menin Road about 7.30am which holds up all traffic and makes it impossible to proceed by that route.

At sunrise we were in Ypres. I never saw ruins look so majestic or imposing as when silhouetted against the beautiful sunrise this morning. We visited Lille Gate, particularly beautiful in the calmness of the new day, with the torn trees and ruins reflected in the placid mirror-like moat.

Of course everything is so blasted and shelled, that had one not known that before him lay Ypres, it would have been mistaken for a giant brick dump.

We took the car via the Menin Gate, and left it a little out of Ypres, as the road was being shelled and unsafe for transport. The way had been shelled the previous night and was littered with broken limbers and horses. In the centre lay a motor lorry almost cut in halves and burnt by a shell hit.

Australian wounded on the Menin Road, near Birr Cross Road on 20 September 1917

The Menin Road is one of the, if not *the*, most ghastly approach on the whole front. Accretions of broken limbers, materials and munitions lay in piles on either side, giving the road the appearance of running through a cutting.

Any time of the day it may be shelled and it is absolutely impossible, owing to the congested traffic, for the Boche to avoid getting a coup with each shell.

The Menin Road is like passing through the Valley of Death, for one never knows when a shell will lob in front of him. It is the most gruesome shambles I have ever seen, with the exception of the South Georgia Whaling Stations, but here it is terrible for the dead things are men and horses.

from *Hurley at War: The Photography and Diaries of Frank Hurley in Two World Wars*

Through the entrance of Chateau Wood to the battlefield of Ypres.

Chateau Wood

The beautiful avenue of trees at the entrance to Chateau Wood had been reduced to a place of gloom and death by late 1917.

28 October: The day was foggy so that the Boche balloon observation was bad. Under these conditions the shells are on registered and favourite points and also does a considerable amount of area firing. We succeeded in reaching the infamous Chateau Wood without incident, when a fleet of 14 Taubs and Gothas came over us. They dropped their bombs vigorously a few hundred yards away and peppered the roads with machine-gun fire.

We took refuge close beside a big tree stump and escaped the machine-gun fire, the bullets pelting a few yards off. Our safety was but momentary, however, for a 5.9 shell lobbed only 15 paces off and showered us with mud – a narrow squeak.

Chateau Wood must have been a glorious spot with its lake on one side and heavily foliaged timber. It is now so lonely and desolate that one feels as if death alone dwelt there. The trees are smashed and splintered and only stumps; the ground is heaved up into wave-like ridges with shelling and here and there along the lonely duckboard track lies a stricken soldier.

One does not linger more than necessary in this place over which hangs the pall of gloom and death. Guns boom all around, yet everyone dodges the awful loneliness and hazards of Chateau Wood.

from *Hurley at War: The Photography and Diaries of Frank Hurley in Two World Wars*

Victory at El Alamein

Hurley's final war photos were taken at the Battle of El Alamein. It was here that Montgomery's Eighth Army defeated Rommel's Afrika Korps. The battle began on 23 October 1942 and by 4 November, Allied armour had broken through the German positions.

The Australian 9th Division was heavily involved in the twelve days of fighting in the decisive Battle of El Alamein. This was the Allies' first major victory over the Germans.

Jubilant Australian soldiers after the battle of El Alamein in October wearing captured German helmets and giving a 'Heil Hitler' salute in mockery of the defeated German army.

Damien Parer – front-line cameraman

During World War II, Damien Parer had become Australia's best known war photographer. His documentary *Kokoda Front Line*, which was filmed in 1942, was the first Australian film to win an Academy Award.

Damien Parer was born in Malvern, Victoria, in 1912. While growing up he developed a passion for photography, and after leaving school became a portrait photographer. In 1933 he began working with the renowned Australian film director Charles Chauvel. In the film *Forty Thousand Horsemen*, Parer impressed Chauvel with his outstanding camerawork while filming the famous cavalry charge at Beersheba.

When World War II began, he became the official movie photographer to the AIF and was sent to the Middle East and Greece. His reputation as a film-maker grew as his startling images showed the unpleasant reality of war in the front line of battle. He was next assigned to document the Australian defence of Port Moresby on the Kokoda Trail. Parer's graphic shots of the retreating troops along the muddy, rain-sodden track showed their courage and endurance in the face of death.

On 17 September 1944, Damien Parer's career as a front-line cameraman came to a sudden end, when he was killed in action while filming a landing of US marines on the Pacific island of Peleliu.

Damien Parer.

The cameraman looks at the digger

In the following article, written in 1943, Parer describes the emotions and privations of the digger in New Guinea. He also reflects on the mateship that enabled the Australian troops to inflict the first major defeat on the Japanese, and explains his philosophy of being a cameraman at war.

It is difficult for the average man to understand the job the front-line infantryman is doing up north, and his attitude to it. Even troops working just behind the lines, who frequently get bombed and strafed and shelled, sometimes don't realise the extraordinary hardships besetting the forward sections. They must be seen to be realised.

What is our soldier thinking when he is in the line? If he has been fighting and is tired, his mind dwells on the past or on the future, and his main topics of conversation are when the hell does he get leave, and what he will do when he gets it; the battles in which he has recently fought; the bloody heartbreaking hills; the mail from home, and, of course, that ever-green subject, the tucker.

His whole existence is bound up with his cobbers. His great contact with the outside world are the letters he receives – they are his only touch with home. The family, wife, or girl friend are beauties beyond reach. These men are hard with others who don't measure up to their own Spartan standards. Death is not always their greatest sadness.

Monotony is a great enemy. It is not the monotony that comes to troops who are out of danger areas, the monotony of food and living conditions. It is the monotony of living in the perpetual mud, in continual discomfort. It's hard to tell sometimes whether their shirts and trousers are wet through with rain or sweat. There are long nights of fitful sleep in the wet. The long monotonous strain of waiting day after day, and night after night to fight an unseen enemy in this jungle.

Can you imagine being on guard on a dark night with the Japs a stone's throw away? When every leaf rustling may be a Jap? May prelude a sudden devilish, screaming attack? In any sudden danger I don't think that self-preservation is his first thought. The AIF man's code is to be with this cobbers, to fight beside them and never to let them down. If he is wounded or sick and has to leave his unit, he is like a lost man till he rejoins it.

How can we understand the aching emptiness when a cobber is killed beside him? I have seen a man badly hit; he is lying in a small depression on the damp ground out of the line of enemy fire. The Medical Orderly hastily applies the first field dressing to plug those nasty wounds. Above is an occasional crack of a rifle, and short bursts of machine-gun fire. A cigarette is lit and put between his lips. His face is a blood-drained yellow, but there's no sign of giving-in here. There is a hard-uttered joke about it being a 'Homer' this time. And then there is the untold agony of being moved from the ground to the stretcher. Yes, a half-suppressed cry breaks from him but he smothers it. I had to turn away and hide the tears that came to my eyes but they were tears of pride.

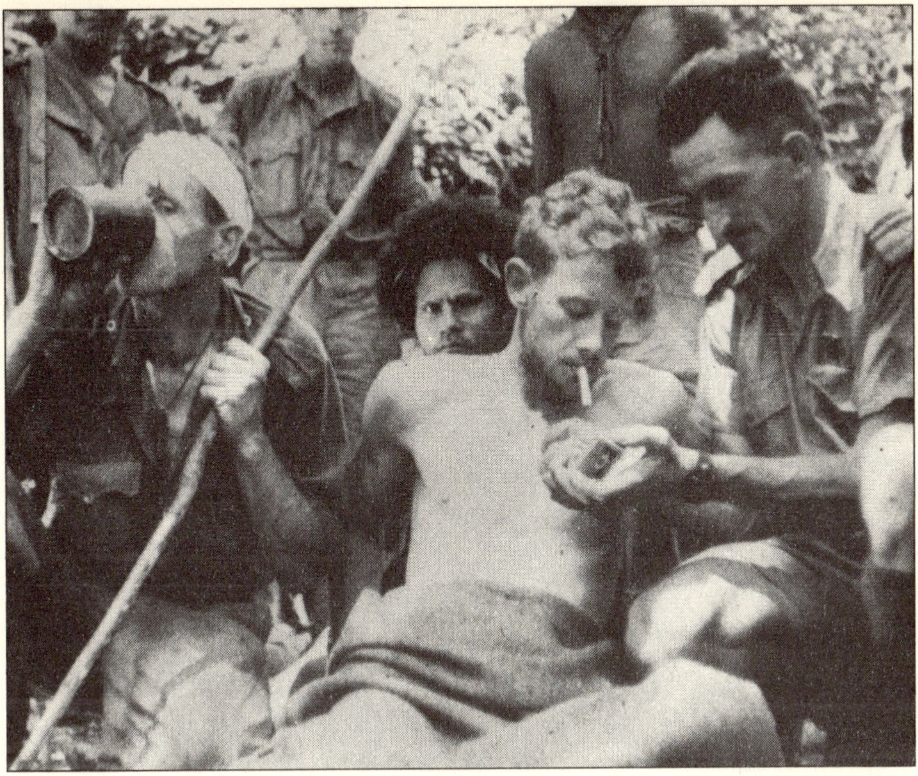

Wounded Australian soldier, Lieutenant Valentine Gardner, has his cigarette lit by Salvation Army Chaplain, Albert Moore, in the still from *Kokoda Front Line.*

But they go on, day after day, until it seems endless. The time comes when, with sheer weariness, all the talk and back-chat are finished. They are beyond that. Silent, they go on; they are beyond all normal thinking, they are not normal. They have almost reached the stage of animals. Animals? You ask the Japs – they know.

The Jap is a fanatic with subnormal, animal cunning, but our infantry has been more than a match for him. The Digger asks no beg-pardons. He has adapted himself from the heavy-equipment desert war with the Germans to this individual war in the jungle, but he had to learn the hard and bloody way. He has outfought the Jap with the same spirit as he held the Hun at Tobruk, and smashed him at Alamein. The Jap can commit his Hari-Kari for the Emperor and the Imperial Nipponese Empire, but the Digger has fought, and

Mekong Delta, South Vietnam, 1967. Australian cameraman Neil Davis crossing a river while out on patrol with South Vietnamese troops.

always will fight for his cobbers; for Bluey and Snowy, for Lofty and Stumpy.

The cameraman going in to film these men and their deeds lays aside his superficial outlook of peacetime reporting. In those days he worked for the sensational picture that was considered if it made a good space on the front page or the weekly newsreel. This is now replanted by an approach that is founded in sympathy. Through his lens he sees those intimate, human details that reveal the true story, where the big spectacle alone would give a cold and lifeless report.

So he doesn't film the war as he would a race meeting or a football match. He goes in with the troops, and for a short time, becomes one of them. To some extent he shares their hardships and dangers, and their grim sense of humour. He gains their confidence, and they will eventually take him and his camera as a matter of course. He must be saturated in the atmosphere of this strange world.

He must look at these men with the open-eyed surprise of a child first seeing the world, and comprehend their greatness as they themselves cannot. To them their stirring deeds are commonplace. It is for the cameraman to see these things and record them. As he works, he plans his story, and his film will be pervaded by a sense of honesty and closeness that may be some contribution to the truth of these fine infantrymen.

from *The Cameraman Looks at the Digger* by Damien Parer 1943

The Kokoda Track

Damien Parer introduced his Academy Award–winning film *Kokoda Front Line* with the memorable words: 'Eight days ago I was with our advance troops in the jungle, facing the Japs at Kokoda.' The first two stills from *Kokoda Front Line* and *Road to Kokoda* show the harshness of the terrain and the difficulties of helping the wounded in the retreat along the Trail.

Neil Davis – in the line of fire

Neil Davis was killed in September 1985 in Bangkok when he was caught in the line of fire from a machine gun of a Thai rebel tank. At the time, he was filming an army coup for the American NBS network.

Davis, born in Tasmania in 1934, was one of the world's most famous cameramen for over twenty years. His repute especially lies in his reporting of the Vietnam War, which he covered from a number of perspectives – American, South Vietnamese and Viet Cong. He often accompanied South Vietnamese forces in action and he filmed the war from the other side, when he was permitted to film the Viet Cong in the field. Davis stayed on in Vietnam to the final days, filming the first North Vietnamese tank to break through the gates of the Presidential Palace in Saigon on 30 April 1975. His scoop symbolised the defeat of America.

Combat Footage

In this description, Neil Davis was with a detachment of South Vietnamese marines, who were making a frontal assault against North Vietnamese regular troops across scrubby sandhills.

A Communist hand grenade was thrown and I put my hands up to my face to try and shield my head. When it exploded, it cut my hands about and took a great jagged piece out of the left side of my jaw, but didn't break the bone. It also severed a minor artery somewhere near my temple, which immediately bled a lot. I fell back stunned, with my camera still in my hand, and I must have looked an absolute bloody mess.

At this moment the North Vietnamese decided to try to overrun our position. As I lay there half-reclining, with blood streaming down from my head and hands, a North Vietnamese soldier appeared literally a metre away over a slight rise.

My first reaction was, 'What a fantastic shot!' I looked down to adjust the focus and swing the turret of the camera on to a wide-angle lens. I mean, there was this man coming to kill me, and my first reaction was to get on to the right lens to get this dramatic shot.

As I tried to do so, I saw he was carrying a weapon, and I thought I was almost certainly dead. I'm a left-hander with a rifle, and if he had been too, he would have swung the AK47 just a little and shot me in a second. But he was a right-hander and his rifle was on the side closest to me, and it was pointing away.

All this of course happened in a second. I was going to adjust my camera, and he appeared to sum it up and decided that the quickest thing for him to do – he could see that I appeared to be badly wounded with blood everywhere – was not to shoot me. He would have had to swing around to do that. So he just swung forward and back with the butt of his rifle and smashed it into my forehead, while I was still trying to swing my lens turret around!

Davis lost consciousness for between one and five minutes, recovered in time to film the figure of a South Vietnamese marine dragging a wounded comrade back and correctly assumed that there had been a successful counter-attack. He managed to crawl back to safety and the shot of the marine rescuing his wounded comrade appears in the documentary film *Frontline*.

from *One Crowded Hour* by Tim Bowden

The VCs – For Valour

The VCs – For Valour

The Victoria Cross has become the most important decoration for valour awarded to the forces of the British Commonwealth in the previous 150 years. The royal warrant instituting the VC was signed by Queen Victoria in 1856, its clause 5 stating: 'It is ordained, that the Cross shall only be awarded to those officers or men who have served Us in the presence of the enemy, and shall have performed some single act of valour, or devotion to their country.' And even more importantly, clause 6 declared that 'neither rank nor long service nor wounds nor any other circumstances or condition whatsoever save the merit of conspicuous bravery shall be held to establish a sufficient claim for the honour'.

The decoration was introduced as a result of circumstances related to the Crimean War of 1853–56. At that time, *The Times* condemned the fact that high-ranking officers who had not engaged in battle were identified for official commendation, and the British press in general were concerned that the deeds of the ordinary soldier should be publicly recognised. After debate in the House of Commons and royal consultation, it was decided to create a new decoration for bravery to be named after the Queen – the Victoria Cross. The royal warrant signed by Queen Victoria was made retrospective to 1854, the year that British troops first participated in the Crimean conflict.

Australia's VCs

Ninety-six Australians have received the VC. Six were won during the Boer War, 66 in 1915–19, twenty during World War II and four in the Vietnam War.

Boer War (1899–1902)
Bell, F.W. 1901
Bisdee, J.H. 1900
Howse, N.R. 1900
Maygar, L.C. 1901
Rogers, J. 1901
Wylly, G.G. 1900

World War I (1914–18)
Axford, T.L. 1918
Beatham, R.W. 1918
Birks, F. 1917
Blackburn, A.S. 1916
Borella, A.C. 1918
Brown, W.E. 1918
Buckley, A.H. 1918
Buckley, M.V. 1918
Bugden, P.J. 1917
Burton, A.S. 1915
Carroll, J. 1917
Cartwright, G. 1918
Castleton, C.C. 1916
Cherry, P.H. 1917
Cooke, T. 1916
Currey, W.M. 1918
Dalziel, H. 1918
Dartnell, W.T. 1915
Davey, P. 1918
Dunstan, W. 1915
Dwyer, J.J. 1917
Gaby, A.E. 1918
Gordon, B.S. 1918
Grieve, R.C. 1917
Hall, A.C. 1918
Hamilton, J. 1915
Howell, G.J. 1917
Ingram, G.M. 1918
Inwood, R.R. 1917
Jacka, A. 1915
Jackson, J.W.A. 1916
Jeffries, C.S. 1917
Jensen, J.C. 1917
Joynt, W.D. 1918
Kenny, T.J.B. 1917
Keysor, L.M. 1915
Leak, J. 1916
Lowerson, A.D. 1918
McCarthy, L.D. 1918
McDougall, S.R. 1918
McGee, L. 1917
McNamara, F.H. 1917
Mactier, R. 1918
Maxwell, J. 1918
Moon, R.V. 1917
Murray, H.W. 1917
Newland, J.E. 1917
O'Meara, M. 1916
Peeler, W. 1917
Pope, C. 1917
Ruthven, W. 1918
Ryan, J. 1918
Sadlier, C.W.K. 1918
Shout, A.J. 1915
Statton, P.C. 1918
Storkey, P.V. 1918
Symons, W.J. 1915
Throssell, H.V.H. 1915
Towner, E.T. 1918
Tubb, F.H. 1915
Wark, B.A. 1918

Weathers, L.C. 1918
Whittle, J.W. 1917
Woods, J.P. 1918

North Russian Force (1919)
Pearse, S.G. 1919
Sullivan, A.P. 1919

World War II (1939–45)
Anderson, C.G.W. 1942
Chowne, A. 1945
Cutler, A.R. 1941
Derrick, T.C. 1943
Edmondson, J.H. 1941
Edwards, H.I. 1941
French, J.A. 1942
Gordon, J.H. 1941
Gratwick, P.E. 1942
Gurney, A.S. 1942
Kelliher, R. 1943
Kenna, E. 1945
Kibby, W.H. 1942
Kingsbury, P.S. 1942
Mackey, J.B. 1945
Middleton, R.H. 1942
Newton, W.E. 1943
Partridge, F.J. 1945
Rattey, R.R. 1945
Starcevich, L.T. 1945

Vietnam War (1959–75)
Badcoe, P.J. 1967
Payne, K. 1969
Simpson, R.S. 1969
Wheatley, K.A. 1965

The first Australian VC of World War I

Albert Jacka was the first member of the Australian Infantry Forces to be awarded a Victoria Cross in the Great War. After winning the VC at Gallipoli in May 1915, Jacka went on to win the Military Cross at the Battle of Pozieres the following year, and a bar to the MC at the Battle of Bullecourt in May 1917. His legendary courage and quick thinking in battle conditions are clearly demonstrated in the following account:

Jacka landed at Gallipoli still with the rank of Acting Lance-Corporal. Although keen for further promotion he was circumspect in his diary about his involvement in the action on 19 May. He recounted:

> Great battle at 3am. Turks captured large portion of our trench. D. Coy called into the front line. Lieut. Hamilton shot dead. I lead a section of men and recaptured the trench. I bayoneted two Turks, shot five, took three prisoners and cleared

the whole trench. I held the trench alone for 15 minutes against a heavy attack. Lieut. Crabbe informed me that I would be recommended.

Albert Jacka VC.

For this action Albert Jacka was awarded the Victoria Cross, the highest award for gallantry in action awarded to members of the British Empire. He was 22 years old and it was the first Victoria Cross awarded to Commonwealth forces in the first world war. Although he was probably unaware of it at the time he would be offered the £500 promised to the first VC winner in the Australian troops by an influential Melbourne businessman, John Wren. Wren would even more drastically affect his life after the war.

At the time of the Turkish attack on 19 May, Jacka was standing on a fire-step cut half a metre into the front of the trench he was occupying with ten other men from his platoon. He was on the extreme left of the trench with the communication trench running up behind him. A party of Turks crept up just short of the trench without being observed by the Australians. At 3.30am, the Turks threw eight bombs into the trench which killed three and wounded most of the rest. Jacka, protected by the narrow indentation of his fire-step, was not injured. The Turks jumped into the trench and the Australians, numbed by the ferocity of the attack, fled past Jacka. Jacka chose to remain in his position and by firing into the back wall of the trench stopped the Turks from proceeding any further. Nevertheless, the Turks now held ten metres of the firing line immediately above the edge of Monash Valley. It was a critical portion of the line and had to be recaptured.

The Turks, blocked by Jacka to the north, were unable to move to the south because the trench passed another communication trench along which other members of the battalion were firing warning shots. By now the Australian officer who had been in the trench, Lieut. Boyle, had managed despite being wounded to raise the alarm that the 'Turks are in the trenches'. Hearing this cry, Lieut. W. Hamilton, a Duntroon graduate from D Company, ran forward and made his way into the reserve trench running parallel to and five metres behind the line. He began firing his revolver but was hit in the head by a bullet fired by a Turk from the front trench.

A quarter of an hour passed with Jacka the only man stopping the Turkish advance to the north. Back at battalion headquarters on the rear slope of the position, Maj. Rankine heard a cry 'officer wanted' and detailed Lieut. Crabbe to investigate. As Crabbe crept up the communication trench Jacka shouted 'back out, Turks in there'. Crabbe stopped just to the left of Hamilton whom he described as being 'in a sitting position, his back resting on the wall of the communication trench, dead'. Crabbe called out to ask whether Jacka would charge the Turks if he could get men to back him up. Jacka replied, 'Yes, I want two or three.' Crabbe returned a little later with three volunteers from A Company, Privates Howard, Poliness and De Arango. He recalled asking them, 'Will you charge, it's a tough job, will you back Jacka up?', to which one of them, Poliness, replied, 'It's sink or swim.'

Jacka vaulted across the front trench from the fire-step into the mouth of the communication trench to join the three men. Crabbe's plan was simple in the extreme. The four would attempt to fight their way into the front line from the communication trench. Jacka did not question the order, trench line meant that Jacka was obscured from their view. Moving towards the Turks he left the front trench near the bend and lay out in no-man's-land. Poliness threw two bombs at the Turks from his position and De Arango fired several shots at the wall to make the Turks think they were coming that way. Jacka leapt to his feet and jumped down into the trench. He shot five with his rifle and bayoneted two more. Poliness shot two more attempting to crawl over the parapet and these rolled out of Jacka's reach. Silence now fell on this part of the battlefield. Unsure of what had happened in the trench, Lieut. Crabbe waited for dawn. During this period Jacka held the trench alone.

As dawn broke, Crabbe entered the trench to find it littered with dead Australians and Turks. Despite the fact that two Turks were still alive, Jacka had an unlit cigarette in his mouth and uttered, 'Well I managed to get the beggars, Sir.' Crabbe, in his account, stated that 'his face was flushed by the tremendous excitement he had undergone during the previous hour'. The front line was reoccupied and held by members of the battalion. Jacka spent the next day 'resting' in Monash Valley at the rear of Courtney's Post but was back in the front trench by the late afternoon.

from *Jacka, VC* by Ian Grant

Syria – World War II

Artilleryman Lieutenant Roden Cutler received his VC in the Syrian campaign, for outstanding bravery during a period of eighteen days from 19 June to 6 July 1941. He was fighting with the 7th Division against the Vichy French. His contribution to Australian society after the war was no less impressive. In 1966, Roden Cutler was appointed governor of New South Wales and during his fifteen-year term of office he became known as 'the people's governor'.

The following incident took place at Damour on 6 July 1941, when he was an artillery observation officer attached to the 2/16th Battalion.

Roden Cutler VC.

Roden crouched with the rest and waited for the command to move forward, aware that all he had was an officer's revolver. No one had a spare weapon to donate to him, one of the finest shots in the army. And it was terrifying. The waiting always is.

The sky was alight with gunfire but the first streaks of genuine dawn hadn't yet appeared when the company stood up to loosen its muscles and took off at a run up the north bank of the wadi. Ahead was barbed wire; Roden hung back until it was cut and the men were away again, still running, then he followed with revolver drawn. But the pace was too precipitate. No one saw the machine-gun nest save Roden. Its inhabitants were stirring, as they too had grown used to sleeping through barrages; it was the sound of boots that aroused them. Everybody in the company was ahead of him, everybody was going to be mown down. Waving his revolver, Roden leaped feet first into the nest among the three legionnaires it contained. Confronted by six feet five of steel-helmeted Australian, the Vichy French put their hands in the air and were shepherded outside.

These were French Foreign Legion, the most professional of troops, yet presence of mind on a battlefield is rare, even among professionals. No one tried to overpower Roden, who had spied a second nest. He called out to its occupants to surrender in his atrocious French, whereupon three more men emerged, hands in air.

By now the rear men in the Australian company had noticed what was going on; the six prisoners were disarmed and pushed off to one side. A third and bigger nest opened fire, its crew wide awake. Roden grabbed at a Bren gunner's arm.

'You've got your gun, so give me your Mills bomb,' he said. 'Cover me while I try to get close enough to toss it in.'

As Roden wriggled, prone, towards the nest, the Bren gunner noticed someone moving the machine gun around, and fired a short burst. One bullet went straight through the legionnaire's cheek. That gave Roden time to throw the Mills bomb into the nest, which was a big one built on a zigzag principle; the blast which followed injured no one. The five legionnaires inside had had enough, however, and came out with arms up, a senior NCO in the lead. Even in the midst of so much action, a corner of Roden's mind was busy being amazed at how the pie slices of cheek in the wounded man's face flipped and flapped as he breathed.

There were now eleven prisoners no one knew what to do with. Labouring over his French, Roden told them to walk back to the wadi and give themselves up to the Australians there. They clearly thought that the battle was lost.

Every man going into action carries two things: a water bottle and a field dressing. As the eleven prisoners shuffled off Roden gave his water bottle to the wounded one, for their water was still inside the nest.

But there were more machine gun nests ahead, too many of them too well dug in and positioned to take front on. This was the kind of situation where drawing down artillery fire became a vital necessity. The laggards of the 2/16th Company took refuge inside a small, circular animal pen surrounded by a high stone wall. They had no idea what was going on, whether the assault had succeeded or failed, but it seemed to them that failure was more likely than success. That they were isolated among the enemy. One of them went off to find out what was happening; when he didn't return, another man followed.

There were twelve of them left inside the sheepfold, sure they were surrounded on three sides.

'Look,' said Roden, 'I'm just lumber you have to carry, so I'll take a tack through the bananas and see if I can find my officer and the telephone. Once I call down fire you'll be able to get out.'

The edge of the nearest banana grove was scant yards away; Roden sped to it and ran along its edge. The morning was wearing on, the time about 11am.

He didn't see this machine gun nest, just inside. Nor did he feel the bullet which smashed his right leg apart below the knee. Blood was spraying everywhere! He saw before he felt a thing, spread-eagled on the ground, the enormous gaping wound on full display because he was, like all the Australian troops in Syria, wearing shorts, his socks slipped down around his ankles.

Two men bearing hand-held machine guns came out of the nest and headed towards him – to finish him off, Roden was sure. But then, close enough to observe their victim's condition, they said a few words to each other and returned to the almost invisible nest. No point in wasting a bullet, the *cochon* was nearly dead.

The first thing to do was to stop the bleeding. His field dressing was no use, couldn't hope to plug or cover the hole in his leg, its bones sheared and splintered, flesh mangled. A tourniquet. A tourniquet – *what*? His lanyard! He detached the thick piece of cord connecting the butt of his revolver with his shoulder and wrapped it about his thigh just above the knee, then twisted it until the blood stopped spurting. After that he managed to squirm out of his shirt, tore it into strips, used some of it as a pad and the rest as a bandage.

There was no shade where he lay and the sun seemed to stay at its zenith forever and ever; the heat was intense, his shirt no longer shielding his skin. Thirst raged, but he had given his water bottle away. And the pain! Oh, God Jesus, the *pain*!

Every so often he loosened the tourniquet, understanding that the shattered leg had to have its share of oxygen lest it died. But *he* couldn't die!

The sky whirled, consciousness began to slip away, yet he knew the moment it did he would lose control of the tourniquet; he would bleed to death unknowing. Whatever he did – however he did it – he *had* to stay conscious.

Despair came as the unbelievable, unbearable pain grew even worse; his head turned, his eyes contemplated the revolver. One shot to the temple and it would all be over, this terrible, remorseless, ghastly pain . . . Then he thought of his mother. What would she do if he died? How would she manage if she was cut off from the allotment automatically deducted from his army pay because he was dead? What would happen to Geoff, to Rob, to Doone if he died? His father had died, and think how dreadful that had been. If he died, who was there to look after them?

Darkness fell, the damp chill of night invaded his almost bloodless body. The pain ground on, the gunsmoke reeking the air was gradually dwindling before the eternal mystery of the stars. How long had it been? How long would it go on? He couldn't die, he *couldn't* die!

The machine gun nest was utterly silent; perhaps the men in it had stolen away, though Roden never knew that answer. But suddenly the eleven soldiers from the sheepfold were gathered around him in the night.

They had heard the machine gun fire, heard Roden cry out in a great voice, 'My God, they've got me!'

Someone had actually brought his army greatcoat into battle with him; the men buttoned it and slipped a rifle through each arm, then lifted Roden onto this makeshift stretcher.'

from *Roden Cutler, V.C.* by Colleen McCullough

Bomber pilot – World War II

On 28–29 November 1942, Flight Sergeant Rawdon (Ron) Middleton was piloting a Stirling bomber in a raid on the Fiat works in Turin, during which the plane was hit and he was badly wounded. Enduring terrible pain, Middleton managed to fly the bomber back to the English coast and allow five of his crew to parachute to safety. Ron's body was recovered from the shore at Dover's Shakespeare Beach two months later.

For his courage and self-sacrifice in extreme circumstances, Middleton was awarded the Victoria Cross. The following extract pieces together the final hours of the raid, with contributions from two of the survivors, Cameron and Skinner:

Rawdon Hume Middleton VC.

By the time Middleton reached the outskirts of Turin he was at a height of 2000 feet and about to begin the search for the Fiat works on the southern side of the city before attempting to bomb from a low level as he had been instructed. By then, Royde, who was the bomb aimer as well as the navigator, had gone into the bombing well in readiness for the run on to the target, when the aircraft was heavily engaged by anti-aircraft guns while crossing the marshalling yards.

Middleton had difficulty identifying the Fiat works at first despite the bright light from the flares, and made two passes over the target area before making a positive identification.

Douglas Cameron recalls the circumstances:

> When we went down to identify the target Ron didn't think it was the right one so he made a second run. He finally identified it and said, 'We're running on,' and as we were doing so, with the bomb aimer about to let the bombs go, Ron suddenly said, 'Oh my God, I've been hit!' and then collapsed. A shell had burst in the cockpit between the pilots taking out his right eye and part of his face – what terrible pain the man must have been in. We had never expected it to be like that.

Hyder, too, had been severely wounded by the bursting shell, mainly in the body and legs, while Skinner had sustained a leg wound and at the same time the windscreen had been shattered. With Middleton now unconscious, the aircraft immediately went into a dive with the fuselage and wings being hit continually by flak, but Hyder managed to level the Stirling out at a height of 800 feet despite his injuries and the difficulty of maintaining lateral control because of the damage to the port wing. Realising that it would be impossible under the circumstances to attack the target effectively, he took the aircraft up to 1500 feet and when over the outskirts of the city dropped the load of incendiary bombs.

By this time Middleton had regained consciousness, although he was still in a dazed state when he gave an order to abandon the aircraft, but fortunately Hyder, showing great presence of mind considering his injuries, countermanded the order immediately. Meanwhile the three gunners were continuing to fire against ground targets when the rear turret was suddenly put out of action by a direct hit. And when well clear of the target area Middleton took over the controls, sending Hyder back to the aircraft bed where Cameron was able to provide first-aid treatment.

Skinner recalls the injuries sustained by Hyder:

> Hyder had been badly hit. The wounds on his face were dried with gauze and his hand, which had been torn, was dressed with a pad but he refused to have a tourniquet put on his wounded leg. 'I want to go back and help Ron,' he said, knowing Middleton might lose consciousness again and he shambled past me, head forward, looking in his determination like a wounded bear. I could see the blood stains on his flying suit as he passed the lights on the engineer's panel and I could not imagine how he kept standing.

Hyder was then helped into the second pilot's seat, where he was to remain in silence and in great pain for the rest of the flight and close to unconsciousness for much of the time. Crew members suspected that Middleton, too, was wounded in the body or legs as well as having sustained a very serious facial injury, but despite being given an injection of morphine to reduce the intense pain, he was finding it difficult to speak and asked his crew to speak to him only when it was absolutely necessary. The crew discussed the possibility of flying to North Africa to avoid the climb over the Alps, or alternatively baling out over Switzerland or crash-landing the aircraft somewhere in the flat country of northern France, but Middleton was determined to get his aircraft and crew back to England.

Douglas Cameron continues:

> It's not very pleasant if you have to bale out over the target especially knowing there are still more incendiaries to be dropped. Besides the Italians wouldn't take you alive then –

> they were either shooting our chaps or hanging them at that stage. We had a big job to climb again with the Alps so close, even though we were no longer carrying a bomb load, but we managed to get through. The Swiss, who were neutral, would put up a few shots if you ever went near them otherwise it would be an offence to Italy, but we were miles away. When we were near Lyon we suggested to Ron that we head for Spain as there were known escape routes and we all carried photographs for identification and special compasses sewn into our uniforms, but Jeffery said he thought we had enough fuel to make it back to England. To lighten the aircraft and so conserve petrol we had begun to throw out everything possible – my guns had to go as well as the huge boxes of ammunition stacked the full length of the fuselage on both sides and we even threw out the seats. We had two tomahawks and hacked the aircraft to bits – it took a couple of hours to get rid of everything we possibly could.

Skinner continues:

> We jettisoned everything we could – the camera, armour-plating, oxygen bottles, flares, fire extinguishers and even the sextant. Royde crawled around the aircraft with a fireman's axe chopping off things to jettison. We had a four-hour flight ahead of us and both our pilots were seriously wounded and they were sitting in an icy gale because their windscreen had been smashed. Mackie, the front gunner, had come back to stand near the pilots, setting the compass and helping them weave their way through the passes. We thought the time spent in bombing Turin had reduced fuel to such an extent that we would be lucky to reach the sea in order to ditch, but we kept our dinghies.

In the hours that lay ahead, Skinner was to have the task of keeping Middleton and Mackie informed of the bearing that would provide the shortest possible route to the English coast. And despite having a severe leg wound, Skinner remained at his post and sent a number of radio messages giving details of the crew's difficulties and at the same time obtained several fixes which helped the navigator guide the crippled aircraft towards England. More than four hours later Middleton and his crew reached the coast of France in the region of Dieppe, only a few miles off course, where they encountered searchlight activity and were subjected to shelling from the local anti-aircraft defences.

During the interview recorded by the BBC, Skinner recalls the circumstances at the time:

> The north wind had dropped a little so we made better headway than expected. There was still little hope of reaching England safely, however, and Middleton must have realised he could have baled out or crash-landed on the flat plains of France but he had made up his mind to get his aircraft and crew back to England even though his wounds were serious. When we were over northern France I saw a flash of light above me and realised it was a reflection of searchlights on the astrodome. We had been coned by about twelve of them and then more light flak hit the wings. Despite the effort of flying the aircraft for such a long time when he was so seriously injured, Middleton had put the aircraft into a dive to escape from the searchlights and flak and had dropped from 6000 feet to 600 feet by the time we began the Channel crossing. He was an artist at throwing a bomber about.

Knowing that he would need more height by the time he reached the coast of England if the crew were to bale out safely, Middleton was able to take the Stirling up to 2500 feet, but at the same time the escape hatches were opened and preparations made for ditching in case there were further difficulties while the aircraft was still over the Channel. Royde [the navigator/bomb aimer] had warned Middleton there was little chance of reaching an aerodrome and that if the crew were to bale out and avoid parachuting into the sea, he should fly at least two miles inland because there was a strong north-easterly wind. Middleton then stated his intention of flying parallel to the coast while the crew were baling out and then taking the aircraft out to sea.

Skinner continues:

> As we crossed the Channel, Middleton asked about petrol, and just as we sighted the coast of England the flight engineer reported that he could guarantee five minutes more fuel but not ten minutes more. Middleton asked for his parachute and it was passed to him by the navigator, but I believe now that this was no more than a gesture to reassure us. His voice by then was very thick and difficult to understand. I went off the intercom momentarily to get a bearing and when I came on again to announce the result, I was told the order had been given to bale out. I went forward in time to see the second pilot's upturned face disappearing through the escape hatch and then I went out.

Douglas Cameron recalls the events at the time:

> On reaching the coast of Kent, Ron turned the aircraft to port in the direction of Dungeness and in a very weak voice instructed the crew to bale out. I was fortunate because I had done quite a few jumps with paratroops at Manchester early in the war when I was doing a gunnery course there. Pete was already in the fuselage because I think his intercom had been shot away when his turret was put out of action over Turin, but he wasn't used to parachute jumping. I told him to watch out for the long aerials trailing a few feet beneath the aircraft which could tear his arm clean out if he made contact with them during the jump. I said, 'Watch the aerials and when the aircraft sways and the aerials go one way, you go the other.' I told Ron I was baling out but I'm not sure if he heard me. Everything has to go like lightning – you're trained to act that way. And so I went out the aft hatch with Pete following immediately behind me.

★

Meanwhile Mackie had helped the severely injured Hyder towards the forward escape hatch while at the same time making sure that Hyder was grasping the ripcord firmly before easing him out into the darkness below. Skinner and Royde had then followed in quick succession. The five men floating to earth could see only the blackness of the night but they could still hear the sound of the Stirling's engines although it was receding towards the east and over the sea. Just as the first of the crew to leave the aircraft reached the ground the moon shone through a short break in the cloud cover which gave them their last glimpse of the Stirling as it continued its flight out to sea. Those of the crew who had parachuted to safety on land did not know that both Mackie and Jeffery had remained in the aircraft until the last possible moment but were then parachuting towards the sea, and it can only be surmised that Middleton had ordered them once again to abandon the aircraft and not stay with him to assist when he ditched. There had never been any prospect of his leaving the aircraft because the automatic pilot had ceased to function during the Turin attack, so that he, as the aircraft captain and the last person to leave in an emergency, would have no way of controlling the flight of the aircraft while he was attempting to bale out. Moreover, he would not have had the strength to put on his parachute with the speed necessary under those circumstances and escape through the forward hatch, even though it was only a few feet beneath him. And presumably he would have been simply too weak to control a damaged aircraft if he had attempted to ditch without assistance and would have remained at the controls until there was no petrol remaining, when the aircraft would have plunged into the sea. It seems most unlikely that he would have survived the impact.

Once safely on the ground, Cameron and Gough had begun to look for help: 'At the first house we came to, the people shut the door in our faces, probably because there were quite a few Germans about then and it was three o'clock in the morning and pitch black. It was a long time before we could get any help, but it wouldn't have mattered much anyway.'

Next morning Gough went as a passenger on a flight in a Tiger

Moth to look for survivors from the crashed Stirling but none could be found. That afternoon, however, the bodies of Mackie and Jeffery were found in the sea still with their parachutes attached having failed to survive the remaining hours of darkness in the cold water, if indeed they had not drowned almost immediately. There was no sign of Middleton.

Douglas Cameron wonders if Jeffery, at least, may have survived under different circumstances:

> I was told later that Jeffery had gone towards the back of the aircraft to look for me. He shouldn't have done that – those few extra seconds may have cost him his life because he landed in the sea. Both Mackie and Jeffery would have drowned soon after striking the water because they would have come to the surface beneath their canopies, unable to see well enough in the darkness to free themselves.

Middleton's actions throughout this flight reflected in a number of ways the personal attitudes that his close friends had come to recognise. While many considered him to be a very reserved person, and could perhaps be described as a 'loner', he nevertheless possessed a strong team spirit, as anyone who played cricket with him will testify. His endurance for more than four hours in an attempt to help his 'team', despite the severe injuries he had sustained, was the quality he brought to his cricket when at school at Gilgandra and Dubbo, and later when he was playing cricket at Coolatai.

There was a reason, too, why Middleton had flown out to sea after the crew had baled out as Douglas Cameron recalls: 'Once when Ron was staying at my home in Scotland he received a letter from the mother of an Australian colleague. From the letter he learnt that the friend had crash-landed near Cambridge and killed a young woman and her new-born baby. Ron said to me, "If ever I crash it will never be on land." '

from *Middleton VC* by Stuart Bill

Acknowledgements

We would especially like to thank Tom Gilliatt, the Publisher, for his enthusiasm during the development of this book, Julie Crisp for her professional editing and production organisation and Richard Hoskin for his invaluable help in locating resource materials.

Text Acknowledgements

For permission to reproduce copyright material, the authors and publishers would like to thank the following:

Allen & Unwin for extracts from *Nicky Barr: An Australian Air Ace* and *The Silent Men* by Peter Dornan; *Vietnam Fragments* by Gary McKay; *In the Footsteps of Ghosts* by Bill Spencer.

S. & L. Bill for an extract from *Middleton VC* by Stuart Bill.

Commonwealth Copyright Administration for Commonwealth Gazette 23 July 1915 despatch by C.E.W. Bean.

Robert Crack and Nan Bennet for an extract from *Until A Dead Horse Kicks You.*

JM Dent, a division of The Orion Publishing Group Ltd, for an extract from *Guns in the Sky* by Chaz Bower.

Ron Guthrie and Col King for an extract from *Escape from North Korea.*

Hardie Grant Books for extracts from *War on Our Doorstep* by Gabrielle Chan.

HarperCollins Publishers for extracts from *White Coolies* by Betty Jeffrey; *Stoker's Submarine* by Fred and Elizabeth Brenchley;

One Crowded Hour Neil Davis Combat Cameraman 1934–1985 by Timothy Bowden; *The Wells of Beersheeba* by Frank Dalby Davison.

Hodder and Stoughton Ltd UK, an extract from *Anzac* by John Vader, reproduced by permission of the publisher.

Ion Idriess for permission to reproduce sections from *The Desert Column* from the publishers, ETT Imprint.

Mr E. LeCouteur and Mrs A. Carroll for extracts from *ANZAC to Amiens* by C.E.W. Bean.

Ruth Lockwood for an extract from *Bill Harney's War*.

Ian Mckie for extracts from *The Heroes*, *Proud Echo* and *Baron Murchison of Han*.

Pan Macmillan Australia for extracts from *One Man's War* by Stan Arneil; *One Fourteenth of an Elephant* by Ian Denys Peek; *Jacka, VC* by Ian Grant.

Penguin Books and the authors for extracts from *A Fortunate Life* by A.B. Fancy; *The War Diaries Of Weary Dunlop* by E.E. Dunlop.

Random House for an extract from *Roden Cutler, V.C.* by Colleen McCullough.

Andrew Rule for extracts from *A Sniper's Tale*.

Sherry Stumm for an extract from *I Saw Too Much*.

The estate of Peter Firkins for the extract from *Heroes Have Wings* by Peter Firkins.

The Hurley family for the entries from the World War I diaries of Frank Hurley. (The original diary – ML ref. ML MSS 389/5: CY Reel 3134 – is held in the Mitchell Library, State Library of New South Wales.)

The Orion Publishing Group Ltd for extracts from *Tobruk* by Frank Harrison.

Ray Whitecross and Simon and Schuster for an extract from *Slaves Of The Sun Of Heaven* by Ray Whitecross.

Photo credits

ix	Australian War memorial negative 083166
p1	Australian War memorial negative H10363
p11	Australian War memorial negative A02025
p13	Australian War memorial negative A00879
p17	Australian War memorial negative J06392
p21	nla.pic-an23998557 by permission of National Library of Australia
p29	nla.pic-an24574133 by permission of National Library of Australia
p40/41	nla.pic-an23478258 by permission of National Library of Australia
p45	Australian War memorial negative E04623
p51	Australian War memorial negative A03315
p57	Australian War memorial negative J00450
p63	Australian War memorial negative B00010
p65	Australian War memorial negative 042075
p68	Australian War memorial negative 007481
p72	nla.pic-an23816560 by permission of National Library of Australia
p75	Australian War memorial negative 106483
p79	Australian War memorial negative 027081
p83	Australian War memorial negative 070300
p92	Australian War memorial negative 014001
p105	Australian War memorial negative 015515

p107 Australian War memorial negative 042975
p114 Australian War memorial negative 027793
p117 Australian War memorial negative 060696
p125 Australian War memorial negative 067177
p133 Australian War memorial negative A01551
p135 Australian War memorial negative P00305.001
p139 H98.103/3273 Argus Newspaper Collection of Photographs, State Library Victoria
p143 Australian War memorial negative 019327
p153 Australian War memorial negative 019199
p159 Australian War memorial negative 044097
p166 Australian War memorial negative H11559
p173 Australian War memorial negative 006602
p191 nla.pic-an23998546 by permission of National Library of Australia
p194 Australian War memorial negative A05340
p203 H98.103/297 Argus Newspaper Collection of Photographs, State Library Victoria
p211 Australian War memorial negative P00809.002
p213 Australian War memorial negative 013764
p215 Australian War memorial negative 057645
p223 Australian War memorial negative P01035.012
p231 Australian War memorial negative 093451
p245 Australian War memorial negative P00660.001
p248 Australian War memorial negative P03732.001
p252 Australian War memorial negative JK0243
p261 Australian War memorial negative 044748
p267 Australian War memorial negative EKN/67/0130/VN
p273 Australian War memorial negative WAR/70/0026/VN
p277 Australian War memorial negative EKT/67/0046/VN
p284 Australian War memorial negative BEL/69/0556/VN
p287 Australian War memorial negative 027388
p289 Australian War memorial negative P00885.001
p298 Australian War memorial negative 011529/21
p306 Australian War memorial negative 131583

p311 Australian War memorial negative 127971
p313 Australian War memorial negative E01059
p315 nla.pic-an24539406 by permission of National Library of Australia
p316 Australian War memorial negative E01237
p318 Australian War memorial negative 013356
p319 nla.pic-an11845931 by permission of National Library of Australia
p321 Australian War memorial negative 013287
p322 Australian War memorial negative P00508.010
p327 Australian War memorial negative 013971
p331 Australian War memorial negative A02868
p333 Australian War memorial negative 134905
p337 Australian War memorial negative 100641

Index

Page numbers in *italics* indicate an illustration.